dictionary of
EDUCATION

DENIS LAWTON *and* PETER GORDON

Hodder & Stoughton

A MEMBER OF THE HODDER HEADLINE GROUP

British Library Cataloguing in Publication Data

Lawton, Denis
  Dictionary of Education
  I. Title   II. Gordon, Peter
  370.3

  ISBN 0-340-53179-7

First published 1993
Impression number   10 9 8 7 6 5 4 3 2 1
Year   1998 1997 1996 1995 1994 1993

Typeset by Rowland Phototypesetting Limited, Bury St Edmunds, Suffolk.
Printed in Great Britain for Hodder & Stoughton Educational, a division of Hodder Headline PLC, Mill Road, Dunton Green, Sevenoaks, Kent TN13 2YA by Page Bros (Norwich) Limited.

CONTENTS

Foreword   v
Acknowledgments   vii
Note about the authors   viii

Section 1   Discussion of some key concepts   1

            Introduction   3
            1 Education and educational theory   4
            2 Aims, values and ideologies   7
            3 Culture and curriculum   10
            4 Accountability, standards and inspection   12
            5 Assessment and examinations   15
            6 Education, schooling and pedagogy   20
            7 The language of education reform: the Education
                Reform Act (1988)   23
            8 Politics and education; the politics of education 28
            9 Changes in the language of post-compulsory
                education and training   31

Section 2   The Dictionary: An alphabetical list of definitions 35

Section 3   Acronyms and abbreviations   191

FOREWORD

The intention of this book is to provide a guide to the language of education. It is divided into three sections: the first provides brief *discussions* of some key ideas in education in the form of short papers which explore concepts and relationships between concepts; the second is intended to give short *definitions* (and where necessary cross-references to other terms in Section 1 or Section 2); the third contains an up-to-date list of acronyms and abbreviations.

Non-professionals, including some politicians, sometimes complain about the existence of 'jargon' in educational writings. Sometimes such criticisms are justified, but it would be very difficult to avoid technical terms completely. If newcomers to the field of architecture want to appreciate it fully, they will find it necessary to acquire an understanding of such words as Romanesque and Gothic. Similarly, in education, there are new ideas and concepts to be grasped in order to understand current issues and problems. We hope that this book will enable parents, governors and others (as well as teachers and students of education) to understand and participate in education debates.

Less excusable than the use of technical terms in education is the profusion of acronyms, and education is no better than most specialisms in this respect. We include an up-to-date list of acronyms and abbreviations in Section 3 on page 191.

ACKNOWLEDGMENTS

In collecting material for this book, the authors relied heavily on the expert knowledge of many individuals. We would like to thank the following for providing information and answering questions on a range of topics: Alaric Dickinson, Althea Efunshile, Simon Grigor, Trevor Male, Jon Ogborn, Charles Plummeridge, Dr C. Pond, Alex Porter, John Robinson, Mark Thomas and Meryl Thompson. We also gratefully acknowledge the help of the numerous organisations which readily offered their advice.

Finally, we are especially grateful to Joyce Broomhall, Pauline Gordon, Joan Lawton and Patricia Thomas for their help in preparing the manuscript for publication.

NOTE ABOUT THE AUTHORS

Denis Lawton and Peter Gordon are both Professors at the Institute of Education, University of London. Professor Lawton is in the Curriculum Studies Department; Professor Gordon is in the History and Humanities Department.

Section 1

DISCUSSION *of* SOME KEY CONCEPTS

INTRODUCTION

The following short papers or essays are intended to explore the particular meanings of some key words in education, and to analyse the relationships between those words. We feel this Section to be an essential preparation for the definitions we offer in Section 2.

In some cases it is helpful to get to grips with the technical meaning of a word by seeing it in the context (or contexts) of other terms. The most obvious example of this is included in Essay 7 with the discussion of the profusion of new technical terms generated by the Education Reform Act (1988): Attainment Targets, Levels of Achievement, Statements of Attainment, can all be defined correctly in isolation, but their full meaning only emerges in a description of their relation to each other. All the essays contain examples of that kind, and although we make cross-references (shown in bold type) to dictionary items in Section 2, we feel that a preliminary reading of Section 1 may be helpful.

ONE

Education and educational theory

'Education' is a difficult word, partly because it has a wide variety of meanings, partly because it involves not one but several complex processes. Richard Peters (1966), who did so much to clarify educational concepts, has suggested that education is not a word to which a single precise meaning can be attached: it is not a word like 'running' which conjures up an image of one single kind of activity. You can run quickly or very quickly, but all running is essentially of the same kind. Education is a different kind of word: it must be associated with learning, but no specific type of activity is required. Education is in the same category as words like 'reform'. Reform is not associated with any particular process: people may be reformed by imprisonment, or by listening to a sermon. And students may be educated by reading books, by listening to lectures, and by conversation with others. In each case we think that the word 'reform' or 'education' is properly used if certain criteria are met.

One of the criteria for both words is that something worthwhile should be achieved – improvement is involved. It would make no sense to say, 'Prison has reformed him but he is a worse criminal than ever.' Nor would it be meaningful to say, 'He has been well educated, but he has learned nothing of value.' Some beneficial change must take place. Education must involve learning, but not all learning is educational: Oliver Twist learned from Fagin how to pick pockets, but that could not be described as 'education'; what he learned was not something which made him a better person. Oliver was *trained* as a pickpocket and given *instruction*, but he was not being educated.

The last example also illustrates the fact that value judgements are inevitably involved in talking about education. When we say someone is 'educated', it implies that we value certain aspects of the process. But it does not necessarily imply total approval of that individual's character or behaviour. It is quite possible to say, 'He is well educated but eats like a pig', but it would not make sense to say, 'He is well educated but knows nothing.' Education is concerned with transmitting something that is worthwhile.

Peters inserts an additional condition, namely, that the transmission must be carried out in a morally unobjectionable manner. The person being educated must know what is happening to him or her, and must accept the process rationally: learning, even of worthwhile content, would not be educational if it were imparted by using techniques involving cruelty, or by brainwashing or conditioning.

That brings us to a distinction between education and schooling (see also Essay 6 for a further discussion of schooling). Education can take place outside schools or other formal institutions, and not everything that is learnt in a school is necessarily educational. There is some dispute, for example, about what students learn from operating within a prefect system or a cadet corps. Are these educational even if students and teachers are unaware of what is being learned? Hence discussions about the 'hidden' curriculum.

Our discussion of the meaning of 'education' has inevitably led us into the area of educational theory, involving value judgements about worthwhile activities and educational processes. One of the strange features of discussions about education in recent years has been the hostility shown by politicians and the media towards educational theory. Some have suggested that there is too much theory involved in the training of teachers; others have blamed fashionable theories for poor reading standards and for other alleged failures in the education system.

It may be worth beginning with the fairly obvious statement that in education, medicine or any other kind of professional service, it would be impossible to have practice which was completely free from theory. Theory may be seen as convention, or professional tradition, or even as common sense, but practice will always be guided by some set of principles.

The problem with educational theory is that it attempts to deal with issues of great complexity whilst it is still in a relatively early stage of development. Education theory has passed through a series of stages and some of them have been seen by practitioners as possessing relatively little relevance to their practical classroom activities. An early stage of education theory consisted of an account of the views of the great educators – perhaps Plato, Comenius, Rousseau or Dewey. At a later stage theory developed into extracting from philosophy and psychology aspects which had some bearing on education. At this stage it was common to have lectures on philosophy of education, educational psychology, history of education and somewhat later, sociology of education. During the 1960s, efforts were made to 'integrate' and apply that kind of knowledge to specific educational issues and problems.

During the 1970s, there were further developments. It was suggested that a better approach would be to identify the real-life problems of teachers (and student teachers on practice in schools) and to see what light theory could throw on these problems. It may be that this was the stage which caused hostility from politicians and others. Some of the problems put forward for discussion were controversial. For example, problems of social class and inequalities in educational opportunity, gender differences in educational achievement, or the difficulties of some ethnic minority students.

The current state of educational theory is much influenced by the idea that theory should be generated by teachers themselves out of their own enlightened practice. Donald Schon (1983) in the USA has invented the useful expression 'the reflective practitioner'. A little earlier, Lawrence Stenhouse (1975) spoke of 'the teacher as researcher'. Paul Hirst (1984) was originally committed to the idea of applying 'disciplines' such as philosophy and psychology to education, but eventually changed his mind and advocated theory generated from practice.

References

HIRST, P.H. (1984) *Educational Theory and its Foundation Disciplines*. Routledge and Kegan Paul.

PETERS, R.S. (1966) *Ethics and Education*. Allen and Unwin.

SCHON, D. (1983) *The Reflective Practitioner*. Temple Smith.

STENHOUSE, L. (1975) *An Introduction to Curriculum Research and Development*. Heinemann.

TWO

Aims, values and ideologies

There have been, from time to time, philosophical discussions on whether or not education needs to have aims (for example, Peters, 1966; White, 1982). The main principle underlying arguments against aims is that education, appropriately defined, is concerned with worthwhile activities and is therefore good in itself. The discussion may then shift to an examination of those kinds of knowledge and experience which are regarded as worthwhile. This may seem like a backdoor approach to aims, indicating a need to distinguish them and recognising their importance, implicitly. Some aims may be universal but others will be culture specific. In this sense, an analysis of the educational aims of any society will involve a study of the values of that society. Educational aims change (to some extent) from place to place as well as from time to time in accordance with differences in values and changes in values over time. (This is not to beg the question about whether there are or could be absolute values.)

In the UK, for example, discussion of education in the nineteenth century would have usually been much more concerned with religious values than would discussions in the 1990s. Similarly, the emphasis on science and technology in the National Curriculum as specified in the Education Reform Act (1988) is an obvious reflection of the dominance of scientific values in the late twentieth century. In the nineteenth century there was quite a struggle to have science admitted as a curriculum subject at all. And whilst acknowledging the appropriateness of according science such high priority now, it may be a mistake to think of this change as a simple account of linear progress. Many, not only reactionary advocates of a return to traditional values, have sounded warnings about too much emphasis on this aspect of contemporary culture – for example, the German philosopher, Marcuse, has written of 'one-dimensional man', and the Canadian novelist, Robertson Davies has drawn attention to the similarities between science and theology: 'science is the theology of our time . . . a muddle of conflicting assertions.' This should not be taken to indicate a denial of the importance of science, only a warning that we need to be cautious about rejecting other kinds of 'truth'.

Certainly, many educational reforms and much educational legislation can be seen in terms of a change in values. In the nineteenth century the extension of educational provision to all social classes, and eventually to girls; in the twentieth century attempts to equalise the quality of provision and to diminish inequalities of access and opportunity in education. Many would see more recent reforms such as the Education Act referred to above as an attempt to modernise British industry and to make it more competitive, hence the greater attention paid to international comparisons of educational achievement, especially in mathematics and science (there appears to be much less concern about how well our schools may be doing compared with Germany and Japan on moral development, aesthetic awareness or political understanding). Education in the 1990s is dominated by science and technology, and indirectly by industrial and commercial values. This may not be a permanent condition.

Those who might wish to criticise the values dominating education in the 1990s might use another concept: 'ideology'. The word ideology implies a distorted, or at least a limited, perception of reality. Human beings see the world through the distortion of their own values and beliefs which will be partly cultural or societal and partly sub-cultural – that is, caused by such factors as social class or religious affiliation. We tend to think that other people's perception may be distorted by their ideology but we are probably more reluctant to admit that we might be misled by our own beliefs. One definition of the educated person might be one who is sufficiently aware of the distorting effects of values and beliefs to be conscious of the danger of distortion in his or her own perceptions and judgements.

Within the UK, ideology is said to distort discussions of many social issues, including education. Those from the upper classes, it is alleged, will tend to have arguments which justify inherited wealth and privilege; they will also tend to justify private schools, and favour competition rather than cooperation, stressing standards rather than equality of opportunity. By contrast, it may be said that those on the left politically may tend to over-value (or exaggerate the importance of) enjoyment, participation, equality rather than quality, opportunity rather than excellence.

Another aspect of ideological distortion is particularly concerned with the language of education: the same words are used with different meanings (or different shades of meaning) according to ideology. For example, 'standards', 'quality' and 'excellence' are 'approval' words (that is, it is difficult not to regard them as 'good things'). But their precise meaning depends on ideological context: does quality in education mean high quality education for an elite with something else provided for the majority, or does it mean high quality for all? The answer has to be found, with examples of that kind, in the ideological context of the statement.

References

DAVIES, R. (1985) *What's Bred in the Bone*. Penguin.
PETERS, R. S. (1966) *Ethics and Education*. Allen and Unwin.
WHITE J. (1982) *The Aims of Education Restated*. Routledge and Kegan Paul.

THREE

Culture and curriculum

All societies have the task of passing on to the next generation the values, knowledge and skills regarded as particularly worthwhile; some societies achieve this by means of formal education.

When we talk of values, knowledge and skills, we are touching upon a concept which is much used by anthropologists and sociologists – **culture**. Anthropologists developed the culture concept to convey the idea of the whole way of life of the communities they studied – often preliterate societies with simple technology, but with highly complex social structures. Sociologists have found the culture concept equally important in making distinctions between modern societies or even between social groups within a society, in which case they may use the term 'sub-culture'.

Culture is a useful but difficult concept. It is difficult for a number of reasons. First, in English the word 'culture' is often used, in a misleading way, to describe the tastes of the upper classes (or probably a minority of the upper classes); in everyday speech 'culture' tends to be used to denote 'high culture' rather than popular culture, and individuals might be described as 'cultured' if they like literature, classical music, art and architecture. A second difficulty is that although it comparatively easy for anthropologists to describe the culture of, say, the Trobriand Islanders at a given time, it is much more difficult for a sociologist to differentiate between working-class and middle-class culture in any modern, industrialised society.

The link between education and culture is important because those involved in the education service make decisions about the aspects of culture considered to be important enough to be included in school programmes – that is, in the school curriculum. The definition of curriculum as a selection from the culture of a society is uncontroversial (what else could a curriculum be?). But exactly what should be selected from the culture to constitute a curriculum may sometimes be disputed. There may also be disputes about what should be compulsory (in a **core**, **common** or **national curriculum**), and what should be left to choice – perhaps in the form of **options**. Such debates will involve, explicitly or implicitly, discussions of culture, although the disputes may sometimes be couched in narrower terms, such as the need to prepare the young for work (vocationalism), or the need to inculcate habits of obedience and respect for authority.

Another possible contentious issue occurs in those modern societies which possess ethnic minorities whose children become part of the responsibility of the education service. These children may possess cultural differences which pose problems for educational planners. If a national curriculum is based on notions of a common culture, to what extent should the curriculum be adjusted for ethnic or religious minorities? Or is it important for all children to be exposed to the common culture curriculum of the society in which they are growing up, even if they are also encouraged to celebrate their cultural differences inside and outside the school in other ways? An alternative – pluralistic – view is that ethnic minorities, and other groups such as working-class children, would be better served by being given a curriculum specific to their own culture or sub-culture. For example, some have advocated a 'working-class curriculum', denying the feasibility of a common curriculum based on a common culture. Such prescriptions tend to break down when detailed specifications are attempted for the content of the curriculum. They have tended to produce programmes which would limit the horizons of the young people exposed to it. And one of the functions of an education system in a democratic society should be to open up opportunities rather than to restrict them.

In practice, however, it would be difficult in any society with a class structure to avoid giving the children of the privileged some educational advantages. All that an education service can do is to endeavour to provide, for example, by means of a national curriculum, general access to worthwhile knowledge and skills.

The advantage of discussing the core curriculum in terms of a 'national curriculum' rather than a 'common curriculum' is that some disputes about the precise nature of the common culture can be avoided by focusing on what all young people 'need' in order to live in a given society, rather than upon aspects of cultural values and beliefs, which will tend to be more controversial.

References

LAWTON, D. (1989) *Education, Culture and the National Curriculum*. Hodder and Stoughton.

FOUR

Accountability, standards and inspection

Lessinger (1971) traces the use of the word 'accountability' in education to the USA in the late 1960s, but the notion of educational accountability is much older. Callahan (1962) identifies the accountability tradition with the claim that US culture is dominated by the world of business, and that soon after 1900 business values and practices were being adopted by educational administrators who modelled themselves on business executives rather than on academics. Bagley's *Classroom Management* (1907) saw schools as a 'problem of economy'. Soon after, Bobbitt wrote *The Elimination of Waste in Education* (1912) which was very influential. Whilst not using the word accountability, Bobbitt wrote of the need for a system of 'accounting' which would need to be very elaborate.

Many of these ideas about applying business efficiency to education were revived in 1963 when President Lyndon Johnson asked Robert MacNamara to apply the business efficiency methods of the Ford Motor Company to the Department of Defense and then to other government spending departments. From 1965 to 1967 seminars were held to encourage education administrators to learn such techniques as management by **objectives**, cost benefit analysis, and planned programme budgeting (PPB). This use or management ideas and terminology spread to other parts of the English-speaking world, and some of the ideas were taken up, or at least discussed, by most developed education systems.

It has gradually been recognised, however, that it is not appropriate for education simply to take over the methods of the business world (House, 1978). Sockett (1980) also attacked the concept of accountability on the grounds of lack of clarity. The world of education is also much more complex than the world of business and commerce, at least in terms of objectives. Nevertheless, the term accountability has now become part of the language of education, and all that can be hoped is to urge caution in its usage. Eraut (1981) distinguished between three kinds of accountability in education: the moral, the contractual (or legal) and the professional accountability of teachers. Teachers are legally accountable only to their headteachers and to their employers, but they have moral obligations to pupils and parents. Professionalism and professional accountability are complex and controversial issues.

Maclure (1978) has also discussed four concerns closely associated with accountability: standards, curriculum, parental participation and managerial responsibility.

Many members of the public, including politicians, would assume in a commonsense way that when large sums of money are given to schools and colleges, that there ought to be a means of assuring 'value for money'; part of this assurance comes in the form of maintenance of standards. Maclure and Eraut both point out, however, that one of the dangers of discussions of standards, especially in the context of accountability, is that testing and test results will be given undue prominence. Similarly, accountability when applied to curriculum, tends to over-emphasise basic skills, examination and test results and publishing such results as **league tables** of good and bad schools. The appropriateness of those warnings were confirmed ten years later by the English experience following the **Education Reform Act (1988)**.

Since 1988 the market metaphor has increasingly been applied to education: parents are 'customers' who choose; in order to choose between schools parents must have data about the schools – hence the publication of National Curriculum Assessment results (and examination results) in the form of league tables. Many have pointed out that this kind of accountability is not only over-simplified but misleading: the quality of schools cannot be judged merely on results – their test performance will depend on what the children were like to begin with. It is doubtful whether any simple formula will ever be able to provide a single index of **quality**; but attempts are now being made to use much more sophisticated methods of analysis, such as the 'multi-level' approach favoured by Goldstein (1987). Meanwhile in England other kinds of **performance indicators** (PI) are being recommended by government as measures of quality and standards: for example, **truancy rates**, the percentage of secondary pupils staying on beyond the compulsory stage, and the first destination of leavers.

Much of that kind of accountability is alien to an older means of schools being called to account – the process of **inspection**. Whereas the 'business efficiency' kind of accountability relies on outputs in the form of the kind of measures or indicators discussed above, inspection tends to focus on the quality of inputs and of recommending desirable processes or practices. There is, of course, no reason why both kinds of accountability should not be combined, provided the balance between them is right and the complexity of education is accepted.

References

BAGLEY, W. L. (1907) *Classroom Management*. Macmillan.

BOBBITT, F. (1912) *The Elimination of Waste in Education*. Houghton Mifflin (Boston).

CALLAHAN, R. E. (1962) *Education and the Cult of Efficiency*. University of Chicago Press.

ERAUT, M. (1981) 'Accountability and Evaluation' in SIMON, B. and TAYLOR, W. (eds) *Education in the Eighties*. Batsford.

GOLDSTEIN, H. (1987) *Multi-level Models in Educational and Social Research*. Charles Griffin.

HOUSE, E. (1978) 'An American View of British Accountability' in BECHER, A. and MACLURE, S. (eds) *The Politics of Curriculum Change*. Hutchinson.

LAWTON, D. (1992) *Education and Politics in the 1990s*. Falmer.

LESSINGER, L. M. (1971) 'Accountability for Results' in LESSINGER, L. M. and TYLER, R. W. *Accountability in Education*. C. A. Jones (Washington, Ohio).

MACLURE, S. (1978) 'Background to the Accountability Debate' in BECHER, A. and MACLURE, S. (eds) Accountability in Education, NFER.

SOCKETT, H. (1980) *Accountability in the English Education System*. Hodder and Stoughton.

FIVE

Assessment and examinations

Assessment is, or should be, closely associated with curriculum. Nearly all writers on curriculum and assessment stress the importance of seeing assessment as an aspect of curriculum design, rather than a process which operates independently. Assessment should be 'curriculum driven'; but one complaint about some kinds of curriculum is that they are assessment driven. An example of an assessment-driven curriculum, or more specifically, an examination-dominated curriculum, was the secondary curriculum in England and Wales prior to 1988. Because there was officially no national curriculum, teachers tended to use the public examination syllabuses for **General Certificate of Education** (GCE), and later the **General Certificate of Secondary Education** (GCSE) as their curriculum guidelines – what should have been a means of assessment became the curriculum.

Whilst acknowledging that assessment should be seen as an aspect of curriculum planning, a number of writers have pointed out that assessment in schools has a number of different, sometimes conflicting, functions. Gipps (1990) has, for example, put forward a six-fold classification of the uses of assessment: **screening** (testing to detect special needs); **diagnosis** (identifying strengths and weaknesses); **record-keeping** (often based on **standardised tests**); **feedback** on performance (to teachers, headteachers, local education authorities); **certification** (providing a qualification); **selection** (for entry to secondary school, further education or higher education.)

Gipps and Stobart (1993) and others have also made a distinction between professional and managerial functions of assessment. Professional use of assessment helps teachers educate children and complements curriculum planning; managerial or 'bureaucratic' means using assessment (especially testing) to manage the education system efficiently, perhaps producing the kind of test results that can be used to compare the performance of teachers, schools or local education authorities (perhaps by means of **league tables**).

Examinations are only one of many methods of assessment, but they are often considered to be of major importance in the eyes of parents, employers and politicians. A serious limitation of public examinations is that they are usually exclusively **summative**. Much more important for diagnostic or **formative** purposes is the kind of continuous assessment carried out by teachers on a day-to-day or week-to-week basis; but in the view of the public, continuous assessment lacks the prestige and credibility of a public examination which normally operates with standards which are well established, and include checks on **reliability** and **validity**. Because examinations are used for selective purposes, they are less useful for improving educational performance of individual students. The **GCE Advanced level** in England, the **Baccalauréat** in France, and the **Abitur** in Germany, are all used as entry qualifications for university: this selective function gives them high prestige but they cannot be used diagnostically – they are exclusively terminal and summative.

Not all examinations are terminal public examinations; many schools have end-of-year, or end-of-term examinations as part of their record-keeping and formative assessment programme. These examinations can be used for feedback and diagnosis, but in the past, examinations have tended to be managerial rather than professional devices. Examinations are distinguished from other kinds of assessment in that they tend to be more formal: having a fixed time limit (for example, one-hour, two-hour papers), with 'unseen' questions designed to test a student's performance on content which has been specifically taught as part of the preceding course. Because the examination questions cannot cover the whole of the course, examiners have to 'sample' content – that is, set questions on some parts of the syllabus only. This introduces an element of chance into what should be a completely rational process: candidates can be 'lucky' in revising what 'comes up' in the examination. In public examinations students and their teachers can waste time in trying to predict and cover the answers to likely questions, leading to the unfortunate custom of teaching to the test (and learning for the test) rather than covering the curriculum in an educationally desirable way. To offset the disadvantage of examinations on their own, there has been a tendency in recent years with university and public examinations, to use examinations in conjunction with other assessment methods such as **coursework** of various kinds, and the continuous assessment of the teacher (with or without **moderation**).

In England and Wales, the **General Certificate of Secondary Education** (GCSE) provides some interesting examples of changes in examination procedure. The GCSE began in 1988 as a combination of two other exams for 16-year-old pupils: the **General Certificate of Education** (GCE) 'O' level (originally intended, in 1951, for only the most academic twenty per cent of the age group) and the **Certificate of Secondary Education** (CSE) which was introduced in the 1960s as an examination for the forty per cent below the top twenty per cent (deliberately leaving forty per cent of 16-year-olds as non-examinable). The division of 14- to 16-year-olds into these three categories was, however, administratively inconvenient, and many felt that it offended against the principles of comprehensive education. After several trials and committees, the new examination was established in 1986 to make its first awards in 1988.

One problem to be overcome was that of control: the CSE was regionally organised and locally controlled by Boards created by groups of local education authorities; on the other hand, for 'O' levels, schools could choose from one or more GCE Boards which were locally based (often historically linked with universities). The Secretary of State required the new GCSE examinations to be run by Groups of Boards, with GCE Boards being responsible for monitoring standards of the top grades (A, B and C), and the CSE Boards being responsible for the other standards. The result was a national system of four GCSE Groups (in England) which were regionally based but offered their examinations to schools anywhere in the country. Competition prevailed, but coordination and some cooperation was maintained by a Joint Council for GCSE. There was also much greater central control over syllabuses and procedures by the **Department of Education and Science** (DES) through the Secondary Examinations Council (SEC), which after the Education Reform Act (1988) was replaced by the **School Examinations and Assessment Council** (SEAC). The **Secondary Examinations Council** (which was, in turn, superseded by the **School Curriculum and Assessment Authority** (SCAA) in 1993) organised the groups to work out general criteria for the GCSE which had to be approved by themselves and the Department of Education and Science. The general criteria included references to the following: all subjects had to have statement of **aims** (the educational purposes of the subject), together with assessment objectives. Although each group offered different syllabuses, all had to contain a 'common core' of content for each subject.

The new examination had its fair share of difficulties – some of them technical, some of them questions of control and organisation. The technical problems were partly concerned with the difficulty of setting papers for the whole ability range, and this was sometimes solved by setting '**limited grade**' examinations (that is, examinations in which the range of grades which may be awarded is restricted by stopping short either of the highest or of the lowest grades). Another technical difficulty was that Sir Keith Joseph, when Secretary of State, had demanded an examination which was more **criterion-referenced**. This was found to be very difficult to achieve, and instead, the compromise of '**grade descriptions**' was adopted (descriptions of expected standards for each grade were provided for examiners and teachers, but not criteria strictly defined). The organisational difficulties included too little training for those teachers involved, before the introduction of the new examination and, perhaps more importantly, the controversy that developed out of the proportion of marks to be given to course assessment as compared with traditional examination papers. Some teachers argued for a high percentage of **continuous assessment** (even one hundred per cent in some subjects) on the grounds that increasing motivation and continuous assessment were more appropriate for some kinds of work. But pressure developed from some politicians, including Kenneth Clarke when he was Secretary of State, to limit continuous assessment to about twenty per cent on the grounds that written papers were a superior method of assessment. There is no evidence that examinations are better in terms of reliability, and the **validity** of continuous assessment is almost certainly higher. The view that examinations were preferable, however, seemed to be firmly fixed in some minds, and traditional examinations won the day for GCSE.

There is, of course, plenty of evidence, much of it from the Examining Boards themselves, showing that the traditional written paper type of examination is by no means flawless in terms of **reliability**, **validity** and the **comparability** of results between Boards. Despite the evidence, politicians and apparently the general public, retain great faith in written examinations, such as GCE 'A' level (sometimes referred to as the 'gold standard' against which all other assessment should be compared) and the GCSE so long as it resembled the traditional GCE 'O' level type of examination rather than the more innovative CSE which had also encouraged the development of continuous assessment.

Wherever a formal system of education exists, there tends to be assessment of some kind, probably involving examinations. But the style of examination varies considerably from one society to another. For example, in the USA, much more use has been made of so-called **objective tests**, involving **multiple choice** and other techniques, whereas in England there has been an emphasis (outside maths and science) on 'essay-type' examinations. This contrast probably reflects cultural differences in the societies concerned, but the forms of assessment used will also have interesting effects on the education system and on the performance of students. Successful students in England and Wales, for example, tend to find writing essays and reports easier than their American colleagues of the same age and ability.

In those countries where both kinds of examination are used, the advice sometimes given to candidates is 'for multiple choice, guess; for essay questions, bluff!' There are ways of improving the reliability and validity of both kinds of assessment, but it can be safely stated that few examinations are as good as they pretend to be or as the public think they are. In England, for example, there is great faith in the GCE 'A' level examination as a method of selecting 18-year-olds for higher education. But the **correlation** between 'A' level results and university degree performance is only about 0.4. Even so, it is as good as, or better than, other predictive measures. However, one of the complaints made in recent years about the English secondary system is that the domination by the 'A' level examination has distorted the curriculum and limited access to higher education.

References

GIPPS, C. and STOBATT, G. (1993) *Assessment*. Hodder and Stoughton.

Education, schooling and pedagogy

Oscar Wilde once said that education begins when a person leaves school. This may have been an over-cynical view, but it does alert us to the need to distinguish carefully between the two concepts – education and schooling. Earlier we endeavoured to establish the principle that education should be regarded, by definition, as good in itself, since it is concerned with developing the young in desirable ways and with worthwhile knowledge and experiences. Unfortunately the gap between education and schooling is a good example of what sociologists sometimes contrast as 'ideal and reality'. Whereas education is concerned with development, schools often appear to be more concerned with conformity and obedience; and while some educationists speak of education as 'emancipation', the reality of schooling may be closer to 'oppression'.

Why is there such a serious gap between ideal and reality – between education and schooling? There are many reasons, and some of them are connected with the third concept – 'pedagogy', or what teachers do in order to meet the aims of education. Although there have been many books and articles written on 'the role of the teacher', Brian Simon (1981) has complained that little has been written about pedagogy in the UK. How a teacher transforms, or attempts to transform, ambitious ideals into practical reality is a neglected area. What we do know is that the task is an extremely difficult one, and one which is becoming more rather than less difficult. In the twentieth century more and more is expected of teachers, but at the same time, the authority of teachers has been increasingly questioned and has become less easy to enforce.

A related problem area is that 'society' expects schools to do much more than educate the young. (This problem is, of course, not unconnected with the discussion of the role of the teacher, and the problem of over-loading, referred to above.) Schools, and therefore teachers, are expected not only to be concerned with children's intellectual, moral and social development by means of opening up access to worthwhile knowledge and experiences, they are also expected to be involved in the socialisation of the young – that is, inducting them into the customs, conventions and accepted practices of society. Some of these aspects of socialisation may be entirely in harmony with educational ideals, but there may be some 'grey areas', and there are certainly occasions when, for example, the demands of some employers for young workers to be trained to be unquestioningly obedient, may be in stark conflict with the educational aim of developing **autonomy**.

The grey areas are the ones most likely to be the subjects of dispute and often of media reporting (and misreporting). For instance, it is clearly part of the responsibility of a teacher of English to develop the powers of communication in pupils: this will involve improving achievement in listening, speaking, reading and writing. But does it involve insisting upon standard English and received pronunciation? The teacher of English might argue (and some would) that those are mere conventions which have nothing to do with education. The response to this 'idealist' teacher might be that to deny children the social advantage of 'correct' English (in addition to the uncontroversial 'communicative competence') may be to prevent young school leavers from access to certain kinds of employment. Our teacher might then reply that he or she is not concerned with preparation for the labour market, only with education.

In other words, we are concerned with the extent to which it is reasonable to expect schools (and therefore teachers) to be responsible for preparation for adult life which is not, strictly speaking, educational, but is (at least in the case of preparing for employment) a highly desirable activity. The problem is a real one, and there are many others of a similar kind. For example, is it part of the function of a teacher to encourage the young to be proud of their own country – even to be patriotic? Is it a legitimate aspect of the teacher role to encourage the development of 'good citizenship'? Can 'real' history be taught without encouraging the young to be critical of some aspects of their own social system?

In recent years in the UK attempts have been made to give guidance to schools and to teachers: the Education Act (1986) requires governors to be responsible for preventing political indoctrination in schools. But these are only the fairly obvious 'surface' problems; at a deeper level, one of the problems is that twentieth-century teachers are facing twentieth-century problems of curriculum and pedagogy in institutions (schools) which were developed in the nineteenth century within a framework of socialisation which was much more authoritarian, even repressive, than would be acceptable publicly today. But the deep structure of society retains social class attitudes and authoritarian expectations just below the surface. When teachers are asked to cope with curricular and pedagogical innovations, they not only have to adjust their own behaviour, attitudes and beliefs, but also have to deal with the powerful resistance to change which is inherent in the institutional structure. Much of the literature on educational change is highly relevant to these discussions – for example, Michael Fullan (1991).

References

FULLAN, M. *et al*; (1991) *The New Meaning of Educational Change*. Cassell.
SIMON, B. (1981) 'Why no pedagogy in England?' in SIMON, B.
and TAYLOR, W. (eds) *Education in the Eighties*. Batsford.

SEVEN

The language of educational reform: the Education Reform Act (ERA) 1988

Until 1988 the major piece of educational legislation in England and Wales had been the 1944 Education Act which made secondary education free and compulsory, and established a system which was centrally governed but locally administered (by local education authorities). By the late 1970s some educationists were complaining that new legislation was needed, but it was not until 1987 that a reforming Secretary of State, Kenneth Baker, began to prepare the 'Great Education Reform Bill' (GERBILL) which after much debate in both Houses of Parliament and elsewhere, became the Education Reform Act (1988). (The purpose of this essay is not to summarise the Education Reform Act – a task which has been admirably carried out by Stuart Maclure (1989) – but merely to highlight some of the educational terminology which emerged from the discussions of reform.)

The dominant ideology behind the Act is 'consumerism' in the particular form of increasing parental choice and introducing market forces into the education service. But there were other pressures as well: not least the desire for more central control (or the desire to diminish the powers of local education authorities). This 'centralism' is sometimes clearly in conflict with the dominant market ideology, and it has been argued that it is difficult to find a coherent set of principles which guide the Act. What it is possible to find, however, is a number of new powers for the Secretary of State (more than 300) and a number of educational terms which gained currency as a result of being associated with the new legislation. All such terms will be in bold type in this essay, and further definitions will be found in Section 2.

Sections 1–25 of the Act were concerned with the National Curriculum and its Assessment. Section 3 gives priority to three subjects – mathematics, science and English – to be known as **core subjects** and seven other compulsory **foundation subjects** (history, geography, technology, music, art, physical education, and a modern language in secondary schools). In Wales, Welsh became a core subject for Welsh-speaking schools, and a foundation subject for non-Welsh-speaking schools (a distinction not always easy to apply in practice). Religious education, the only compulsory requirement under the 1944 Act, continued to be required, but not as part of the National Curriculum: religious education became the responsibility of **Standing Advisory Councils on Religions Education** (SACRE) to be set up by local education authorities.

The Act required that for each foundation subject, there should be a specification of knowledge, skills and understandings, in the form of **Attainment Targets** (ATs) which all pupils of different abilities and maturities are expected to have learned by the end of each **Key Stage** (that is, at age 7, 11, 14 and 16). The curriculum, as opposed to the assessment arrangements, would be specified in **Programmes of Study** (PoS) details of which, like Attainment Targets, would be contained in **Orders** rather than in the Act itself. The National Curriculum and its assessment are legal requirements for all **maintained schools** (but not for private, independent schools).

Section 14 requires the Secretary of State to set up two curriculum councils: the **National Curriculum Council** (NCC) for England and a **Curriculum Council for Wales** (CCW). In addition, the **School Examinations and Assessment Council** (SEAC) was required to cover both countries. The Act obliges the Secretary of State to refer Orders about the curriculum to the National Curriculum Council which is, in turn, obliged to consult local education authorities, teachers' organisations and others about the proposals on or changes to the National Curriculum. The Secretary of State has to publish the National Curriculum Council advice, and if he/she does not follow it, he/she has to say why. The Act also gives the Secretary of State power to demand information from schools and local education authorities, and to insist on the publication of such information. (Later on this was to give rise to the publication of '**league tables**' of local education authorities and of schools – lists in **rank order** showing performance scores on the National Curriculum Assessment.) The original intention was that performance would be reported in terms of subjects and of **profile components** (that is, clusters of Attainment Targets) within each subject, but there was some confusion about how specific Attainment Targets should be; in 1992 Attainment Targets in maths and science were reduced in number and became more like the original idea of a profiles component.

The detailed arrangements for setting up a national scheme was entrusted to a small group chaired by Professor Paul Black – the **Task Group on Assessment and Testing** (TGAT) which produced its first report for the Secretary of State in December 1987. This was eventually accepted by government and became the guidelines for the separate Subject Working Groups set up for each foundation subject. The Task Group on Assessment and

Testing recommended a system of assessment which would rely heavily on teachers' **continuous assessment** (teacher assessment or TA). This would be used in conjunction with **Standard Assessment Tasks** (SATs), which would be externally set but marked by teachers. Standard Assessment Tasks were envisaged not as conventional, paper and pencil tests, but as normal class-room assignments with built-in assessment. But by 1992 a later Secretary of State, Kenneth Clarke, had decided that the Standard Assessment Tasks were 'elaborate nonsense' and demanded a return to more conventional testing. The assessment procedures were intended to be used both **formatively**, to assist teachers in their classroom tasks, and **summatively** at ages 7, 11, 14 and 16 (the end of key stage 1, 2, 3 and 4) to inform parents and others about pupils' progress. The Task Group on Assessment and Testing further recommended that the relation between National Curriculum and assessment should be in the form of **criterion-referencing**: children would be assessed on what they knew and could do in terms of **Statements of Attainment** (SoA) which would define each of ten **Levels** of Attainment for every Attainment within each subject. (In the past, pupils' progress had often been stated in the form of **norm-referencing** – placing a pupil's achieve-ment not in relation to criteria or **standards**, but in terms of how that pupil achieved compared with others in the same class or age group. The new criteria were sometimes (misleadingly) referred to as **bench-marks** (that is, not as rigid age-related standards, but as indicators of desirable goals at ages 7, 11, 14 and 16.

Sections 26–32 of the Act are concerned with the change in policy regarding the admission of pupils to county and voluntary schools – the new doctrine of 'open enrolment'. The purpose of these sections was to increase the power of parents to choose a school. All maintained schools were now compelled to admit pupils up to the limit of their physical capacity, rather than up to a maximum agreed with the local education authority as part of a planned distribution policy. This means that schools have to admit pupils up to their maximum capacity, if parents so choose, even if the result is that other schools are left with non-viable numbers. (The theory is that such 'unpopular' schools will eventually be driven by market forces to close down; in practice, this rarely happens, but unpopular schools become even less attractive.) Parents are recommended to choose schools on the basis of the National Curriculum Assessment results referred to above.

Sections 33–51 are concerned with finance and staffing – in particular with financial delegation away from local education authorities to schools them-selves by means of **formula funding**. The term used by the Department of Education and Science in Circular 7/88 was **local management of schools** (LMS) which some say really means 'less money for schools' because the formula used resulted in many cases in less generous payments to schools than the previous local education authority allocations. As for staffing, the

Act gives more powers to school governors, and removes from local education authorities the power to establish a staff complement for each school.

Sections 52–104 deal with the controversial issue of **grant-maintained schools** (GMS). This is a new category of school which is directly funded by the Department for Education, and is therefore free from local education authority controls and inspections (see Section 2 for more details). Local education authorities, and many others, have opposed grant-maintained schools, because they threaten the whole system of partnership between central and local government in education established by the 1944 Education Act. In practice some local education authorities, where a large number of schools **opt out** and seek GM status, find it impossible to play their traditional role: for each school opting out, the LEA loses a percentage of its own central budget, and eventually loses the ability to pay for some central services.

Section 105 provides a legal basis for the Secretary of State to enter into agreements with sponsors of another new type of school: **city technology colleges** (CTCs). (Strictly speaking there are two new types: Section 105 also refers to 'city colleges for the technology of the arts'.) The Secretary of State is empowered to make grants and provide capital for city technology colleges whose main funding was originally intended to come from industry and commerce (in practice a good deal of the funding has had to come from the Department for Education).

Sections 106–11 define 'free education' and clarifies local education authority responsibilities regarding charges in maintained schools. The legislation had been preceded by a consultative document issued in October 1987.

Section 115 gives governing bodies the responsibility for deciding the length of a **school day**, but certain conditions have to be observed, including consulting parents and the local education authority.

Sections 120–38 deal with changes in **higher education** (HE) and **further education** (FE) and their funding arrangements. The **University Grants Committee** (UGC), a body dominated by senior academics, was replaced by the **Universities Funding Council** (UFC) dominated by lay members, including representatives from industry and commerce. A parallel body for non-university higher education was created: the **Polytechnics and Colleges Funding Council** (PCFC). By 1992 both of the above funding councils had been replaced by a new system of national funding councils (see Section 2): there will be separate **Higher Education Funding Councils** (HEFC) for England, Wales and Scotland (see entry in Section 2).

Sections 139–55 deal with the proposed changes in the finance and government of locally-funded further and higher education. The aim was to increase the autonomy of such institutions (or to decrease the power of local education authorities). It proved to be a short-term measure, because more radical changes (complete independence) came in the early 1990s.

Sections 162–96 were concerned with a dramatic example of restricting the powers of local education authorities – the abolition of the **Inner London Education Authority** (ILEA), the largest of the authorities. The responsibilities of the Inner London Education Authority were divided between the thirteen inner London boroughs.

A number of other sections deal with a variety of other minor reforms – for example, Sections 214–17 outlaw 'bogus degrees' (making the award of such degrees a criminal offence, to be enforced by Weights and Measures Officers). The remaining sections do not, however, entail the use of new terminology.

References

LAWTON, D. (1989) *Education, Culture and the National Curriculum*. Hodder and Stoughton.
MACLURE, S. (1989) *Education Re-Formed* (second edition). Hodder and Stoughton.
Note: NCC and SEAC were replaced by the School Curriculum and Assessment Authority (SCAA) in 1993.

EIGHT

Politics and education; the politics of education

We often hear pleas for education to be kept out of politics. Superficially, this sounds attractive, particularly when examples are given of educational issues being used as 'political footballs'. But on closer analysis it becomes clear that education is essentially a political matter and a legitimate concern of non-educationists, including politicians. To some extent the language of politics is also the language of education.

Education is necessarily a political issue for a number of reasons. First, in all modern societies the education budget takes a large share of the gross national product (GNP): not only do large amounts of money have to be justified (see Essay 4 on accountability), but they also have to be argued for in competition with other political priorities such as the National Health Service and expenditure on defence. Education is 'political' in the sense of being a disputed priority; and within the education budget there will be 'political' debates about competing priorities.

Education is also necessarily political in another sense. The meaning of 'education' and the meaning of many educational terms vary according to ideological context (see Essay 2). The purpose of education and the publicly declared priorities within education are not only the subject of ideological and political debate, but also have different connotations according to who is addressing whom, for what purpose.

In our essay title we have made a distinction between 'politics and education' and 'the politics of education'. The second half of the title implies that we can regard political discussions of education in the same sense as history of education, sociology of education or philosophy of education – that is, a sub-section of educational studies in which political concepts may be applied to the study of education and where the politics of education is regarded as an important aspect of political studies. The politics of education is, however, less well established than most of the other sub-disciplines.

Within the politics of education, one interesting example of political terminology being used to throw light on the education system is 'the control of education'. In this context we would be dealing not necessarily with party politics but with 'politics' with a small 'p' which might be more concerned with power relations within the **Department for Education** (DFE) and **Her Majesty's Inspectorate** (HMI) than with politicians (although it is possible that party politicians might play a role in this struggle). Similarly, the politics of education is often used to include much more local studies of power and control – in which case the term would be, for example, the *micropolitics* of the school (as compared with the *macropolitics* of the whole system).

A remarkable feature of both 'politics and education' and 'the politics of education' has been the emergence in the 1970s and 1980s of a number of political pressure groups (with one exception, right-wing groups) which have set out to influence public opinion on education by publishing papers, tracts and books in a deliberately polemical style.

Perhaps the best known of the right-wing groups is the Centre for Policy Studies (CPS) established by Sir Keith Joseph and Margaret Thatcher in 1974. Even earlier than this, the Critical Quarterly Society (CQS), under the leadership of Brian Cox and Anthony Dyson, had published the first of the **Black Papers** (1969) which was extremely influential in the 1970s. The Adam Smith Institute (ASI), a free market publishing group, was set up in 1977 (two years before the first Thatcher government); as its name suggests, it is primarily concerned with economic issues, but has been greatly influenced by the ideas of F. A. Hayek and has applied *laissez-faire* philosophy to a number of social targets, and its well known *Omega Projects* included an important paper on education.

The proliferation of these groups in the 1980s is puzzling, because many of them purveyed exactly the same message, and had overlapping member-ship: for example, Roger Scruton was a member of the Conservative Philos-ophy Group (CPG) in the 1970s, and has contributed frequently to the publications of the *Hillgate Group*, and is also prominent in the *Education Research Centre*, as well as editing the *Salisbury Review*. It is, however, possible to distinguish two main strands of right-wing 'radicalism' in education: the neo-liberal, free market writers favouring the privatisation of education (the Social Affairs Unit and the Institute of Economic Affairs (IEA) as well as the Adam Smith Institute) and the more traditional neo-conservatives, including Scruton and the Hillgate Group, who are closer to the tradition of 'Tory paternalism' on education. On some questions, such as opposition to com-prehensive education, both strands tend to agree, but on other matters, such as the **National Curriculum**, free marketeers such as Stuart Sexton (Head of the Institute of Economic Affairs Education Unit and formerly Education Advisor to Keith Joseph), would see no need for such an infringe-ment of parental rights, whilst Scruton and others would view the content of education as too important to be left to parental choice and the vagaries of the market.

The only left of centre 'Think Tank' or pressure group to emerge in this period, was the Institute for Public Policy Research (IPPR), headed by Tessa

Blackstone. The IPPR has published a number of moderate, reformist documents on education.

Whilst education is, we suggest, essentially political, there are many educationists who hope that in future years more effort will be made to establish as much consensus as possible within education – that is, try to reach a level of agreement deeper than the ideological conflicts which were so prominent in the period 1979–92 (Lawton, 1992).

References

BALL, S. (1987) *The Micropolitics of the School*. Methuen.
BALL, S. (1990) *Politics and Policy Making in Education*. Routledge and Kegan Paul.
LAWTON, D. (1992) *Education and Politics in the 1990s*. Falmer Press.

NINE

Changes in the language of post-compulsory education and training

The **Education Reform Act** (1988) left a number of problems unsolved, not least in the field of the education and training of young people who would have followed the National Curriculum from age 5 to 16. In 1988 a major problem was the fact that most children not only left school at 16, but many of them then received no further education or training for the rest of their lives.

Sections 120–55 of the Education Reform Act (1988) were concerned with higher and further education, but a number of issues were left unsettled by the Act, necessitating further legislation in 1992. The Act removed polytechnics from local education authority funding and control, and made them part of a national system of higher education: the **binary** line had been destroyed. Larger colleges of further education were similarly removed from the local education authorities.

During 1991 two **White Papers** were produced to take post-compulsory education and training further in the direction of government policy – one clear aim was to make both further education and higher education more competitive and open to market forces. The content of the two White Papers (*Education and Training for the 21st Century* and *Higher Education – a New Framework*, both May 1991) became law as a result of the Further and Higher Education Act passed on 16 March 1992, just before the General Election on 9 April 1992.

Higher education The distinction between university and non-university higher education was abolished, and polytechnics were allowed to be renamed as universities. Funding was no longer to be separated, but regional funding was developed by having separate higher education funding councils for England, Wales and Scotland (with Northern Ireland being kept in close relation). Higher education funding was to be a mixture of market competition (with 'old' and 'new' universities competing for students and for research money, for example) and much tighter central control from the funding councils. **'Quality Assurance'** became a new key term, with a number of interesting sub-categories: **'quality control'** (mechanisms within the universities); **'quality audit'** 'external scrutiny of internal controls' – thus the **Committee of Vice-Chancellors and Principals** (CVCP) own Academic Audit Unit together with the Polytechnics' Council for National Academic Awards (CNAA) were replaced by a **'quality audit unit'** 'which would be independent of funding councils). Part of the function of the new quality audit unit would be to make available 'performance indicator' information about universities to potential students and employers.

Further education/education and training 16 to 19   Another aim was to increase access to higher education. The **age participation** rate was lower in the UK than in most developed countries, and it was government policy to increase the percentage of young people gaining higher education qualifications (as well as vocational qualifications 16 to 19) by the end of the century.

Part of the problem was that the major academic route for young people after the **General Certificate of Secondary Education** (GCSE) was the **General Certificate of Education** (GCE) 'A' level which had existed since 1951 and was regarded by traditionalists (including the Conservative Government) as the 'gold standard', that is as a qualification which was so well established that it should not be changed. On the other hand, for many years this narrow, usually over-specialised curriculum of two or three 'A' level subjects had been criticised not only by educationists but also by employers. There was another disadvantage: 'A' levels produced a diet which was not only unbalanced but also part of a failure system. Although only the most able 16-year-old students begin 'A' level courses, about a quarter of them fail to achieve a pass of any kind after two years' study, and have nothing to show for their two years' full-time course.

Throughout the 1960s a number of abortive attempts had been made to reform the 'A' level curriculum: Qualifying and Further **(Q and F)** examinations in 1969; Normal and Further **(N and F)** in 1979; Intermediate (I) examinations in 1980. All had been rejected for various reasons, one of them being the problem of retaining three-year Honours degree programmes in universities if the standards at age 18 were lowered. In 1984 the Department of Education and Science proposed its own solution: 'A' levels would remain, but would be supplemented by courses of the same standard but which would require only half the content and study time – **'Advanced Supplementary'** (AS) syllabuses were drawn up by the Examination Boards. The intention was that 'AS' papers would be used partly to contrast with 'A' levels and partly to complement 'A' level subjects in a way which would provide a broader curriculum by means of four or more subjects being taken (a mixture of 'A' and 'AS').

There was another complicating factor for the 16 to 19 age group: since the mid-1960s there was an increasing number of students who wanted to continue studying beyond age 16 but who were regarded as insufficiently academic for 'A' level courses ('the new sixth form'). Schools were faced with the problem of offering something worthwhile, and in 1976 a Certificate of Extended Education (CEE) was established experimentally, but it did not meet with the Department of Education and Science's approval, was abolished in 1983 and replaced by the **Certificate of Pre-Vocational Education** (CPVE). Some students, especially those in further education, may also have taken a variety of vocational qualifications. In 1986 the **National Council for Vocational Qualifications** (NCVQ) was established by government to coordinate the 'jungle' of vocational courses and to preserve standards.

The 'A' level route, however, was still regarded as unsatisfactory, despite the 'AS' innovation (which was not proving to be very popular with schools and colleges). A committee was set up under Dr Gordon Higginson which recommended (in the *Higginson Report*, 1988) a five-subject structure – a mixture of 'AS' and 'A', but the 'A' levels would be leaner and tougher, with less detailed content but without lowering standards. This proposal was generally thought to be a modest step in the right direction, but was vetoed by the Conservative Government on the grounds that it was a threat to the 'gold standard'.

The Government's solution (in the White Paper 1991 and the Education Act 1992) was to preserve the 'A' and 'AS' route but to promote the development of an alternative, more vocational, pathway by means of courses under the aegis of the NCVQ. Some students already reached university by means of **Business and Technology Education Council** (BTEC) qualifications (which were now part of the responsibility of NCVQ), but the numbers were extremely small. The proposed solution was to develop a new kind of **National Vocational Qualification** (NVQ) which, unlike existing NVQ qualifications, would be available in schools on a full-time basis: this was to be called the **General National Vocational Qualification** (GNVQ). Pilot courses were rapidly developed, starting in 1992 in the hope that this alternative would quickly become popular. At the same time, it was proposed that the provision of vocational courses should be extended and upgraded to standards set by NCVQ.

These reforms were welcomed in principle, as a means of extending education and training for the 16 to 19 age group and increasing access to higher education, but were generally considered to be unsatisfactory as a long-term solution. The academic 'A' level route is still very unsuitable (lacking breadth and balance) even for academic students, and there will inevitably be problems of comparability with the new GNVQ. Many educationists would have preferred an integrated route post-16 rather than two sharply divided routes. The existing plan provides for 'switching' from 'A' to GNVQ and vice versa, and even for common modules, but for most students the likelihood is that they will be labelled as 'A' level or vocational. The Institute for Public Policy Research (IPPR) had in July 1990 recommended a much more radical reform on the grounds that tinkering with the present system would be doomed to failure. *A British 'Baccalaureat': Ending the Division between Education and Training* (IPPR, 1990) recommended that 'A' level and vocational courses should be abolished and that all young people would study in **tertiary colleges**, and their curriculum would consist of three areas: social and human sciences; natural sciences and technology; and arts, language and literature. This proposal would have been much closer to the broader curriculum required in many European countries. This kind of solution, although supported by many other organisations, including the Confederation of British Industry (CBI), was not accepted by government. It remains to be seen how well the dual system ('A' levels plus GNVQ) 16 to 19 will develop.

The world of NCVQ has its own language derived from the policies and practices of training rather than education. (It is financed by the Department of Employment.) There is a basic notion of occupational competence which can be assessed at an appropriate level by 'outcomes' which will be 'performance-based' often in the form of skills or clusters of skills, some of which will be assessed by supervisors in the workplace. The extension of these terms (and practices) to GNVQ courses as a route to higher education is interesting.

References

CONFEDERATION OF BRITISH INDUSTRY (CBI) (1990) *Investors in People*. CBI.
FINEGOLD, D. *et al.*, (1990) *A British Baccalaureat: Ending the Division Between Education and Training*. Institute for Public Policy Research.
HIGGINSON COMMITTEE (1988) *Advancing 'A' Levels*. HMSO.

Section 2

THE DICTIONARY: AN ALPHABETICAL LIST *of* DEFINITIONS

INTRODUCTION

Here in Section 2 we provide a list of words, in alphabetical order, which are either peculiar to education or have a specific, technical meaning when used in educational contexts.

We have called this section 'A dictionary of educational terms'. It would be pretentious to call such a slim volume 'An encyclopaedia of education', but our intention is to be as comprehensive as space allows, and in order to achieve greater coherence, and where we think it helpful, we have made cross-references (words shown in bold type) to other items in Section 2, and sometimes we have advised reading one of the essays in Section 1.

a

ability The 1944 Education Act stated that children should be educated according to age, aptitude and ability. Age caused little difficulty, but it was never clear what precisely was meant by aptitude and ability, although the phrase was occasionally used to justify selection for different kinds of **secondary school**. It may have been the intention to link ability with **academic** ability, and aptitude with a more specific aptitude for a technical **curriculum**. There is now a tendency to use ability in a more general way and to confine aptitude to more specific kinds of ability; both words are closer to 'capacity' than to 'attainment' – it is quite possible to have high ability but low **attainment**, achievement or performance.

ability groupings Most education systems group children mainly according to their age. Some countries e.g. Japan make the assumption that it is reasonable to expect uniform achievements; other countries, including the UK expect differences. (*see also* **mixed-ability grouping, setting, streaming, unstreaming**)

Abitur The German examination for 18- to 19-year-old school leavers. Like the **GCE** 'A' level in England, it is a university entrance qualification as well as being recognised as a general educational qualification for entry into some kinds of employment. Unlike the 'A' level it is a broadly based examination, more like the French **Baccalauréat**.

academic (1) A teacher or researcher in higher education. (2) An adjective applied to scholarly activities, sometimes as a term of abuse.

Academic Audit Unit (AAU) Responding to political demands for greater **accountability** in UK universities, the **Committee of Vice-Chancellors and Principals** (CVCP) set up its own independent AAU in 1989. It was based at the University of Birmingham with a small permanent directorate and about twenty-five temporary academic staff seconded from universities to form academic audit teams to visit universities to scrutinise documents and check records. The overall purpose of the AAU was to look at existing methods for monitoring academic standards, to spread 'good practice' and to keep the whole system under review notionally, including the operation of the external examiner system. Early in its history, the AAU was also concerned to ensure the maintenance of standards at a time of expanding student numbers; and also to develop **performance indicators** for good teaching. The AAU, together with the **Council for National Academic Awards** CNAA, were replaced by a single quality audit unit as a result of the **Further and Higher Education Act** (1992). (*see* Section 1, Essay 9)

academic board A group of academic staff in a college or university normallly elected in order to regulate academic affairs; usually one of the most senior committees possibly responsible only to the senior governing body of the institution. Academic boards rarely exist in schools, but it is sometimes suggested that such an organisation would be highly desirable.

academic disciplines (*see* **disciplines, academic**)

Access course Many universities and polytechnics are prepared to accept students without 'standard qualifications' (i.e. a minimum of two **'A' levels**) provided that they can be satisfied that the students have reached appropriate standards by other means. One of the alternative routes is an 'Access' course, run either by the higher education institution itself or by another approved college. (*see also* **Access Course Recognition Group**)

Access Course Recognition Group (ACRG) The ACRG was set up by the **Committee of Vice-Chancellors and Principals** (CVCP) and the **Council for National Academic Awards** (CNAA) in 1989, at the invitation of the Secretary of State for Education and Science, to provide a framework of national 'recognition' of Access courses to **higher education**. The ACRG authorises certain higher education institutions to be 'Authorised Validating Agencies' (AVA). AVAs can approve Access courses which are regarded as an appropriate preparation for admission to higher education. ACRG does not scrutinise courses, but oversees processes of **validation** and awards 'kitemarks'.

accountability A word imported from business and commerce into education during the 1960s, especially in the USA. Accountability reflects an increased public concern over educational issues such as **curriculum** and not simply the large sums of money involved. (*see* Section 1, Essay 4)

accreditation A process by which one academic institution, perhaps a university, officially approves the awards of another institution and guarantees that they are of a certain standard. For example, the **National Council for Vocational Qualifications** (NCVQ) (which does not itself offer courses) gives public recognition to the awards of other bodies such as the **Business and Technology Education Council** (BTEC).

action research A study of a particular social situation (which might or might not be concerned with education) in which the intention is not simply to understand and report, but to bring about certain improvements. A well-known educational example concerned the study of educational priority areas (EPA). (*see also* **research and development**)

active learning Learning that encourages the student to do more than receive information from a teacher or textbook, memorise the information and reproduce it. Active learning would require the student to make something, be involved in a **project** or experiment. When revising, for example, students are often advised to 'do' something such as construct their own notes, rather than just read. (*see also* **experiental learning, passive learning**)

active vocabulary The words that a child (or adult) is able to *use* in speech or writing (or both), not just recognise and understand. (*see also* **passive vocabulary**)

admission to school See 'rising fives'.

adult education Courses of an informal character provided for adults in a range of interests: these are usually held in institutions different from colleges and universities attended by school leavers. They range from leisure pursuits to higher degree qualifications. (*see also* **community college, continuing education, recurrent education, village college**)

adult literacy The setting up of an Adult Literacy Research Agency in 1975 was the first official recognition of the large proportion of the adult population in need of **literacy** skills. A national campaign was mounted and local authorities and voluntary agencies were given short-term financial assistance in starting their schemes. In 1978, an Adult Literacy Unit was established but was replaced in 1980 by an **Adult Literacy and Basic Skills Unit** (ALBSU), which covers other areas such as English as a second language and numeracy. (*see also* **National Institute of Adult Continuing Education**)

advanced level examination ('A' level) The advanced level of the **General Certificate of Education** (GCE) is an examination taken by more able pupils, usually after a two-year period of study following the **General Certificate of Secondary Education** (GCSE). It is closely associated with the traditional sixth form of a school. A wide range of subjects is available at 'A' level, though candidates normally choose two or three to study. This specialisation and narrowness has been criticised, but attempts at its reform have not been successful. Passes in at least two 'A' level subjects are normally required for admission to university. (*see* Section 1, Essay 9)

Advanced Supplementary (GCE) (AS) In 1984 the Department of Education and Science proposed a new kind of **GCE** examination – Advanced Supplementary or AS. AS courses were designed to be at **'A' level** standard but covering only 50 per cent of the content. The intention was to broaden the typical student's curriculum by encouraging a programme of two A plus two AS subjects in place of the traditional three A programme. Originally two kinds of AS were envisaged: complementary and contrasting, but that distinction did not survive the test of time.

Advisory Centre for Education (ACE) Founded in 1960, ACE is a non-profit making organisation, stemming from the Consumers' Association, which disseminates information on many aspects of schooling.

advisory teachers Experienced teachers who are appointed or seconded for a short term by a local education authority to advise school staff. They work closely with advisers but have the advantage of recent classroom experience. (*see also* **advisers** for changes since 1992)

aesthetic A term increasingly used in discussions of a balanced curriculum to indicate those subjects or areas of experience by means of which a pupil is introduced to the world of 'beauty' (e.g. art, music, literature). The basis for this distinction dates back to the German philosopher, Immanuel Kant (1724–1804). An opposite point of view was taken in England by William Morris and John Ruskin, who did not wish to accept the separation of art and morality.

affective In Benjamin Bloom's *Taxonomy of Educational Objectives* (1956) a distinction is made between the **cognitive**, the **psychomotor** and the affective domains; the affective being concerned with emotions, feelings and attitudes rather than with cognitive processes or physical skills.

after-school activities Extra-curricular activities which often take the form of clubs, societies and groups and form an important addition to the normal school day. The range is very wide and can include music, drama, sports as well as homework clubs. Teachers play a leading role in this work.

age: chronological and mental Chronological age is the every-day usage of an individual's age defined in terms of time since date of birth. For educational purposes, it is sometimes useful to compare chronological age with mental age or **reading age**. Mental age is calculated by comparing a child's score on an **intelligence test** with the average scores of children. For example, a child might have a chronological age of 8 and a mental age of 10, that is, she/he is mentally advanced for her/his years and is capable of reasoning at the same level as the average 10-year-old – she/he would thus have an above average IQ. (*see also* **intelligence**)

age of transfer Up to 1964, the age of transfer from primary to secondary schools was between 10½ and 12 years of age. The Secretary of State in 1964 encouraged experiments in different sorts of schools, especially the middle school, which recruits pupils of between 8 and 12 or 13. The present situation is very confused: throughout the country, transfer occurs at many different ages according to the educational planning of local education authorties. The problem has been mitigated, to some extent, by the **National Curriculum** (1988) structure which introduces the concept of **'Key Stage'**; Key Stage 2 finishes at age 11 and Key Stage 3 (age 11 to 14) prescribes a 'secondary curriculum' for all pupils.

age participation rate (APR) A term used in calculating demand for higher education (and sometimes further education). The age participation rate for higher education is calculated by showing the number of 18-year-olds who enter higher education as a proportion of the whole group.

aggregation The process of converting several scores on smaller objectives into a single score. (For example, in the field of National Curriculum Assessment, the scores for the **Statements of Attainment** within **Attainment Targets** have to be added up (aggregated) in order to arrive at the appropriate **level** of **attainment**.)

agreed syllabus The **1944 Education Act** stipulated that local education authorities, together with Church and teacher representatives, should draw up an agreed non-denominational syllabus in religious education. Authorities were not restricted to using their own syllabus: they could borrow a syllabus developed by another authority. (*see also* **Standing Advisory Conference on Christian Education (SACRE)**)

aims Statement of educational intentions or purposes of a more general nature than **objectives**. Although all three terms (aims, goals and objectives) are sometimes used synonymously, they are increasingly used distinctively to represent three levels of intention from the most general aims to more specific objectives. 'Aims' became unfashionable with educational theorists in the 1960s and were avoided in the **Plowden Report**, but in the 1980s philosophers have returned to the concept. (*see* Section 1, Essay 2)

allowances Allowances are given to teachers who meet one or more criteria, usually connected with additional responsibilities. The allowances are graded A to E.

alternative schooling A general term used to indicate a form of schooling which is different from that offered by the state or other traditional agencies. Alternative schools are usually, but not necessarily, associated with radical and progressive views of education, such as the avoidance of a formal curriculum and formal teaching methods. (*see also* **compulsory education, deschooling, free schools, home schooling**)

ancillary staff Non-teaching staff (NTS) of an institution who assist in its everyday running, for instance, media resources officers and laboratory technicians or **information technology** (IT) officers.

annual maintenance grant (AMG) The annual sum provided to **grant-maintained schools** for running costs. The direct AMG is equivalent to what a school would have received from its local education authority under local management; to this is added the central AMG to pay for the services previously provided by the local education authority before the school opted out.

appraisal A system for assessing the work of teachers, headteachers, as well as the teaching staff in universities. Appraisal may be connected with schemes of staff development; they may or may not be connected with promotion and/ or pay increases.

aptitude An individual's potential **ability** to acquire skills or knowledge (i.e. not existing achievement or ability). For example, there are tests which are designed to indicate mechanical aptitude or mathematical aptitude. One problem of such tests is, however, that although they are intended to be predictive (i.e. indicating potential rather than actual achievement), they necessarily involve performance now, which may be partly dependent on **skills** or techniques already learned. In practice it is difficult to distinguish between aptitudes and abilities, despite the conceptual differences between them and the desirability for some purposes of establishing potential (i.e. aptitude) rather than present achievement (ability). (*see also* **attainment test, performance test, vocational guidance**)

articled teachers (AT)   The articled teachers scheme was introduced by the Department of Education and Science in 1991 partly as a way of encouraging a more school-based version of initial teacher training (ITT), and partly to offer an alternative to the two established routes – **Bachelor of Education** (BEd) and **Postgraduate Certificate of Education** (PGCE). The scheme was available to suitably qualified applicants – graduates or those with at least two years of higher education in 'teaching subjects'; most of their training would be school-based but some 'theory' would be involved. In some respects the course resembled a part-time PGCE course spread over two years. At first local education authorities were responsible for some of the costs involved, but in 1992 the Department for Education (DFE) announced that from April 1993 the AT bursary would be entirely covered by government funding under the Local Education Authority Training Grants Scheme (LEATGS) (*see* **teacher training**).

Assessment of Performance Unit (APU)   Established by the Department of Education and Science in 1974, its terms of reference were 'to promote the development of methods of assessing and monitoring the achievement of children at school and to seek to identify the incidence of under-achievement.' Much of the work of the Unit has been concerned with the first task. It set out to assess children's development in seven areas – aesthetic, mathematics, science, social and personal, physical, language and modern languages. In 1978 tests were administered covering the performance in mathematics of 11- and 15-year-olds in England and Wales, followed by tests in foreign languages, English and science. It was decided not to proceed with tests of social and personal development or aesthetic development. The Unit was eventually abandoned because it was replaced by much of the assessment work connected with the National Curriculum.

assignment   A task given to a pupil or student by a teacher either as part of a learning programme or as a means of **assessment** (or both). Assignments are usually set out as individual exercises, often for **homework**, but cooperative assignments are sometimes set for completion by two or more students. In primary schools 'assignment' tends to be used with much the same meaning as **project**.

assistant   A person from abroad, either a student or a graduate, attached to a secondary school for a period of a year in order to help in the teaching of a foreign language. There is an official system of exchange for assistants sponsored by the Department for Education (DFE).

Assisted Places Scheme (APS)   This scheme, which was first included in the 1974 Conservative Party manifesto, became part of the 1980 Education Act and was designed to assist academically able children whose families could not otherwise afford the tuition fees to attend one of the independent secondary schools in the scheme. The age of entry is usually 11 to 13, though many are admitted at sixth form stage. The scheme came into operation in September 1981 and has been criticised by advocates of **comprehensive schools** on the grounds that it 'creams off' some of the most able pupils from those schools. (*see also* **independent school**)

Association for Colleges (AFC) A new organisation representing further education colleges. The AFC absorbs the Association of Colleges for Further and Higher Education (ACFHE), the Association of Principals, the Association of Principals of Sixth Form Colleges (APVIC), the Further Education Campaign Group, and the Tertiary Colleges Association.

Association of County Councils (ACC) The forty-seven member counties of the ACC provide the major services for nearly thirty-one million people living in England and Wales. The Association, founded in 1974 and formerly the County Councils Association, puts forward policies for county government after receiving approval from its executive committee. It discusses issues with ministers, civil servants and MPs and appears before select committees. Central to the ACC's work is the problem of finance. It argues its case with the government through the Consultative Council on local government finance and at officer level through technical working groups. It also takes part in national negotiations on pay and conditions of service for local authority employees. (*see also* **Council of Local Education Authorities**)

Association of Masters and Mistresses Association (AMMA) *See* **Association of Teachers and Lecturers**.

Association of Metropolitan Authorities (AMA) The AMA, which was formed in 1974, is funded by subscription from the metropolitan authorities. Its task is to keep them informed of what is happening in government circles and to represent the authorities at governmental and parliamentary levels. Each major area of interest has its own service committee, and specialist staff deal with education, planning, housing, social services, and legal matters. (*see also* **Association of County Councils, Council of Local Education Authorities**)

Association of Principals in Sixth Form Colleges (APVIC) During the 1970s and 1980s the idea of a sixth form college taking students aged between 16 and 18 from several comprehensive schools in a district grew in popularity. The heads of such colleges tended to be called **Principals**, and formed themselves into a discussion group/pressure group to ensure their specialist requirements were kept under review.

Association of Teachers and Lecturers (ATL) The Association originated from an amalgamation of the Assistant Masters Association and the Association of Assistant Mistresses in 1978 when it took the name Assistant Masters and Mistresses Association (AMMA). In 1993, to reflect the growing number of members from the further education sector, it changed its name to the Association of Teachers and Lecturers. Membership consists of about 120,000 teachers. It is non-party politically and is not affiliated to the Trades Union Congress. The Association lays great stress upon professionalism and equal opportunities for men and women. (*see also* **teachers' unions**)

Association of University Teachers (AUT) In 1909 a meeting was called in Liverpool 'to consider a proposal to form an association for bringing the members of the junior staff more in touch with one another and with the life of the University.' From this sprang the AUT, which now represents the majority of university teachers and related associated administrative grades in professional and salary matters. (*see also* **teachers' unions**)

attainment The present (i.e. achieved) learning of a particular skill or area of knowledge as demonstrated by evidence of some kind, including the evidence of teacher assessment. 'Attainment' should be regarded as different from 'aptitude'.

Attainment Target (AT) In the National Curriculum (1988) each subject is sub-divided into meaningful areas (e.g. in English, speaking and listening, reading, writing). These sub-divisions of a subject are referred to as Attainment Targets. Each AT is divided into ten levels, and each **level** is identified by one or more **Statements of Attainment** (SoA). (*see* Section 1, Essay 7)

attainment test A test which is designed to measure the degree of **learning** which has already been achieved in a particular subject area or skill, rather than the potential ability of an individual which might be measured by a specific **aptitude test**. (*see also* **performance test**)

audio-visual aids (AVA) Equipment for using recorded sound and visual images in schools and other educational institutions. A distinction is sometimes made between AVA hardware (equipment such as film projectors, television screens and audio players) and the software (e.g. films, audio tapes, film strips, slides). Posters, wallcharts and other display materials are included in AVA, but not books. (*see also* **educational media, education technology, educational television**)

audit A term borrowed from the world of commerce and accounting to indicate a means of publicly checking standards in education institutions, especially universities. English universities have tended to stress their tradition of independence or autonomy, despite the fact that (with the exception of Buckingham) they now all receive large sums of money from the State. In the early 1980s the **Committee of Vice-Chancellors and Principals** (CVCP) set up its own review – the Reynolds Committee – to make recommendations about procedures for monitoring and maintaining standards. The Reynolds Report drew up a code of good practice which was discussed by all universities and largely adopted by them. Part of the code was a set of recommendations about the duties of **external**

examiners (a central part of the university system for degrees of all kinds). In addition, an **Academic Audit Unit** (AAU) was established in 1990, based at the University of Birmingham, with a brief to audit each university every three years. Twenty-three senior academics were seconded to the AAU to visit universities and to comment on the structures and mechanisms by which universities themselves 'assure the quality' of their courses and awards. The AAU did not inspect teaching, but scrutinised the documents relating to programmes to see what steps were taken to review the courses, including feedback from students and external examiners. After each three-day audit, a confidential report was sent to the **Vice-Chancellor**. The audit system seemed to be working well, but the AAU together with the very different **Council for National Academic Awards** (CNAA), which had been concerned with polytechnics, were replaced in 1992 by the Government's own system of quality assurance. (*see also* **Audit Commission, quality audit**)

Audit Commission An independent body established by the Government to scrutinise publicly funded services in order to encourage greater effectiveness and accountability.

auditor/auditor-moderator The school assessment arrangements for 1993 require local education authorities to appoint auditors to be responsible for setting and maintaining standards at **Key Stage** 1. It seemed to be felt that in the past local education authority moderators had not been sufficiently authoritative. From 1993 the auditor's role included developing teachers' assessment skills as well as adjudicating where there is disagreement within a school. In addition to local education authority auditors there are independent agencies for grant-maintained, independent and overseas schools. Any independent school participating in Key Stage 1 assessment must have its **Standard Assessment Task** results validated by an agency.

aural Aural refers to the ears and to hearing: as in 'aural training' which is designed to teach partially-hearing children to identify speech sounds. Because the two words have the same pronunciation, 'aural' is sometimes confused with 'oral' (which refers to speech).

autistic Autistic children appear to be unable or unwilling to communicate with other individuals including their own parents. Even if such children are of average or above average intelligence, they are likely to be educationally **retarded**; in the past they would probably have been considered to be mentally sub-normal or classified as feeble-minded. The causes of autism are not known, but researches in the field of special education have established improved methods of teaching autistic children, some of whom have been able to make considerable progress. Considerable claims have been made for the Hungarian Peto method, and in February 1992 the Spastics Society set up a Peto Centre in London. (*see also* **retardation, special needs**)

autonomy One of the aims of education in a democratic society is said to be the development of a pupil's ability to make rational decisions for him or herself 'autonomously' rather than to simply carry out instructions. 'Moral autonomy' is the highest level of moral development. (*see also* **moral development**)

b

baccalauréat A school leaving examination in French secondary schools. General *lycées* offer a general *Baccalauréat* and the technical *lycées* offer the *Baccalauréat Technologiques*. These general and technological *Baccalauréates* are not of equal prestige. In 1985 a third type, a four-year vocational course followed by the *Baccalaureat Professionnel* was introduced. (*see also* **International Baccalaureate, Technological Baccalaureate**)

Bachelor of Education (BEd) It was recommended in the **Robbins Report** (1963) that teaching should become an all graduate profession. By the end of the 1970s Teacher's Certificate courses had been replaced by three- or four-year courses leading to the award of a Bachelor of Education **degree**. This degree includes a professional teaching qualification and may be taken at a large number of colleges of higher education and **university departments of education.** Courses must be approved by the **Council for the Accreditation of Teacher Education** (CATE); they will include curriculum subject studies, educational and professional studies, school experience and **teaching practice**. Most students preparing for teaching careers in primary schools follow this 'concurrent' pattern of initial teacher education and training. Applicants for BEd courses are expected to have a good general education and will normally be required to have passed GCSE in English and Mathematics, at an appropriate level, together with two subjects at GCE 'A' level. Some BEd degrees have been renamed Bachelor of Arts (BA) with professional qualifications. Several institutions of higher education also offer a BEd degree for serving teachers who hold a certificate qualification but wish to achieve graduate status. In-service BEd courses focus largely on the academic study of education. Such courses have also proved to be suitable for teachers from overseas who are seeking to upgrade their professional qualifications.

backwardness Educational backwardness refers to a child whose attainment in the basic skills of reading and arithmetic falls below the levels of achievement of those in his or her age group irrespective of intelligence. Backwardness should, therefore, be distinguished from educational **retardation** which arises, in the main, from low intelligence. Backwardness is capable of remediation but teachers have to be alert to a wide range of causative factors which may be physical, emotional and environmental. (*see also* **retardation, special educational needs**)

banding The division of a school year group into two, three or four bands, mainly on the criterion of ability, such as verbal reasoning or reading tests. Each band is sub-divided into a number of classes, though not necessarily of equal **ability**. Aimed at giving schools a balanced intake, in practice, there are often widely different proportions of pupils between the bands. (*see also* **mixed ability groupings, setting, streaming**)

basic English A phrase which ought to be used as a technical term rather than as a parallel to basic maths, basic science, etc. Basic English was developed between 1926 and 1930 by C. K. Ogden as a possible international language. Its basis was the listing of 850 commonly used key words which could communicate all ideas and any kind of message. However, it was increasingly used as a means of teaching English to foreigners rather than as a complete language in its own right. It was also used in some studies of '**readability**' and graded reading.

basic skills Normally used to refer to those skills, especially in the three Rs, which provide the kind of competency such as being able to add up and multiply, which are thought to be necessary for participation in everyday adult life. The fallacy of this approach, for example in reading skills, is that skills are divorced from content, so that first the child is taught to read and at a later stage is taught to read something useful. A more correct use of 'basic skills' would be to refer to those skills in any subject which are necessary to proceed to more advanced skills in the same area.

behavioural objective A specific statement of intent by a teacher about the changes in behaviour that a student must show as a result of a teaching programme. The emphasis is in pupil or student behaviour rather than teacher behaviour or teacher intention. An essential feature of a behavioural objective is that the behavioural change must be specified in advance, in terms of student behaviour which can be measured. Opponents of the behavioural objectives approach criticise this view of **curriculum** planning for a number of reasons, including the suggestion that teachers will tend to concentrate on what is easily tested, that is, the most trivial aspects of a subject. Another criticism is that human learning is a much more complex process than this simplified view would appear to suggest. (*see also* **objectives**)

benchmark A term used in education to indicate a certain kind of **standard**, but which was originally borrowed from surveying. The original meaning was a mark cut into a rock (or other permanent feature) which could be used as a point of reference for levelling. In education a benchmark normally means a standard which is easily recognised and about which little dispute is possible. Few exist in education.

bilateral school A school in which any two of three main elements of **secondary**

education, i.e. grammar, technical or modern, were organised in clear defined sides. Pupils, though on the same site, remained in their allocated courses during their secondary school life. Some local authorities after the Second World War retained separate grammar schools, confining bilateral schools to the technical and secondary modern streams. (*see also* **bipartitite system**, **tripartite system**)

bilingualism A term used for pupils who are fluent in more than one language. Bilingual may also be a euphemism for children who begin school knowing little English.

binary system In a speech given at Woolwich Polytechnic in 1965, Anthony Crosland, then Secretary of State for Education, announced the Labour Government's acceptance of a plan to develop a system of **higher education** within the further education sector, separate from the university sector. In 1966, the Government's White Paper, *A Plan for Polytechnics and Other Colleges: Higher Education in the Further Education System* substantially added weight to the argument, leading to the establishment of thirty **polytechnics** in the next six years. Margaret Thatcher's White Paper *Education: A Framework for Expansion*, published in 1972, endorsed the binary policy, recommending that polytechnics should play a leading role in the development of higher education in the 1970s. The Further and Higher Education Act (1992) granted university status to polytechnics. However, **colleges of higher education** seeking university status under the Act have to meet stricter criteria than existing polytechnics and argue that a new binary divide has been created. (*see* Section 1, Essay 9)

bipartite system A system consisting of selective and non-selective schools, usually of the **grammar** and **secondary modern** type respectively.

Black Papers The title adopted for a series of occasional publications which first appeared in 1969 attacking modern teaching methods, the **Plowden** philosophy, the alleged decline in educational standards and **comprehensive** schools. They advocated the retention of selection for secondary education, and the provision of super schools for the gifted. Contributors consisted of academics, teachers, writers, and politicians holding right-wing views, including G. H. Bantock, Rhodes Boyson, C. B. Cox, A. E. Dyson, Kingsley Amis, Cyril Burt and Jacques Barzun. Many of the issues aired in the Black Papers have subsequently been taken up and amplified by such organisations as the National Council for Educational Standards (NCES), the Centre for Policy Studies (CPS), the Institute of Economic Affairs (IEA) and the Hillgate Group. (*see* Section 1, Essay 8)

block release A period of time granted by employers to their workers in which to pursue study leading to a vocational qualification. These courses are usually held in **colleges of further education**.

boarding school Predominantly found in the independent sector of education, boarding schools normally require their pupils to be resident during term-time.

Special houses belonging to the school accommodate the pupils under the supervision of a master or mistress. In recent years the strict division between boys' and girls' boarding schools has been weakened: now accommodation is often provided within a school for both sexes. A recent survey by **Her Majesty's Inspectorate** (HMI) has shown that of the seven million pupils in England, fewer than two per cent are boarders. Weekly boarding is becoming increasingly popular. In the State sector, the majority of such provision is for children with special needs. (*see also* **day school, house system**)

Board of Education Set up in 1900 in order to meet the need for a single central authority in education, one of its main functions was to put into effect the provisions of the 1902 Education Act and ensure that the new **local education authorities** provided well maintained and efficient schools. It also administered grants, withholding them from authorities failing to comply with the Board's requirements. The Board was also responsible for establishing schemes for the constitution of education committees and making orders for voluntary school managers. In 1944, the Board was superseded by the **Ministry of Education**.

borderline (1) Those points on a scale of marks near (i.e. on either side of) cut-off points. For example, if the pass/fail cut-off point is a mark of 40, then the range of marks 36 to 44 might be regarded as borderline. Similarly, in the marking of **honours degrees** there would be a cut-off point or mark for first class-upper second, but the range of marks either side of the cut-off point would be regarded as borderline and normally subject to special scrutiny. (2) Candidates who fall into the category near the cut-off point are sometimes referred to as borderline.

brain drain A tendency for highly educated professionals to leave the home country in order to work abroad. There are a variety of reasons for such a move, including improved salary, working conditions, or the opportunity for recognition of one's achievements. In recent years, the term has been extended to cover those highly qualified graduates who leave the country because they are unable to find suitable employment within the UK.

brain storming A technique, originating in the USA, designed to encourage creative solutions to a problem or series of problems. A group of colleagues meet to discuss a problem, but agree to suspend criticism until the concluding session. The theory is that by removing the fear of criticism, ideas flow more readily and much more creative solutions are generated.

British and Foreign School Society The first public meeting of 'The Society for Promoting the Royal British or Lancasterian System for the Education of the Poor' was held in 1808. Joseph Lancaster's system, embracing a complete scheme of primary instruction, was unsectarian though Christian, and attracted many influential supporters, including Lord Byron and James Mill. It included provision at Borough Road for training monitors. The Society was reorganised as the British and Foreign Society in 1812. Flourishing societies were established not only in Great Britain but on the continent and throughout the Empire. (*see also* **British Schools**)

British Association for the Advancement of Science (BAAS) Commonly called the British Association, it was established in 1831 by a small group of scientists who were concerned to ensure that science and technology made their maximum contribution to the life of society. Its main platform is the annual conference, held in different centres of Britain, which meets in seventeen different sections. The conference proceedings, which are published, are intended to inform people of recent scientific advances and to stimulate public debate.

British Council The Council was established in 1934 to develop closer cultural relations and to promote a wider knowledge of Britain in other countries. The majority of its funding is provided by the Foreign Office and the Commonwealth Office. A large part of its activities is devoted to education, such as the teaching of English, providing educational assistance in developing countries and maintaining and running libraries. The Council is represented in more than eighty countries.

British Education Index (BEI) A quarterly publication listing and analysing by subject content all articles on education appearing in periodicals published in the British Isles

British School A shortened term for nonconformist schools established by the **British and Foreign School Society** from 1814. The majority of them became state schools after the 1870 Education Act.

British Standard BS 5750 The British Standard on ' quality systems' was originally devised for contracts in which two parties were involved either with the manufacture of a product or the delivery of a service. It is now being awarded to **colleges of further education** and training organisations who match up to the criteria. The scheme affords the opportunity for institutions to raise **standards**.

Bryce Report A Royal Commission was appointed in 1894 'to consider the best methods of establishing a well organised system of secondary education in England.' The Commission, chaired by James Bryce, recommended in its Report the following year three major reforms: the need for a central authority for secondary education under a **Minister for Education**; the extension to local authorities of responsibility for secondary as well as elementary education; and the provision of scholarships to provide a **ladder of opportunity** for elementary pupils. It also noted the comparatively meagre supply of secondary school places for girls. Although the recommendations were not adopted, they were influential in subsequent changes made at the beginning of this century. (*see also* **eleven plus examination, girls' education**)

bulge A metaphor used to indicate the increase in the number of pupils reaching a stage in the educational process. The term was used in the UK to indicate the growing demand for school places resulting from the increased number of births immediately following the Second World War. The bulge was responsible for the shortage of teachers and overcrowded classrooms in the early 1950s; but when the bulge passed out of the system, the problem of falling rolls produced the reverse effect, namely too many teachers and schools having to be closed. The bulge also caused problems subsequently in the higher education sector. There was a second but less dramatic bulge beginning in 1958.

Bullock Report The Committee of Inquiry appointed in 1972 by the Secretary of State for Education and Science chaired by Lord (then Sir Alan) Bullock was given three tasks: to consider, in relation to schools, all aspects of teaching the use of English, including reading, writing and speech; to report on how present practice might be improved; and to suggest ways in which arrangements for monitoring the general level of attainment in these skills could be introduced. In the Committee's Report, issued in 1975 under the title *A Language for Life*, it stated that every teacher should be a teacher of English, but linked this with the need for a systematic policy in schools. Language across the curriculum was advocated, starting with pre-school children and continuing through the secondary stage. Together with a recommended increase in resources for English, especially in secondary schools, greater in-service facilities for teachers were necessary. (*see also* **language deficit**)

bullying A survey of 4000 English children carried out between 1984 and 1986 claimed that over one-third of them had been bullied at school. The Elton Report on Discipline (1989) stated that bullying was 'a problem that is widespread and tends to be ignored by teachers.' It recommended that school staff should be more alert to signs of bullying and should take firm appropriate action: systems should also be devised to support the victims. Evidence about bullying is vague and contradictory, but it tends to take place outside the classroom; boys rather than girls are more likely to be the targets; and bullying is less common in schools where there is order and **discipline**. (*see also* **disruptive units, exclusions**)

bursar (1) Originally a treasurer of a college, the term now applies to a school or college post which involves financial responsibilities and other duties such as the maintenance of the buildings of an institution. Since the introduction of **local management of schools**, the scope of the post has been widened to include income generation, public relations and the organisation of in-service work and conferences. Now a key member of staff, the bursar is often a full member of a school's senior management team (*see also* **registrar**). (2) Holder of a monetary award, a **bursary**, for maintenance on an education course.

bursary An award, granted by an educational institution such as an independent school or other body, which assists the student in covering expenses for a course of study. (*see also* **entrance award**)

Business and Technology Education Council (BTEC) Set up in 1974 as the Business and Technician Education Council by the Secretary of State for Education and Science, it plans and approves a national system of courses in business and public adminstration below degree level in England and Wales. There are two main types of BTEC qualifications – certificates and diplomas, both of which are available at three levels. Courses can be on a full or part-time basis. The first level is normally taken by school leavers or sixth formers; the second level by junior managers and technicians and the third level by managerial or supervisory grades. The awards called respectively, First, National and Higher National Certificates or Diplomas are equivalent to the **General Certificate of Secondary Education** (GCSE), **Advanced level** and degree level. Courses are strongly vocational in character, for example, in such fields as agriculture, business and finance, computing, design, hotel and catering, leisure and service. In 1991 the Council changed its title to the Business and Technology Education Council to emphasise the changing nature of the enterprise. (*see also* **business education**)

business education A number of reports since the Second World War, such as that by Haslegrave on technician courses and examinations (1969) led to the establishment of business studies degrees and diplomas in polytechnics and colleges. The subject has since flourished. In schools, with the advent of the National Curriculum, all pupils from age 5 to 16 are recommended to take a component in education and industrial understanding, and business education tutors will have a key role to play in the technology team. **General Certificate of Secondary Education** (GCSE) courses in business education have also undergone much change in recent years; the narrow content-based course has been replaced by one which includes the skills, knowledge and values of economics and business studies and information technology. Awards in business education are made by a number of bodies including the **Business and Technology Education Council** (BTEC), **City and Guilds of London Institute** (CGLI), the **London Chamber of Commerce and Industry** (LCCI) and the **Royal Society of Arts** (RSA). Many of their awards are accredited by the **National Council for Vocational Qualifications** (NCVQ).

Butler Act The name given to the 1944 Education Act, after its architect, R. A. Butler, then President of the Board of Education. Devised during the Second World War, the Act made many important changes in the system of schooling. It stipulated that public education should be reorganised in three progressive stages: primary, secondary and further education, and children were to be educated according to their age, ability and aptitude. A **Ministry of Education** was to be formed, replacing the existing Board, with a Minister possessing much greater powers to ensure that the local education authorities carried out their duties. The **dual system** continued. County colleges, for continuing education, were to be set up nationally. The school leaving age was to be raised from 14 to 15 and then to 16 as soon as was expedient. No mention of the curriculum appears in the provisions of the Act. The raising of the school leaving age was delayed for two years and the provision of county colleges has never materialised. Nevertheless the spirit of the Act allowed for innovations and advances in education which were previously not possible. It determined the nature of educational administration for the next four decades, being superseded in many of its aspects by the **Education Reform Act** (1988).

C

Campaign for State Education (CASE) A **pressure group** set up in 1960 to improve the quality of local maintained schools, consisting of parents and others interested in education. Local groups operate within the framework of national CASE policy.

campus The grounds in which a school, college or university is situated, forming a self-contained entity. The term originated in the USA in the late nineteenth century at Princeton University.

capitation allowance An amount given each year by a **local education authority** to a school in order to buy such things as books and stationery. The amount a school receives depends on the number of children in the school (capitation, therefore, refers to an amount 'per head'), but the amount usually increases with the age of the children. Normally authorities give more for secondary school pupils than for primary school pupils, and are more generous for **sixth formers** in secondary schools. Since the 1988 Education Act local education authorities have been obliged to pass on much higher sums of money (at least 85 per cent of the total education budget) to schools. The major element in the funding formula is 'capitation' – i.e. the number of pupils enrolled at the school.

case study (1) A method of teaching in which a situation ('case') is presented to students by means of film or sets of documents as a basis for discussion and analysis. (2) A method of 'holistic' research or **evaluation** in education relying less on statistical measurement and more on other kinds of data gained by means of interview or content analysis of documents.

catchment area A geographical area from which a school or institution draws its pupils or students. One view of the comprehensive school is that it should be a **neighbourhood school** drawing pupils from the catchment areas of a small number of **primary schools**. The 1980 Education Act changed the picture, for under Section 5, parents could state a preference for schools and also express a preference for schools in other local education authorities. The 1988 Education Act went further in this direction of **parental choice**, by obliging schools to respect parents' preferences so long as the school was not completely full.

Central Advisory Councils These Councils, one for England and one for Wales, which replaced the Consultative Committee under Section 4 of the 1944 Education Act, differed from the former in that they included persons of experience from outside the education field. The Councils' functions were to advise the Secretary of State in matters of educational theory and practice referred to them, and to offer advice on their own initiative. Three important reports emanating from the Councils were: the *Crowther Report* (1959) on the education of 15- to 18-year-olds; the *Newsom Report* (1963) on the secondary modern school curriculum; and the **Plowden Report** (1967) on the state of primary education. The Councils have not been reconstituted since the Plowden Report was issued. (*see also* **Royal Commission**)

Centre for Educational Research and Innovation (CERI) Created in 1968, the Centre functions within the **Organisation for Economic Cooperation and Development** (OECD). It is concerned with the promotion and development of educational research, the testing of innovations in education systems, and promoting cooperation between member countries in the field of educational research and innovation. It has published reports such as *Education at a Glance, OECD Indicators* (1992).

Certificate of Pre-Vocational Education (CPVE) In May 1982, the Department of Education and Science published a statement *17 Plus – A New Qualification* giving details of this award. It was designed as a one-year course for young people at 16 plus who had few examination successes. The course, which began to operate from September 1983, was intended to prepare them for work, preferably with a training component, or to follow a particular vocational course at a later stage. The CPVE was administered by a joint board of **Business and Technology Education Council** (BTEC) and **City and Guilds** (CGLI), together with representatives of the **Royal Society of Arts** (RSA), and the GCE and CSE boards. It was superseded by **National Vocational Qualifications** (NVQ). (*see* Section 1, Essay 9)

Certificate of Secondary Education (CSE) An examination introduced in 1965 as a school leaving examination for pupils for whom **GCE 'O' level** was considered unsuitable. In 1988 the two examinations were abolished and replaced by a single examination for all (or nearly all) 16-year-olds – the **General Certificate of Secondary Education** (GCSE).

certification The process of awarding a certificate or diploma which indicates the achievement of certain specified standards of proficiency. One of the purposes of assessment or types of assessment is certification: i.e. **summative** assessment which results in a public award of some kind.

chancellor The nominal head of a university. The post was formerly vested with wide administrative powers, but these have diminished over time. The chancellor is normally present on formal occasions, such as degree ceremonies and university foundation days. (*see also* **honorary degree, Vice-Chancellor**)

change of character Schools may only increase their enrolment significantly (i.e. by 20 per cent or more), take children of different ages, or begin to select pupils by ability with the approval of the Secretary of State.

charitable status Bodies calling themselves charities have to be registered with the **Charity Commission** and are governed by rules laid down by the Commission. The advancement of education is accepted as one of the objects of charity. Those who raise funds for schools, such as parent-teacher associations, may wish to register as a charity. One benefit would be that where parents are encouraged to contribute to a covenant scheme, the tax can be reclaimed for the benefit of the school. The 1992 Charities Act made important changes in charitable status and the investment and care of charity funds.

Charity Commission The Commission, established in 1853, consisted of four charity commissioners, at least two of whom were to be barristers, and was charged with the investigation of any charities in England and Wales. Their scope was extended in 1860 and an important aspect of their work was the making of new educational schemes and checking abuse of existing charitable funds.

chief education officer (CEO) The principal officer of a local education authority responsible for advising the local council on a range of educational matters, writing reports for the Education Committee and carrying out its policies. The post dates from the 1902 Education Act when local education authorities replaced school boards. In some authorities the chief officer is called director of education. (*see* **society of education officers**)

child-centred education A version of **progressive education** which places the child rather than the teacher or subject matter at the centre of the educational process. In its milder versions, child-centred education may be regarded as little more than a reaction against the inhumane practices of some nineteenth-century schools: but extreme versions of the doctrine would suggest that the child's interest alone should determine what is taught in class, and therefore any kind of curriculum planning would not be appropriate. (*see also* **teaching methods**)

child guidance clinic Child guidance clinics are centres for the **diagnostic** assessment and treatment of children with behavioural problems and other developmental disorders. They are usually administered by local education authorities and staffed by psychiatrists, educational psychologists, and psychiatric social workers. Many clinics work on the basis of family therapy. The main referring agents are schools and family doctors but some clinics have an open-door policy; parents and adolescents may be self-referring. (*see also* **school psychological service**)

child in need Broadly defined in the **Children Act** (1989) to include children with disabilities and any child unlikely to achieve a reasonable standard of health or development without help. The social services department of a local authority has responsibility for children in need under 5, and for all children in need outside school hours and in school holidays. For children in need of school age, the local education authorities share responsibility: the Act encourages collaboration between local authority departments.

childminding Childminders look after other people's pre-school children in their own homes and receive payment. The requirements to be complied with by persons providing day care for young children were closely prescribed in the **Children Act** (1989). Local authorities were also given a larger supervisory role.

Children Act (1989) The Children Act came into operation in October 1991. One of its purposes was to coordinate existing private and public law about children: its dominant principle was that the child's welfare should be the major consideration in any decision relating to upbringing; it is assumed that upbringing is normally best within the child's own family. The main responsibility for implementing the Act (which is a complex document of ten parts and fourteen schedules) lies with the social services department, but it is recognised that cooperation with other departments – including health and education – is essential. A key concept of the Act was the **child in need**.

chronological age see **age: chronological and mental**.

circular Issued by the Department for Education and signed by the Secretary of State or the Permanent Secretary for the guidance of local education authorities and others on matters concerning government educational policy. Circulars do not have the force of a legal requirement but represent the policy of the central authority and cannot be ignored completely by local education authorities.

citizenship (education for) The Education Reform Act 1988 acknowledges that the aims of education should extend beyond imparting knowledge of, and expertise in, a number of subject disciplines to embrace aims which involve preparation for adult life. A manifestation of such aims is the identification of a number of 'cross-curricular themes' most of which address aspects of personal and social development. One of these, 'Education for Citizenship' which is outlined in the National Curriculum booklet *Curriculum Guidance Number 8*, encourages teachers to deal with the following eight 'essential components' of citizenship: community; a pluralist society; being a citizen; the family; democracy in action; the citizen and the law; work, employment and leisure; and public services. Although 'Education for Citizenship', as described by the **National Curriculum Council** (NCC), is a new provision for the school curriculum, very many secondary schools had included in their curriculum, prior to 1988, courses on 'political literacy', an issues-focused and skills-based form of political education. The NCC's approach to 'Education for Citizenship' ignored this experience and reverted to an approach which bears a closer resemblance to those civics courses which were prevalent in elementary schools from 1900 and in particular between the two World Wars, and which sought to inculcate attitudes of national loyalty and patriotism into children.

City and Guilds of London Institute (CGLI) Founded in 1878, the CGLI is the UK's largest awarding body. It specialises in developing vocational, general and leisure qualifications and awards certificates in over 400 subjects, many of which are **National Vocational Qualifications** (NVQs): more than 250 CGLI awards have NVQ status. General National Vocational Qualifications (GNVQ) are offered at levels 2 and 3 in five areas each with a broadly based vocational curriculum: art and design; business; health and social care; leisure; and tourism and manufacturing. (*see also* **business education**)

city technology college (CTC) A new category of schools which are independent although partly funded by the Department for Education. CTCs were established as part of the **Education Reform Act (1988)**. The original idea of CTCs, as conceived by Kenneth Baker, then Secretary of State for Education, was that they would be financed by industry and commerce and would provide an alternative to local education authority schools, whilst not being selective schools. In practice, it has been difficult to attract sufficient money from the private sector and considerable state funds have been provided for these schools. (*see* Section 1, Essay 7)

civic universities See **universities, history of**.

class (1) A group of pupils or students of varying size, but usually between twenty-five and thirty-five in number. Members of a class are normally of the same age group, except where **family grouping** is adopted. A class may, however, consist of a range of abilities. The term is interchangeable with form. (2) Refers to the division of an **honours degree**, according to performance: normally first, second (upper or lower), and third.

clearing house An information-gathering unit to enable, for example, applicants for university places to make a general application in order of choice rather than having to apply individually to each institution. In the UK the **Universities and Colleges Admissions Service** (UCAS) processes the applications from students in terms of their priorities and the response gained from the universities, passing on 'offers' to successful applicants. Another example in the UK of a clearing house is the **Graduate Teacher Training Register** (GTTR).

cloze The cloze procedure is a method of testing **readability** of a text by requiring students to show their comprehension of a passage where a proportion of the words have been deleted. It is claimed that this process tests both the reading ability of the student and the difficulty of the passage: this is one of the limitations of the procedure.

coaching Special tutorial help given to a student or students, often in preparing for an examination. (*see also* **crammer**)

co-education The education of boys and girls together in the same school and in 'mixed' classes within that school. In England, the term 'co-education' tends not to be used for institutions of further or higher education. Nearly all **primary schools** are co-educational, and there has been a steady trend towards co-education in **secondary schools**, particularly since 1944. It is usually thought that co-educational schools are better for boys, but there is some evidence to support the view that girls achieve better academic results in single-sex schools. (*see* also **girls' education**)

cognition/cognitive Cognition is the act of knowing, perceiving or conceiving, as opposed to emotional (affective) experiences. In Bloom's *Taxonomy of Educational Objectives* (1956) cognitive is one of three kinds of objectives, the other two being affective and psychomotor.

cognitive development The gradual growth of a child's ability to understand concepts, relationships and complex patterns of ideas. Piaget in *The Development of Logical Thinking From Childhood to Adolescence* (1958), Bruner in *The Process of Education* (1960), and others, have theorised about stages of cognitive development, for example, sensory-motor, preoperational, concrete operations and formal operations (Piaget); enactive, iconic and symbolic (Bruner). (*see also* **cognitive map, iconic and symbolic thinking**)

cognitive map The mental picture or diagram that an individual has of a particular environment. A cognitive map will differ from one individual to another in terms of being more or less complete; individuals will also differ from their viewpoint of the same environment.

college of education Following the recommendations of the *Robbins Report* in 1963 the 155 teacher training colleges were renamed colleges of education. A **White Paper** entitled *Education: A Framework for Expansion* published in 1972 revealed that a substantial reduction in the number of teacher training places was necessary to avoid a surplus of teachers in the near future. It proposed that colleges should merge with **polytechnics** and other further education colleges; some, however, joined universities or became institutes of higher education. The shrinking number of students led to the closure of many colleges.

college of higher education (CHE) Colleges of higher education emerged from the reorganisation of teacher education and advanced further education in the 1970s. Many colleges of education were merged with universities or polytechnics but about fifty became self-standing diversified colleges of higher education. The principals of these colleges of higher education formed the Standing Conferences of Principals (SCOP). When polytechnics became universities in 1992 the future and the status of the CHE was questioned, but it seems likely that those offering specialist courses not available in universities will probably survive.

College of Preceptors Incorporated by Royal Charter in 1849, it promoted the in-service training of teachers both in the UK and overseas. It is probably best known for its work as an examining body for practising teachers. During the second half of the nineteenth century, the College made a number of unsuccessful attempts to become a registration council for teachers. The College awards an Associateship (ACP), a Licentiateship (LCP), both graduate level qualifications as well as diplomas in Advanced Study in Education. Two more recent classes of membership are Member (M Coll P), to recognise good professional practice, and Ordinary Fellow (F Coll P), reserved for those who have made an outstanding contribution to education. (*see also* **General Teaching Council**)

collegiate university From the middle ages, the colleges of Oxford and Cambridge Universities were established by money given by pious founders. Each college has considerable autonomy. It controls its own property, elects its own **Fellows**, chooses its own head and, subject to university regulations, admits its own **undergraduate** students. The hallmark of such a college is its corporate identity, in contrast to that of a **federal** system. Durham University is also organised on a collegiate basis. (*see also* **universities, history of**)

Command Paper A document presented 'by Her Majesty's Command' to either House, the Command Paper is in fact the responsibility of a minister. It may be for example, a **White Paper** or a Blue Book and is not in pursuance of an Act of Parliament. All Command Papers bear a number, such as the White Paper, *Higher Education: A New Framework* (1991), cm 1541.

Committee of Vice-Chancellors and Principals (CVCP) This Committee was established in 1918 and reconstituted in 1930. As the title suggests, it represents heads of university institutions. The Committee is a standing body with its own secretariat. It keeps in touch with, and expresses its views to, government departments, research councils and other agencies concerned with higher education. (*see also* **Principal, Vice-Chancellor**)

common entrance examination An examination taken by pupils wishing to enter some of the **independent schools** at 13 years of age. Begun in 1904, it is set by a boys' common entrance committee and a girls' board. Some 14 000 pupils – 10 000 boys and 4000 girls – sit the papers in a complete year. From 1981, joint papers for boys and girls were taken in English, French, mathematics and science. (*see also* **preparatory school**)

community college/school A concept of education which seeks to involve individuals as members of communities in educational activities, regardless of age. This notion, derived from the **village college** and recommended in the **Plowden Report**, has been translated into programmes located in community colleges or schools, with an intake of secondary pupils usually between 14 and 18 years. Parents make use of resources during the day as well as the evening, taking part in academic and recreational activities alongside their children. As well as housing a school, the campus may include a **further education** college, library and sports complex. The buildings are often in use late at night for leisure and cultural activities, and for meetings of local clubs and societies. (*see also* **adult**

education, community education, neighbourhood school, village college)

community education Educational planning which involves educational activities outside the school or beyond the **community college** or **village college**. The concept of community education is related to the ideas of **continuing education**, namely, that education does not stop when a person finishes the period of full-time schooling, but continues into adult life. Many schemes of community education would involve teaching staff venturing into the wider community ('**outreach**') as well as bringing adults into the educational institution. Another of its aims is to improve the environment and the quality of life of the community in general.

Community Service Volunteers (CSV) A national voluntary agency, founded in 1962, with the aim of supporting teachers, youth workers and others interested in developing community involvement projects with young people both inside and outside the formal education system. CSV receives funds from the Department for Education, local authorities and private trusts.

comparability The extent to which the same awards in different examinations represent equivalent **levels of attainment**. For example, GCSE Examining Groups are expected to achieve comparability in four ways: (1) between alternative versions of the same subject provided by a Group in any one year; (2) between examinations in different years in the same subject provided by the same Group; (3) between the examinations of different Groups in the same subject; and (4) between different subjects provided by the same Examining Group.

compensation A process by which a candidate can make up for a lack of knowledge or skill in one area of a **syllabus** (or on one **examination** paper) by better performance in other areas (or in other examination papers).

compensatory education The theory behind compensatory education is that of 'social deficit', that is, that some children come from homes which do not provide early learning experiences or sufficient stimulation to motivate children in the classroom. Working-class children and children from some ethnic minority groups have been singled out for compensatory education programmes such as Head Start in the USA.

competency based teaching (CBT) Aimed at improving teacher performance in the classroom, CBT employs many forms of teaching methods, such as games and **simulations** and **microteaching**, which seek to promote self-awareness and interaction skills. The essence of CBT is that 'competence' must be defined in such a way as to make it measurable.

comprehensive school The **1944 Education Act** legislated for secondary education for all, but did not specify any one type of secondary school organisation. Circular 144/1947 set out various forms of organisation and defined a comprehensive school as 'one which is intended to cater for the secondary education of all children in a given area.' After many local education authority experiments with **tripartite systems** (grammar, technical and secondary modern schools) in the 1950s and 1960s, the comprehensive alternative rapidly gained in popularity during the 1970s. The 1976 Education Act attempted to make comprehensive schools the only kind of permitted secondary school, but was repealed by the 1979 Act, after the election of the Conservative Government under Margaret Thatcher. Nevertheless, by 1988 comprehensive schools were catering for 86 per cent of pupils in England, 98 per cent in Wales and 99 per cent in Scotland; Northern Ireland still retains a mainly selective secondary system.

compulsory competitive tendering (CCT)   The 1988 Local Government Act requires some services such as school cleaning and school meals to be opened up to competition by inviting other organisations to tender for the contract. Local education authorities are required to ensure that complete fairness is observed. The list of services was extended by the 1992 Local Government Act. (*see also* **Local Government Acts**)

computer assisted learning (CAL) Sometimes also referred to as computer aided instruction (CAI). The use of a computer is not only to present instructional material to students, but also to react to their responses. (*see also* **information technology**)

conditional offer Best exemplified by the **Universities and Colleges Admissions Service** (UCAS) procedure for pupils wishing to proceed to university. Such an offer is made by the appropriate university department, conditional upon the pupil obtaining stipulated grades in GCE 'A' level examinations which have yet to be taken at the time of the offer. (*see also* **entry qualification**)

continuing education A term which overlaps adult education, permanent education and recurrent education, but is not synonymous with any of them. With continuing education the emphasis is on the idea that education in its true form proceeds throughout an individual's life. Thus the emphasis in continuing education is to break down the barrier between formal and informal education, institutions of education and real life. (*see also* **University of the Third Age**)

continuous assessment The assessment of a student's work throughout a course instead of (or in addition to) a formal terminal examination. The purpose of continuous assessment is **formative** rather than **summative**, providing useful feedback to the student in order to improve future performance, but the marks awarded may also count towards a summative assessment. (*see also* **coursework**)

convergent thinking A way of thinking or problem-solving which concentrates on finding only one solution to a problem. This assumes that there is only one best or correct solution to any given problem. A person habitually inclined to convergent thinking may be referred to as a 'converger'.

corporal punishment Once common in primary and secondary schools (maintained and private), the practice was already diminishing rapidly by 1986 when it was made illegal in state schools as part of the Education (No. 2) Act (1986). **Independent schools** may still use corporal punishment, but not for those pupils whose fees are paid by the State. (*see also* **discipline, punishment: philosophy and psychology of, Society of Teachers Opposed to Physical Punishment** (STOPP))

correlation (correlation coefficient) The relationship between two sets of data; for example, individual candidates' scores in two papers or the scores given by two examiners to the same set of scripts. Correlation coefficients are expressed on the scale +1.0 to −1.0 where +1.0 indicates perfect correlation, and −1.0 indicates a complete inverse relationship. Coefficients between different components in the same subject **examination** tend to fall in the range +0.5 to +0.8. If the correlation coefficient were +0.4 or lower, there would be grounds for a full enquiry.

correspondence course A course of study, conducted by means of written work, between student and tutor through the post. (*see also* **distance learning, Open University, self-instruction)**

correspondence theory A view put forward by some sociologists which suggests that the major purpose of schooling is to service the needs of industrial society. Pupils are taught in schools to be punctual, obedient, and to work hard under supervision, so that they may become docile factory workers and clerks when they leave school.

Council for Education in World Citizenship (CEWC) Founded in 1939, the Council provides information, projects and practical help on international issues, without political bias or geographical limits. The Council holds national conferences for secondary school students on topics such as world health; organises teachers' seminars to discuss crucial questions relating to education for international understanding; provides speakers for schools; has a London resources centre of teaching material on world studies; and disseminates information through its information service on topics of current or recent international concern.

Council for National Academic Awards (CNAA) A body set up by government in 1964 to validate courses, especially degree courses, offered by colleges and polytechnics. At that time the CNAA was the only non-University body in the UK permitted to award degrees. The Council was abolished in 1991 as part of the reform of higher education.

Council for the Accreditation of Teacher Education (CATE) CATE was established in 1984 'to advise the Secretaries of State for Education and Science on the approval of initial teacher-training courses in England and Wales.' Unless courses are 'approved' they do not carry **qualified teacher status**. In order to be recommended for approval by CATE, courses need to have been recently inspected by **Her Majesty's Inspectorate** and to comply with criteria, known as the CATE criteria, although they were established by the Secretary of State. The original criteria included procedures concerning the selection of students, the qualifications and experience of staff, the course organisation, minimum amounts of time devoted to subject studies and subject method, as well as education and professional studies. In 1989 the Secretary of State issued a consultation document proposing different terms of reference for CATE. A new CATE was established in January 1990 with a smaller council, but more secretarial, administrative and professional support. The new criteria were designed to benefit from the experience of the first five years of CATE as well as to cater for the **National Curriculum**. The requirement of 100 hours for English and mathematics was extended to science; tutors have to have a minimum of thirty-five days school experience in each five years of service; the phasing of students' teaching practice is spelled out; there is more detail about teacher involvement; the subjects that primary-phase students should be prepared to teach are stated; and some of the competencies that students should have acquired by the end of their course are specified.

Council of Europe An organisation established in 1949 with the aim of achieving greater unity between its members, safeguarding and realising their ideals and principles and facilitating their economic and social progress. Its headquarters are in Strasbourg and committees of ministers from the member countries meet there as well as in the Parliamentary Assembly. A Council for Cultural Cooperation was established in 1962 to promote cultural and educational programmes. Conferences, seminars and symposia on many issues including education are held from time to time and their proceedings are published.

Council of Local Education Authorities (CLEA) In 1975, the **Association of Metropolitan Authorities** (AMA) and the **Association of County Councils** (ACC) formed this new Council so that the education authorities of England could speak with one voice. The Council deals with a large range of matters, from discussing teachers' conditions of service to making representations to the Secretary of State on issues affecting local education authorities.

counselling Counselling has been defined as helping people to understand their own motives and reasons for actions, so that they can come to their own conclusions about what they will do and how they can do it. It means helping them to define their needs and discover what resources are available to them to work out the best ways of making and sustaining satisfactory relationships with others. In a school setting, counselling is focused on personal, educational and **vocational guidance**. The first full-time courses for experienced teachers in Britain were established in 1965 and were much influenced by the ideas and work of Carl Rogers, the American psychotherapist.

county school See maintained school.

course The most common usage refers to a 'course of study' meaning a series of lessons, lectures or seminars, of specified duration (often a year). Thus a

programme of studies would consist of several courses. Ambiguity arises, however, when reference is made, for example, to a 'degree course' when the more appropriate terminology would appear to be 'degree programme'. In recent years, some degree programmes have been organised on a **modular** basis.

coursework Work carried out by a student during a course of study. Its nature may range from essay writing to practical tasks. According to the course regulations, such work may be compulsory and taken into account in forming a final assessment of the student's merit.

crammer A name given to an independent college of further education where students of 16 years of age and over attend to prepare for school examinations and special examinations with a view to entering the professions and universities. There are often short intensive courses for those wishing to improve **'A' level** grades.

creativity Partly as a reaction against the use of intelligence tests, which were said to measure **convergent thinking**, some psychologists developed tests which would test **divergent** thinking or creativity, for example 'write down as many uses as you can think of for a brick.'

credit In USA universities a student is awarded one or more credits on successful completion of a course. Usually about 120 credits are needed for the award of a degree. In the UK, most academics object to this cafeteria or fragmented system, prefering a degree programme which is more carefully planned around a central core of knowledge. The **Open University** credit system is very different from that of USA universities since credits are awarded for much longer blocks of study (only six are required for an ordinary degree and eight for an honours degree). In Open University terminology, a credit is awarded for a year's work for a part-time student who works for about ten to twelve hours a week. In 1983, the Department of Education and Science set up a study of credit transfers, that is, facilitating the acceptance of credits gained in one higher education establishment by other establishments. (*see also* **Credit Accumulation and Transfer Scheme**)

Credit Accumulation and Transfer Scheme (CATS) CATS aims to provide a national framework for the recognition of academic credit at first degree and taught masters levels. The main aim is to facilitate the transfer of students (with **credit** for units of work/modules completed) from one institution to another. The CATS system assumes that awards are made up of units/modules each of which carries a credit rating of four or more. A degree is made up of 360 credits; a diploma 240 credits; a certificate 120 credits. Credits can be accumulated on a full-time or part-time basis (normally 120 per annum). Approved work experience can also be credited.

credit transfers See **credit**; **Credit Accumulation and Transfer Scheme**.

criterion-referenced test A test designed to establish a candidate's performance in terms of a given **level** or **standard** rather than being better (or worse) than other candidates. In England, the driving test is often quoted as the most familiar example of a test which demands perforance at a certain level on a number of known criteria. A criterion-referenced test may express the notion of 'pass' either in terms of a 'cut-off point' or test score, or in terms of reaching a standard of competence on a number of related criteria (such as the use of mirror and braking in the driving test). (*see also* **norm-referenced** test)

critical learning period One theory in child development suggests that there are limited times in childhood when individuals may acquire particular skills. If that opportunity is missed during the 'critical period' it is then thought to be difficult or perhaps impossible to acquire the skill at a later stage. Critical learning periods are likely to exist in other animals, but some psychologists doubt their existence in human beings. Language acquisition is sometimes suggested as the most important example of a critical learning period, but this is by no means established.

culture By definition any society possesses a culture or way of life which members of that society share. Culture refers to knowledge, beliefs and attitudes, passed on from one generation to the next. In a complex industrial society this transmission process is much more complex than in a technologically and economically simple society. In a complex society not all values and beliefs are held in common – there are sub-cultures within the major society. But there are always some cultural features held in common, that is, a common culture, as well as sub-cultures. (*see* Section 1, Essay 3)

curriculum A narrow definition would limit curriculum to a 'programme for instruction'; wider definitions would include all the learning that takes place in a school or other institution, planned and unplanned. In recent years curriculum has been defined as a selection from the culture of a society; and the curriculum is planned by a process of cultural analysis. (*see also* **syllabus**, **curriculum (national)**, **National Curriculum**)

curriculum, common A curriculum planned to cater for all pupils in a school. It is 'common' in the sense that all pupils study certain subjects or have certain educational experiences 'in common' by the end of the period of compulsory schooling. 'Common curriculum' can also be used nationally to indicate the desirability of all children in the country having certain planned experiences 'in common'. Both uses depend to some extent on the idea of a common **culture**. (*see* Section 1, Essay 3)

curriculum, compulsory The idea that a properly planned curriculum would either be wholly compulsory or that there would be compulsory elements distinguished from the optional. The term is sometimes used without making clear whether the curriculum would be compulsory for schools (that is, a national curriculum) or compulsory for pupils within a particular school.

curriculum, core Often confused with common curriculum, but is usually used as a weaker term to indicate that there are some subjects which are more important than others, and therefore should be compulsory, or given priority in some way. (*see* Section 1 Essay 3)

curriculum, hidden An ambiguous term. One meaning implies that there are certain kinds of learning which are not included in the timetable, but which will be transmitted by institutional arrangements, such as a prefect system or the cadet corps (CCF). A related meaning refers to the possibility of pupils acquiring attitudes and behaviour patterns not intended by school authorities. (*see* **time-tabling**)

curriculum, national A national curriculum for England and Wales was introduced as part of the **Education Reform Act (1988)**. It is essentially a list of ten **foundation subjects** in England: three core subjects (English, mathematics and science) plus seven other foundation subjects (technology, a modern foreign language, history, geography, art, music and physical education. In Wales there is an additional subject – Welsh – which is taken either as the mother tongue or as a compulsory second language. For most subjects there are statutory Attainment Targets (ATs), Programmes of Study (POS), and a system of assessment which was drawn up by the Task Group for Assessment and Testing (TGAT). This requires the assessment of all children in maintained schools at the end of Key Stage 1 (age 7), Key Stage 2 (age 11), Key Stage 3 (age 14) and Key Stage 4 (age 16) when the main form of assessment (but not the only form) is GCSE. Children in private schools are not obliged to follow the National Curriculum, although they are encouraged to do so. (*see* Section 1, Essay 7)

curriculum, spiral Learning planned in such a way that a pupil encounters important concepts at a number of stages – concrete before abstract, simple before complex, easy before difficult. The intention of the originator, Jerome Bruner, was to indicate that important concepts should not be regarded as something to be learned on a single occasion and then taken for granted; concepts need to be encountered in a variety of contexts, over a period of time, and gradually assimilated.

curriculum control Part of the study of the politics of the curriculum. In any society there are decision makers who control or influence the content of what is taught in schools.

Curriculum Council for Wales (CCW) The Welsh equivalent of the **National Curriculum Council** (NCC). The CCW advises the Secretary of State for Wales on the National Curriculum, and advises schools in Wales on statutory requirements and non-statutory advice. In 1993 CCW was replaced by the Curriculum and Assessment Authority for Wales (ACAC).

curriculum development project A study of a particular subject or area of the curriculum often with a view to improving that part of the curriculum by supplying teachers with attractive teaching materials, sometimes in the form of 'packages'. In recent years there has been less emphasis on 'materials' but greater effort to encourage teachers to rethink aims and methods for themselves. (*see also* **dissemination, Man – A Course of Study project**)

curriculum planning The process of designing and organising the whole curriculum either at national level or within a single school.

cut-off point A point on a mark list or rank order which is used to separate 'passes' from 'failures' or first class from second class, etc. For example, a group of examiners, after looking at a number of examination papers, might decide that a mark of 40 per cent would be the lowest level of pass and all candidates with 39 per cent would fail. Forty per cent would thus be the cut-off point, but all candidates with marks of, say, 37 to 43 per cent would probably be regarded as '**borderline**', and submitted to special scrutiny. In such a case, the examiners would have certain criteria or **standards** in mind which would justify passing some and failing others: the mark of 40 per cent would be arbitrary, but the standard it represented would not.

d

day nursery Unlike other types of nursery education, day nurseries are normally organised by local authority social services departments. They are for children in need under 5 and have qualified staff. They are open often throughout the year from 8.00 a.m. to 6.00 p.m. Another type of day nursery is that provided by either private enterprise or an employers' organisation for children of parents going to work. They are often heavily subsidised and are registered with a local authority. (*see also* **Children Act (1989)**)

day release A method of organising courses in **further** or **higher education** whereby students on courses are in employment and are released for perhaps one or two days a week during the term for training, general education or to pursue a formal qualification. (*see also* **Youth Training**)

day school A term generally applied to most maintained schools as well as to an increasing number of independent schools. The main characteristic is that pupils attend during school hours and do not normally board at the school.

dean (1) The person resonsible for a faculty or department in a university or higher education institution. (2) A **fellow** or senior member of a university who supervises the conduct and discipline of students.

deficit model A theory put forward to account for the 'under-achievement' of certain minority groups and working-class children. The theory suggests that failure is connected with certain cultural 'deficits' which handicap them in the learning process at school. The theory was implicit or explicit in many of the well known reports on education such as Crowther, Newsom and Plowden. Some sociologists have reacted to this model by suggesting that schools often fail to provide adequate teaching for certain groups of children, or that society itself is at fault in various other ways. Whereas the deficit model 'blames' the family of an under-achieving child, later theories tend to blame teachers or society in general. (*see also* **compensatory education, disadvantage, enrichment programme**)

degrees Awarded by universities and other institutions of higher education as the result of successful completion of a course of study: the candidate may be tested by examination, continuous assessment, a viva, thesis, or a combination of any of these. There are three levels of degrees:
(1) *Bachelor*, usually a first degree, except for degrees such as Bachelor of Philosophy (BPhil) and Bachelor of Literature (BLitt) and for some Scottish universities. The course is normally of three years' duration. Examples are the Bachelor of Arts degree (BA) and the Bachelor of Science (BSc).
(2) *Masters*, are usually higher degrees obtained after one or two years of study and may include an element of research. In Scotland, the Master of Arts (MA) is normally a first degree. At Oxford and Cambridge, it is awarded seven years from the time of matriculation upon payment of a fee
(3) *Doctor*, usually awarded as a result of research, in the form of a thesis. The initials PhD or DPhil (Doctor of Philosophy) indicate such an award. There are also higher doctorates, such as Doctor of Laws (LLD) and Doctor of Literature (DLitt), which are awarded on the basis of the submission of publications. Medical practitioners are, as a matter of convention, entitled to be called doctors on becoming qualified, even without obtaining a doctorate qualification in medicine (MD). Degrees are normally awarded in a faculty and may be indicated by abbreviations following the title. For instance, the Bachelor degree in the faculty of economics at the University of London is written as BSc (Econ).
The majority of degree courses are for internal students, but universities, notably London, offer **external degrees** for both home and overseas candidates. The **Open University** offers degree courses with the assistance of distance learning material. (*see also* **diploma, graduate, honorary degree, honours degree, postgraduate, undergraduate**)

delegacy A group of individuals in a university who are given responsibility for a particular task or organisation. For example, in some universities **extra-mural studies** are organised by a delegacy; in others, school examinations are the responsibility of a delegacy. Although these responsibilities are delegated, they are normally reported back to another university committee, perhaps **Senate**.

delegated budget That part of the budget given to governors of a school or institution to control and manage.

delegated management of schools See **local management of schools**.

Department for Education (DFE) The main government department concerned with education has undergone a number of transformations during the present century. In 1900, the **Board of Education** was established which became the **Ministry of Education** in 1945. In 1964, the Ministry became the **Department of Education and Science** (DES) and in 1992, it changed again to the **Department for Education** (DFE).

From 1944, successive departments have been responsible for formulating policies for government in respect of universities, polytechnics, colleges of further education and schools; for determining priorities in the allocation of resources to the education service; for the supply training and qualification of teachers in England and Wales; and for taking professional advice from **Her Majesty's Inspectorate** (HMI). The Secretary of State, assisted by a minister of state and two junior ministers, are the main political appointments. The Department's powers have been increased in recent years, especially since the Education Reform Act of 1988, while those of local education authorities have diminished. From 1992, the science component of the DFE's work was hived off to form the Office of Service and Technology under the Chancellor of the Duchy of Lancaster, and the Department itself was renamed Department for Education.

Department of Education Northern Ireland (DENI) The Department of Education administers public education – schools, further education and universities – in Northern Ireland. The education system is governed by the Education and Libraries (Northern Ireland) Order 1972 which came into effect as from 1973. The five local education authorities in Northern Ireland created by the Order are called education and library boards. They are responsible for ensuring that there are sufficient schools and other facilities in their respective areas. The boards provide boards of governors for the controlled schools though voluntary grammar, and maintained schools have their own individual boards of governors. The 1978 Education (Northern Ireland) Act established the controlled integrated school to break down barriers between different faiths. This movement received further impetus with the Education Reform (Northern Ireland) Order (1990). Integrated schools are the direct responsibility of the Northern Ireland Council for Integrated Education, not the Department of Education.

departmental committees Similar to **Royal Commissions**, except that they deal with subjects of lesser importance and do not enjoy the same prestige. A departmental committee is appointed by a minister to investigate a topic, drawing on a range of specialist advice. Its report may be either a **Command Paper** or a non-parliamentary publication and is usually referred to by the name of its chairman. (*see also* **Parliamentary Papers**)

deputy head A post in the hierarchy of a school between the head and second master/mistress. There is no one standard job definition, but the holder of the post traditionally acts as a liaison between the head and the rest of the staff and frequently exercises powers delegated by the head. Large schools often have two or more deputy heads. Primary schools normally have one deputy head. With the advent of **local management of schools**, there have been changes in senior management teams in order to carry the many new functions given to schools. One example is the introduction of the school manager or **bursar**. As a result, the post of deputy head has sometimes either disappeared or diminished in importance.

deschooling A term invented by Ivan Illich in *Deschooling Society* (1971) to encourage the idea of developing true education without schools. Schools, according to Illich, are too bureaucratic, expensive, as well as being a very inefficient means of educating the young. Developing countries in particular, in his view, would be better off without schools. Some of his followers have concentrated instead on changing schools by weakening the links between schools and the job market. (*see also* **alternative education, compulsory education, free schools**)

designated courses Local education authorities have a duty to provide grants, called mandatory grants, to all students who are following a course which the Department for Education has listed under this heading. (*see also* **discretionary grant**)

detention A form of **discipline** which involves keeping a pupil in at playtime, lunchtime or after school. Pupils in detention are usually set written work to complete during this time.

development plan Most educational institutions draw up plans which review their positions, set targets and state how these are to be achieved and monitored. The plans may be on a short-term basis, i.e. annually or for a cycle of time.

developmental testing A kind of **formative evaluation** particularly used by the **Open University**. Teaching materials are tried out on students on a trial basis before the final version is put into production. The trial group of students are asked to comment on particular difficulties or confusing passages which are then analysed by educational psychologists and others skilled in textual presentation.

diagnosis The analysis of pupils' abilities and learning difficulties. This may be by using specially designed attainment tests, and diagnostic tests in the basic subjects. Pupils can be referred to **child guidance clinics** staffed by educational psychologists, for an investigation of physical, psychological or emotional dispositions which may affect school performance. Schools are also being urged to establish programmes to meet the individual needs of these children. (*see also* **school psychological service**)

diagnostic test A test designed to discover an individual pupil's strengths and weaknesses in a particular subject area, often arithmetic or reading. Such a test is not designed to find out a pupil's competence or where he stands in relation to the rest of an age group. It is designed as an aid to learning. (*see also* **attainment, diagnosis, child guidance clinic**)

differentiated examinations A method of testing different levels of **attainment** by the use of different examination papers. This may be operated in three ways: candidates may take one or more compulsory papers with either easier or more difficult components; they may take the easier components and some harder components; or they may take two or more components which overlap in difficulty. In the **General Certificate of Secondary Education** (GCSE) there are differentiated papers for weaker and more able students.

difficulty index Measure of the difficulty of an item in a test. It might be measured by the percentage of candidates answering correctly according to some models of test construction. An item with either a very low or a very high difficulty index would be omitted from the final version of the test. (*see also* **facility index**)

dilution A fear that if unskilled or untrained helpers are employed in schools to do some of the less professional work previously done by teachers, then the whole of the profession becomes 'diluted'. For this reason many professional teachers' organisations are officially opposed to the employment of **teachers' aides** or classroom helpers of any kind. The opposing argument is that if more non-professionals were employed in schools this would release teachers for their more skilled professional duties. (*see also* **ancilliary staff**)

diploma (1) A qualification granted by an institution at the end of a course of study. Diplomas may be of sub-degree standard or may be confined to graduates, for example **Postgraduate Certificate of Education** (PGCE). Many professional associations grant their own diplomas. (2) A document describing a candidate's performance following a course of study. (*see also* **degree**)

Diploma of Higher Education (Dip HE) Introduced in 1974, the Diploma was a two-year course of study at first degree standard. There was a wide range of subjects to choose from in education: the arts, humanities and the social and physical sciences. Most students went on to study for a degree, very often choosing between a Bachelor of Education (BEd) or a Bachelor of Arts (BA); some institutions had specially designed courses to which successful Diploma students could transfer. The entry qualification was two GCE 'A' Levels, or by access courses or by special entry arrangements for mature students. With the development of credit transfer, the Dip HE has tended to be replaced by other flexible, usually modular, structures. (*see also* **Credit Accumulation and Transfer Scheme**)

Diploma of Vocational Education (DVE) Formerly the **Certificate of Pre-Vocational Education** (CPVE) available post-16, the DVE now embraces the 14–

19 age range with exemption from an introductory phase if the 14–16 foundation phase has been successfully completed. The general aim is to provide exploratory studies in occupational contexts. Two levels are available post-16: Intermediate (GNVQ Level 2) and National (GNVQ Level 3). DVE is based on nine occupational clusters. It was piloted in the year 1991–2, with the intention of phased introduction from 1992 onwards.

direct grant school A type of secondary school, usually a selective grammar school, first established in 1926, which received a grant direct from the central authority for education. The arrangement included a guarantee that a proportion of places would be reserved for children from primary schools to be paid by local education authorities or the schools' governors in accordance with the direct grant regulations 1959. From September 1976, this arrangement ceased to operate: direct grant schools either joined the **maintained** system or became **independent** schools.

direct method This method of teaching modern languages stemmed from work done in Germany towards the end of the last century. It avoided the analysis of grammar, but stressed that the teacher employed oral techniques, especially conversation and question and answering which allowed the pupil to becomes immersed in the language itself. The direct method was very popular in English schools between 1900 and 1914: by the 1920s it was under attack, to be finally laid low by a staff inspector at the Board of Education, F. H. Collins, between the years 1929 and 1932. (*see also* **language laboratory**)

director (1) Director of education: an alternative title to **chief education officer**, the leading officer of local authority education department. (2) Director of studies: a person in a school or college responsible for a course or advising a group of students in academic matters. (3) A title for the head of an educational establishment, particularly in institutions of higher education.

disadvantaged Those whose life chances are diminished by various social, physical, economic or family handicaps, or a combination of them all. The 'cycle of deprivation' hypothesis is often linked to the 'culture of poverty' argument, both laying stress on family process. Another view is that society and its structure is most to blame. The chances of avoiding disavantage depend much on the individual's external avenues of escape. (*see also* **compensatory education, deficit model, enrichment programme, positive discrimination**)

discipline In schools, usually a term used to indicate 'classroom control' or 'keeping order'. The formulation of school rules is the responsibility of the headteacher. (*see also* **disruptive units, detention, exclusion**)

disciplines, academic An area of human knowledge, for example, history, geography, physics or geology, which has been developed often in universities, as a separate subject area for purposes of teaching and research. A discipline would be associated with **learned journals**, professional associations and perhaps written or unwritten codes of practice. Some philosophers, for example, Paul Hirst, have tried to avoid the ambiguity of 'disciplines' preferring to sub-divide knowledge into forms and fields. (*see also* **disciplines of education, inter-disciplinary studies**)

disciplines of education   The subject areas that, according to one view of pro-fessional teaching, all teachers should be introduced to as part of their initial training. The disciplines were traditionally considered to be philosophy, psy-chology and history of education; but since the late-1950s and early-1960s, soci-ology tended to be included sometimes at the expense of history. (*see also* **academic disciplines**)

discretionary award   In contrast to a **mandatory** award, **local education authori-ties** give discretionary awards according to their own determined policies and cases are considered individually. These are for a variety of courses, usually below first degree level. For example, an award might be given to enable 16- to 18-year-old students from low-income families to attend an **'A' level course** at a local college. (*see also* **entrance award, maintenance grant**)

discrimination index   A measure of the success with which an item in a test can discriminate between 'good' and 'poor' candidates on the test as a whole. The easiest way of measuring the discrimination is to see to what extent success on a particular item correlates with success on the test as a whole. In some test models, items that do not discriminate are omitted from final versions of the test.

disruptive behaviour   The disruption of lessons by pupils either deliberately or from emotional or behavioural difficulties. This also takes the form of violence against other children and the verbal abuse of staff. Schools often exclude such pupils for short or longer periods. Parents have a legal right to demand a place for their child in another school, but in practice this presents difficulties. (*see also* **discipline, exclusion**)

disruptive units   Children who cause undue disruption in ordinary schools may be placed in a disruptive unit, either on a part- or full-time basis. Units may be part of the campus of a school or in off-site provision. There is a high staff-pupil ratio and the aim is to continue therapy with an appropriate curriculum. Although such units are regarded, in the main, as temporary measures, many fourth- and fifth-year pupils do not return to their classrooms.

dissemination   Part of the process of curriculum development. A well-planned scheme of curriculum development would not only consist of planning the desired change, preparing materials and methods to implement change, but also the means of getting these new ideas across to a large number of teachers. In the early days of curriculum development, it was thought that this process of spreading ideas would occur naturally by a process of diffusion, but this proved to be an unwarranted assumption and plans for dissemination in an active way were built into later curriculum development projects. (*see also* **research and development**)

dissertation A treatise based on research submitted in connection with an award or qualification. Although the term dissertation and **thesis** are often interchangeable, the latter might often be more demanding. In some universities, a dissertation is shorter than a thesis. (*see also* **degrees, viva**)

distance learning The most obvious kind of distance learning is the correspondence course, but the term now includes other media besides the written and the printed word such as television, video tapes and radio programmes. Distance learning is based normally on a pre-produced course which is self-instructional but where organised two-way communication takes place between the student and a supporting institution. Distance learning is now seen as a useful adjunct to face-to-face learning. The **Open University** is a good example of this form of learning and it has long been common in Australia. Cable and/or satellite television may prove to be very important in distance learning in the future. (*see also* **PICK-UP, study skills**)

distractor In a **multiple choice test** each question will be followed by one correct answer but several incorrect answers or distractors. The candidate has to choose the correct answer from the incorrect, and at least some of the incorrect answers should be sufficiently plausible to distract the candidate. If all the incorrect answers were too obviously wrong, the candidate would be able to 'guess' at the correct answer without really knowing the right one.

divergent thinking A thinking process which tends to look for a variety of solutions rather than a single correct answer. Liam Hudson in his book *Contrary Imaginations* (1972) contrasted the **convergent** thinking of boys who tended to become scientists and those who, as a result of his tests, were classified as divergers who tended to be better at art subjects. (*see also* **creativity**)

don Originating from the Spanish word 'don', to denote a nobleman, it was later applied to **Oxbridge Fellows**, but has now been extended to include university teachers in general.

Down's syndrome A condition, also known as mongolism, named after the nineteenth-century physician Langdon Down who wrote up cases studies of the condition. The condition is now believed to be caused by chromosome abnormalities resulting in flattened facial features, stubby fingers and mental retardation. Children of this kind used to be taught in **special schools**, but recent attempts have been made to integrate them, especially children with the milder forms of Down's syndrome, into normal classes. (*see also* **special educational needs**)

dual system The existence of Church and state schools alongside each other dates from the time of the 1870 Education Act. Under this Act, Church schools were given building grants for new buildings. By the 1902 Act, rate-aid was extended to Church schools in return for concessions such as the nomination of school managers by the local education authorities and their supervision of non-religious aspects of the curriculum. The 1944 Act modified the system by dividing **voluntary schools** into three categories – aided, controlled and special agreement – according to the type of financial arrangement desired in return for concessions made with the local authority. It should be noted that the Act introduced compulsory religious worship and instruction in all county and voluntary schools. Legislation in 1959 and 1967 allowed for building grants for Church schools for the first time in a century. (*see also* **religious education**)

Duke of Edinburgh Award A scheme began in 1956 to 'help the young generation, first to discover their talents and then how to use them, particularly in the service of others.' The scheme is available to organisations and individuals between the ages of 14 and 25. For each award, young people have to meet the requirements in one activity from each of the following four different sections: service, expeditions, skills and physical recreation. Awards – bronze, silver and gold – are given for a range of interests which includes, for instance, life-saving, youth leadership, drama, sailing and expeditions on land or sea. Between 1956 and 1991, over two million young people have taken part in the scheme.

Dunning Report Published in 1977, this Report complemented the work of the **Munn Committee**. The remit of the Committee, under its chairman, Mr J. Dunning, was to identify the aims and purposes of assessment and certification in the fourth year of Scottish secondary education, the higher grade Scottish Certificate of Education and the Certificate of Sixth Year Studies. The Committee's recommendations were quite radical. The 'O' grade examination should be replaced by a three-level certificate – foundation, general, and credit, according to achievement. Assessment of the examination was to be based on a combination of internal and external marks. Teachers would be assisted in ensuring standards by the recommendation that national guides in each subject were to be prepared. (*see also* **Munn Report, Scottish Education Department**)

e

Economic and Social Research Council (ESRC) Established in 1983 to replace the **Social Science Research Council** (SSRC) because the then Secretary of State for Education, Sir Keith Joseph, objected to the term 'social science' – he did not consider such studies to be 'scientific'. No funds would have been provided unless the title of the Research Council were changed. The ESRC responsibility includes funding for university research in education.

educability A measure or estimate of the extent to which an individual pupil or a group might be capable of responding to or benefiting from a given educational programme. Some educationists concerned with children with **special educational needs** (SEN) have shown their dislike of the concept by declaring that 'no child is ineducable'.

education acts Since the last century, a series of education acts passed by parliament, have signalled reform and reorganisation of all aspects of education. The earliest ones, 1870, 1876 and 1880 were mainly attempts to establish adequate school accommodation and to enforce attendance. The 1902 Act laid the foundations for a coherent education system, bringing hitherto disparate elements under a central body, the Board of Education, as well as creating local education authorities. Welfare aspects were dealt with by the 1906 Act (school meals) and 1907 (medical treatment), whilst the school leaving age was raised by those of 1918, 1936 and 1944, which also organised education in three stages: primary, secondary and further. Since 1979 there has been a succession of Acts, some of greater significance that others:

1979 Education Act Repealed 1976 Act (compelling local education authorities to have comprehensive plans).

1980 Education Act Introduced assisted places scheme; stated that all independent schools should be registered; gave parents the right to choose school; gave parents the right to be represented on governing body; stated that local education authorities and governors now required to provide information on examination results, criteria for admission etc.; greater control imposed over advanced further education pool (capping); restricted local education authority rights to refuse places to outsiders.

1981 Education Act Following the *Warnock Report* (1978) local education authorities were given responsibilities for special education; and parents were given the right to be consulted and to appeal against the local education authority.

1984 Education (Grants and Awards) Act Allowed government to allocate money to local education authorities for specific purposes (reducing local authority control over grant).

1986 Education Act Introduced local education authority training grants schemes (LEATGS) and grant-related inservice training (GRIST) – an extension of the 1984 Act, earmarking funds for specific training

1986 Education (No.2) Act Required every maintained school to have a governing body; set formula for numbers of representatives on governing body (parents' representation strengthened); required governors to present annual report to parents and arrange meeting to discuss it; abolished corporal punishment in state schools; made governors responsible for policy on sex education and for preventing political indoctrination; and made governors responsible for policy document on curriculum which could modify local education authority policy.

1987 Teachers' Pay and Conditions Act Abolished Burham negotiating machinery.

1988 Local Government Act Clause 28 forbade local authorities to 'promote teaching in any maintained schools on the acceptability of homosexuality as a pretended family relationship'.

1988 Education Reform Act (ERA) Introduced publication of information on schools; open enrolment; and **grant-maintained schools** (GMS).

1992 Education (Schools) Act Required schools and local education authorities to publish examination performance league tables and provides for the inspection of all schools every few years.

1992 Further and Higher Education Act Introduced quality assurance and new funding arrangements, abolished the binary line in higher education. (*see* **law of education**)

1993 Education Act The Act was based on the White Paper. *Choice and Diversity* (1992) the main purpose of which was to encourage the development of **grant-maintained schools**. The Act also abolished the **National Curriculum Council** and the **School Examinations and Assessment Council**, replacing them with the **School Curriculum and Assessment Authority**; likewise the **Curriculum Council for Wales** was replaced by the **Curriculum and Assessment Authority for Wales**.

Education Association (EA) Chapter 11 of the White Paper *Choice and Diversity* (1992) attempted to deal with the problem of 'failing schools'. The proposed solution (later included in the 1993 Act) was that inspection reports would identify schools which were 'at risk' of failing to give their pupils an acceptable education. The governing body would then prepare an action plan, and the local education authority provide a supporting commentary. The Secretary of State has the power to appoint an EA to take over the management of an 'at risk' school or group of schools from their governing bodies and local authority. The EA has the powers and funding of a **grant-maintained** governing body. The EA manages the schools until the Secretary of State is satisfied that they have achieved a satisfactory level of performance; the schools are then considered for grant-maintained status.

education committee See **local education authority**.

Education Otherwise (EO) Formed in 1977 by a small group of parents, EO now has a membership of well over 1000 families. EO takes its name from Section 36 of the 1944 Education Act which states: 'It shall be the duty of the parent of every child of compulsory school age to cause him [sic] to receive efficient full-time education suitable to his age, ability and aptitude, either by regular attendance at school *or otherwise.'* Families who join EO are sent a guide to the meaning of 'or otherwise' and a booklet *Suggestions About Learning at Home.* (*see also* **school phobia**)

education vouchers A scheme whereby vouchers are given to parents to enable them to purchase education at schools of their choice. A two-year study of vouchers carried out in the Ashford area of Kent in 1977 showed that apart from the expense of the scheme, it would be difficult to administer. A voucher plan was operated in the Alum Rock school district of San Jose, California, from 1972 to 1976, but was not regarded as a success.

Education Welfare Service (EWS) The Service is required, on the one hand to exercise enforcement powers of school attendance through court proceedings; and on the other hand to provide material benefits, such as necessitous clothing allowances and maintenance grants. Other duties of education welfare officers (EWO) include child employment certification, transport of children and assessment for free meals. Their job descriptions include counselling and guidance with pregnant schoolgirls, monitoring child employment, groupwork with persistent non-attenders or disruptive pupils, and liaising with social service agencies. Section 36 of the **Children Act (1989)** stipulates the conditions under which a local education authority may apply to a court for an education supervision order for a child of compulsory school age who is not being properly educated.

Educational Institute of Scotland (EIS) Represents about 80 per cent of all Scottish teachers in primary, secondary and further education, totalling over 45,000 members. The committees dealing with teachers' salaries and conditions of service have a majority of EIS members and the committee for college lecturers has eight of the nineteen places filled by EIS representatives. (*see also* **teachers' unions**)

educational television (etv) A term with two different but overlapping meanings. The first refers to any television programme that is intended to be educational, for example, documentary films or discussions about politics. The second meaning refers to television films which are made specifically for educational purposes in schools and other educational institutions. The latter may often be referred to as 'school television'. The **Open University** has made some major advances in etv for adult learners.

educationally subnormal (ESN) Children described as educationally subnormal will be intellectually impaired in either a moderate (M) or severe (S) form. Many ESN children will have associated disorders in areas of physical and emotional development. Approximately one-third of mildly mentally retarded children have significant problems in the area of behavioural disorders and may have problems of physical coordination. The severely mentally retarded are usually multi-handicapped and some need nursing and social care rather than educational management. (*see also* **special educational needs, special schools**)

effective schools For some years after the US Coleman Report (1966) the conventional wisdom was that schools made little or no difference to the levels of **attainment** of their pupils – social background was the dominant factor. However, a number of studies in the USA, UK and elsewhere, in the 1970s and 1980s showed that the performance of children from similar backgrounds was different according to the '**culture**' of the schools. An effective school has a number of positive features – for example, collaborate planning, cooperative commitment to **goals**, staff stability, maximum use of learning time etc. But it must always be stressed that these cannot be regarded as separate factors to be treated in isolation – they are features of the culture of an effective school. Changing the culture of a school is very difficult. (*see* **Rutter Report**)

EFL See **English as a foreign language**.

elementary school A type of school which existed until 1944 offering an education for children from 5 to 14 years of age. The **1944 Education Act** made provision for primary education for all up to the age of 11 and secondary education thereafter.

'eleven plus' examination Term commonly used for tests administered by local education authorities for entrance into **selective secondary schools**.

emeritus A title conferred on a **professor** on his or her retirement. In some universities it is also conferred on **readers**.

enactive, iconic and symbolic The American psychologist, Jerome Bruner, put forward a theory of children's intellectual development in which he distinguished three sequential modes of representing experience. First, the *enactive* mode during which a child experienced the world by means of purely motor responses; second the *iconic* which involved pictorial images or models; and third the *symbolic* which involved language or abstract formulae. An example which is often given to illustrate these three modes is that of 'balance'. At a very early stage of intellectual development, a child might experience balance in terms of a see-saw – the enactive mode. Later he/she might understand some of the principles of balance by looking at various pictures and diagrams – the iconic mode. Finally, he/she might be able to make calculations about various kinds of balance by purely mathematical formulae – the symbolic mode. Bruner's modes clearly have much in common with Piaget's stages of development, but some teachers have found them to be more useful in classroom planning. (*see also* **Piagetian**, **stages of development**)

encyclopaedism A view of schooling which suggests that up to the compulsory school leaving age all education should be general and should be planned to cover the major kinds of **knowledge** and experiences. Thus a good education would be a balanced selection from the major forms of human knowledge and experience. (*see also* **essentialism**)

English as a foreign language (EFL) EFL is a commonly used abbreviation describing the teaching of English either to foreign students in the UK or in overseas countries. In the USA English as a second language (ESL) is often preferred, but the two are by no means identical. In recent years an attempt has been made to cover both fields by the term ESOL (English for speakers of other languages), since it is not always possible to make sensible distinctions between those for whom English is a foreign language, and those for whom English is a second language but not a foreign language. The problem is particularly acute in countries such as the UK and USA where large immigrant communities exist using their first, native language but for whom English is not a 'foreign' language. (*see also* **language schools**)

enrichment programme a programme of school activities designed either to compensate children from a deprived background, for example, the American **Head Start** programme or to provide additional stimulating experiences for the able.

entrance award At Oxford and Cambridge, financial awards may be made to certain applicants who are successful at the colleges' entrance exminations. These awards are either **scholarships** or **exhibitions**, the former being of greater value. There are both open and closed awards. Open awards are given solely on the basis of merit, whilst closed awards are restricted to certain categories, either of subject or of students from a particular school. (*see also* **bursary, discretionary award, entry qualification, mandatory award**)

entry qualification Most courses in higher education have prerequisites of some kind in the form of entry qualifications or entry requirements. For example, most masters degrees would require a second class honours degree at bachelor's level: most first degrees would require students to have passed at least two **'A' Levels**.

Equal Opportunities Commission (EOC) The Sex Discrimination Act (1975) (Sections 53–61 and Schedule 3) provided that a commission should be appointed by the Home Secretary to work towards the elimination of discrimination on the grounds of sex or marital status, to promote equality of opportunity between men and women and to keep under review the working of the Sex Discrimination Act (1975) and the Equal Pay Act (1970). The Sex Discrimination Act was amended in 1986 but the main provisions of the first Act are largely unchanged; the amendments being designed to extend its scope though not in relation to education (to cover small businesses or retirement ages). The EOC received nearly 3000 complaints about discrimination in educational provision between 1990 and 1992.

ERIC (Educational Resources Information Centre) An American-based system which issues a monthly abstracting journal *Resources in Education* on various aspects of educational research. Many libraries are also linked into the system. (*see also* **information retrieval, resource centre**)

essentialism (1) The belief that there is an 'essential' body of knowledge that all students should acquire. The term is sometimes employed in comparative education to refer to continental school systems such as the Soviet or the French. The term is also sometimes referred to as **encyclopaedism** which suggests that where there is a compulsory system of education, then this should be general education up to the compulsory school leaving age. (2) In philosophy, the term is used to describe Plato's theory that words only have meaning by reference to the resemblance of a particular object or quality to an ideal form. This kind of essentialism rests on the assumption that ideal forms exist in some meaningful sense. The curricular implications of this theory are that art and poetry are inferior to mathematics: whereas mathematics focuses upon the abstract form; art and poetry are concerned with imitation and, therefore, stray further and further away from ideal forms or 'the truth'.

ethnography, ethnomethodology Ethnographic studies refer to small-scale, micro studies of the school or classroom. Ethnomethodology is a branch of sociology invented by the American Harold Garfinkel in the 1960s which concentrates on the sociology of everyday social life. The stress in these studies would be in the way that participants interpret the situation. There is, therefore, sometimes a link between ethnomethodology and phenomenology. Both concepts have been used in educational research.

European Economic Community(EEC)/European Community (EC) The EEC, now European Community (EC), was established in 1957 with the aim of promoting the development of economic activities, enhancing the standard of living and encouraging closer relations between the member States by creating a Common Market. There is a permanent commission at Brussels. Member states are represented by a council of Ministers as well as a European Parliament. The EC publishes studies and pamphlets on a range of social and economic issues of concern to member States.

evaluation A term which may either refer to the general process of judging the worth of an educational programme, including judgements about the quality of its content, or more specifically to measurements of the effectiveness of learning experiences – what is often described in the UK as **assessment** of student **attainment**. In recent years, evaluation has been divided into two kinds – the more quantitative approach (sometimes referred to as the agricultural or botanical model); and those who declare that the measurement of educational experiences are much more complex and demand interviews and whole studies of the context of the experience.

evening class A class for those of post-school age which provides further education, cultural or leisure facilities. Such classes may be held in local education authority evening institutes, further education colleges or community colleges. (*see also* **continuing education, recurrent education**)

examination boards Bodies responsible for the conduct of public examinations. The best known are the eight **General Certificate of Education** (GCE) boards for 'A' levels, and the four **General Certificate of Secondary Education** (GCSE) groups of boards in England (plus one in Wales). Each of the GCSE boards is associated with the territory covered by the ex-**Certificate of Secondary Education** boards in the group, but accepts entries from anywhere in England and Wales.

examinations, mode of The traditional mode of public examinations in England and Wales is that a **syllabus** is agreed and examination papers set and marked by **examination boards** rather than by teachers themselves in their own schools. However, with the development of the **Certificate of Secondary Education (CSE)** in the 1960s, teachers were encouraged to be more involved at all levels of the examination process. In particular, teachers were allowed to propose their own syllabuses, to set papers for their own pupils and to mark them. This became known as Mode III examining (in contrast to the traditional Mode I). Mode II was a compromise whereby teachers worked out their own syllabus, but papers were set and marked by the board. When CSE examinations were superseded by the **General Certificate of Secondary Education** (GCSE) in 1988, there was a tendency to revert to Mode I as the normal requirement. (*see also* **graded assessment**)

examiner, external (1) At school level, a person responsible for marking the **examination** scripts or **coursework** where the examination has been externally set. For example, **General Certificate of Education** (GCE) and **General Certificate of Secondary Education** (GCSE) boards recruit experienced teachers for this work. (2) At post-school level, particularly in **higher education**, examiners are appointed from other similar institutions to ensure that the standards of students' work are being maintained.

examiner, internal (1) A member of a school of college staff responsible for marking candidates' scripts or other forms of presentation of an internally set examination. (2) At post-school level, particularly in higher education, a member of staff who undertakes the marking of her/his students examinations. They are then **moderated** by an **external examiner**.

exceptional children These can be regarded in one of two ways. The first is that they are markedly different from other children, in that they are, for example, mentally retarded, gifted or physically handicapped. The second regards children as differing in degree rather than in kind from each other, with the differences traceable to the result of the normal process of learning which are made different in their effects by physical, genetic or environmental factors. (*see also* **enrichment programme, giftedness, high flier, special needs education**)

exclusion Headteachers may ban a child from attending school on disciplinary grounds, for a temporary, indefinite or permanent period. Parents of an excluded child have, under the Education (No.2) Act (1986), the right of a hearing before a committee of the school's governing body with a view to the reinstatement of the child. Where this is not achieved, a further appeal can be made to the local education authority.

exhibition See **entrance award**.

expressive Expressive attitudes are contrasted with instrumental attitudes; expressive attitudes satisfying emotional needs rather than gaining some extrinsic or instrumental rewards. In the book *Instructional Objectives* edited by W. J. Popham (1969) Elliot Eisner made a similar distinction between expressive objectives and **instructional objectives**. With expressive objectives, there is no behavioural outcome but there may be a change in pupil attitude which is important but not measurable.

external degree A degree for which the candidate does not follow a formal course of study within a university, but sits the requisite **examinations** to gain a qualification. The University of London external degree system has been widely used throughout the world. (*see also* **degree**)

external examiner See **examiner, external**.

extra-mural department A department of a university which provides courses for the general public, mostly in the field of liberal **adult education**. The names of the departments vary, for example, **continuing education**, **adult education**.

extrinsic See **intrinsic/extrinsic**.

f

facility index A calculation of the ease with which any particular item in a test might be answered. It might be expressed in terms of the percentage of candidates answering that item correctly. (*see also* **difficulty index**)

faculty (1) A large division in a **higher education** institution which includes all the teaching staff, for example, faculty of medicine. Colleges themselves are sometimes organised into faculties which may cover a range of allied subjects, for example, faculty of humanities. Many secondary schools organise their work on a faculty basis. (2) A term once used in psychology to describe mental attributes.

falling rolls Since 1977, there has been a continuous decline in the total number of schools and pupils in England. This has led to lower intakes into all types of schools, a drop in demand for teacher recruitment and the closure or amalgamation of smaller schools. In 1981, the Department of Education and Science issued Circular 2/81 urgently requesting local education authorities to undertake a review of over-provision, and the White Paper on Public Expenditure (March 1982) set the Government's target of removing almost half a million school places by the following year.

In 1992, the **Audit Commission** reaffirmed the need for continuing reduction in school places. However, the 1988 Education Reform Act complicated the picture with its policy of open enrolment. The White Paper *Choice and Diversity* (1992) stated the Government's determination to eliminate surplus places in schools and release the resources for redeployment. The **Funding Agency for Schools** (FAS) and local education authorities will have a duty to keep under annual review the supply of places; and will also have the power to propose the rationalisation of schools.

family grouping An alternative, found especially in lower primary schools, to grouping by age in different classes. Where family grouping operates, a child remains in the same **class**, with the same teacher, for the whole of his or her time in that part of the school or for a period of several years. An alternative name for this system of organisation is **vertical age grouping**. (*see also* **setting, streaming**)

feasibility study A preliminary study which is often undertaken before launching a major research project. Such a study provides the team with preliminary data, and may suggest alternative strategies which can be adopted. It will also test the viability of the larger project before financial resources are committed. (*see also* **pilot study**)

feedback A term borrowed from the field of cybernetics where it has a more precise technical meaning. In education feedback normally refers to the process of giving information about results to the students and their teachers with a view to improving performance.

federal university As distinguished from a **collegiate** university such as Oxford or Cambridge. In a federal organisation, there is central control over the whole university whilst constituent colleges look after their internal affairs. The University of London is a good example. There is a senate consisting largely of teachers of the university which gives approval to boards of faculties' recommendations and sanctions the appointment of professors and readers to the university. There is also a network of other committees which ensures that matters affecting the colleges can be discussed. (*see also* **universities: history of**)

fellow (1) A senior member of an Oxford or Cambridge college who has a voice in the running of the college. Fellows teach and give tutorials to undergraduates. Before the University Test Act of 1871, Fellows had to be unmarried. (2) A member of a learned or professional society, such as Fellow of the Royal College of Physicians or Fellow of the Royal Historical Society. (3) A member of a college or university engaged in funded research with the title of **Research Fellow**.

field study A form of work underaken in an environment outside school or college. For example, geographical and biological studies may involve students in carrying out practical activities in either a rural or an urban setting. (*see also* **field trip**)

field trip A journey or excursion to a particular place by students as part of a **field study**.

first degree An initial **degree**, usually a Bachelor's, obtained by following a course of study at a **higher education** institution or by private study. (*see also* **external degree, undergraduate**)

first governor Appointed by a governing body of school for a period of five to seven years from the local community. First governors, of whom at least two must be drawn from parents of pupils at the school, must outnumber the total parent and teacher governors on the body. (*see also* **governors**)

first school The **Plowden Report** (1967) recommended that primary education should be restructured and that the age of transfer to secondary education should be changed. **Nursery education** should be available for children between 3 and 5 years to be followed by attendance at a first school from 5 to 8 years. From there the pupils would attend a **middle school** from 8 to 12 years. Children should enter the first school in the September following their fifth birthday. Where middle school reorganisation has not occurred, the traditional **infant school** still exists, spanning the age group of 5 to 7. (*see also* **junior school**)

flashcard Cards bearing words or letters used in schools in connection with the teaching of reading, especially word recognition. (*see also* **Gestalt**)

flexible grouping Organising the teaching of a large number of pupils (for example, a whole year group) in such a way that they could sometimes be taught in very large numbers, sometimes broken down into conventional classes of twenty-five or thirty, sometimes working in much smaller groups, and sometimes as individuals. (*see also* **timetabling** and **team teaching**)

form An alternative word for a **class** of pupils in a school. The term is invariably used for the highest class, the sixth form, which caters for those aged 16 and over.

formal assessment Section 5 of the 1981 Education Act required local education authorities to assess children's needs where there are special needs or learning difficulties. A **statement** of how these needs are to be met may then be drawn up. Requests for an assessment can come from a school, though parents can demand one. (*see also* **special educational needs**)

formative assessment The distinction between formative and summative assessment was first made by Michael Scriven in 1967; both terms have now become part of the language of education. Formative assessment is part of the 'formation' or development of a student; it is essentially concerned with providing **feedback** with a view to improving performance. Thus formative assessment has to take place during a course or programme whereas summative assessment occurs at the end.

formative evaluation/summative evaluation The process of making judgements about the value of a new curriculum project or new teaching materials with the intention of improving the project or the materials for the future. Unlike summative evaluation the intention is not to make a judgement about the final value of a project, but is intended to provide useful feedback to those preparing materials or working on the project so that improvements can be made before a summative evaluation takes place. (*see also* **developmental testing, evaluation**)

formula funding The income a school receives from its local education authority used to be governed by various weighting factors, for example, pupil numbers and those entitled to free meals. Local education authorities took into account some local factors in determining part of their schools' formula funding, but did not necessarily disclose the 'formula' on which funding was based. In some cases the normal method of allocating funds was to work from an 'historic' base and simply add on a percentage each year for inflation. This was not always seen to be fair, and in the 1980s there were increasing demands for openness about the way that funding was decided. The solution was to abandon any historic base and work to an open formula. The most important factor in the formula is number of pupils (which may be weighted according to age), but adjustments may also be made to account for additional expenses due to age of school, locality etc.

The **Education Reform Act** (1988) compelled local education authorities to provide for the **local management of schools** (LMS) by giving schools more spending autonomy, giving them at least 85 per cent of the total amount calculated (i.e. retaining only 15 per cent or less for central services).

foundation course A basic, introductory course usually designed to prepare students for more advanced courses. The foundation course may be a prerequisite for more advanced courses in the same area. An **Open University** foundation course may be required, for example, in arts/humanities before students proceed to more advanced work in English literature. (see *also* **general education**)

foundation subjects The Education Reform Act (1988) establishing a **national curriculum** stipulated that mathematics, English and science should form the core of the school curriculum and first priority will be given to these subjects. In addition there are other foundation subjects, namely, history, geography, technology, music, art and physical education. A modern foreign language is included in relation to **Key Stages** 3 and 4 and Welsh in relation to schools in Wales which are not Welsh speaking.

franchising A partnership between **further** and **higher education** institutions in the matter of course provision. This may take the form, for instance, of part or whole of the first year of a **degree** course being taken in a further education college.

free period Can refer either to the time allocated to teaching staff for preparation or marking of lessons or to pupils who undertake private unsupervised study.

free-response question An open-ended question in an examination where, in the absence of a prescribed pattern of response, the candidate is invited to explain or discuss work or material of which he/she is familiar.

free school A type of school which emerged in the early 1970s for parents interested in **alternative education**. It also catered for some children who had made little progress in state schools, having a freer curriculum. A number existed in London, such as the White Lion Street Free School in Islington (opened in 1972) and in other large cities and were largely financed by local enterprise. (*see also* **deschooling**)

full inspection A term used to describe the visit of a team of **inspectors** representing a range of subject or phase interests, to an educational institution. The findings of the team are normally enshrined in a report which, as from January 1983, became publicly available. (*see also* **advisers, Her Majesty's Inspectorate**)

full-time equivalent (fte) In those institutions of **higher education** or **further education** where full-time and part-time students are recruited, it is important from the point of view of staffing requirements and other resources to calculate the whole student body in terms of full-time equivalents. Frequently part-time students would count for half a full-time student. In further education it is frequently possible to convert part-time students into fte in terms of the 'contact hours'. In universities this is rarely calculated since most part-time students can be converted into fte in terms of the length of the course rather than the amount of instruction which they receive.

functional literacy The level of skill in reading and writing that any individual needs in order to cope with adult life. It is clearly very difficult to arrive at a satisfactory definition of functional literacy, but in the USA there have been prosecutions brought by parents against a school or school system for failing to equip a child at school leaving age with functional literacy. The idea behind that view of schooling is that functional literacy would be a right of all normal pupils and that it would be the duty of the school to provide it. (*see also* **literacy**)

funding See **local management of schools** (LMS).

Funding Agency for Schools (FAS) Based on the **Further Education Funding Council** (FEFC) and the **Higher Education Funding Council** (HEFC), this new agency has the task of financing and monitoring grant-maintained schools. It is also concerned with the admission of children.

fund-raising Formerly a fringe activity in schools, fund-raising is widely carried out often to supply basic educational materials such as books, furniture and teaching equipment such as computers. Primary schools which receive a lower level of funding than secondary schools, are much involved in this activity. It has been argued that fund-raising highlights the differences between those schools in affluent, middle-class areas which may raise large amounts as against those schools in deprived areas where the tradition has not been established.

Further and Higher Education Act (1992) This important piece of legislation approved by Parliament in March 1992 changed the pattern of post-16 education. Sixth-form, tertiary and further education colleges were removed from local authority control. The financial aspects would be dealt with by the **Further Education Funding Councils** (FEFC); one for England and one for Wales. It also abolished the **binary** divide and allowed polytechnics to be called universities, those in England sharing a funding agency, the **Higher Education Funding Council** (HEFC), with separate funding councils for Wales and Scotland. During the passage of the Bill, there was much discussion in Parliament on the need for safeguards for academic freedom, which seemed to be under threat by some of the Bill's provisions. (*see* Section 1, Essay 9)

further education (FE) A term covering all types of post-school education apart from that given in universities. Much of it is vocationally orientated though not exclusively so. Much of the teaching is carried on in the 450 further education colleges which, before March 1992, were administered by local education authorities. It has been argued that with their newly gained independence, the colleges should be more responsive to local needs, especially in the training aspect. (*see* Section 1, Essay 9)

Further Education Funding Council (FEFC) The Further and Higher Education Act 1992 established this Council in place of the local education authorities who were previously responsible for the financing of further education colleges. The money for the colleges is now channelled through the FEFC, and bids for all courses must be submitted to it by institutions. Responsibility for funding adult education is divided between the Council and the local education authority. (*see* Section 1, Essay 9)

Further Education Unit (FEU) The Unit was established in 1977 to serve as a focal point for further education curriculum matters. It determines priorities for action to improve the total provision, reviews curricula in this sector and identifies duplication and deficiencies, assists in curricular experiments, contributes to the evaluation of the attainment of objectives and disseminates information on curriculum development. A recent example of its work has been the publication of a three-pronged approach to **quality** measurement which could be used by a funding council to **assess** the performance of colleges. Although the

Unit was financed by and housed in the Department of Education and Science (DES), it was free to operate independently from the Department's policies. From January 1983 the Unit became an agency independent of the DES. In April 1992, it merged with the Unit for the Development of Adult and Continuing Education. (*see also* **PICKUP, profiles**)

g

games and simulations Certain kinds of 'games' are designed to be used in teaching to present occurrences in a given order so that pupils can gain insights into some kinds of human interaction. Simulations involve students taking on roles and may be more open-ended than games such as *Monopoly*. A simulation ought, for example, to involve examining the advantages and disadvantages of siting a new airport: roles might be allocated to students who would proceed to make plans, argue their case and so on.

Gaussian curve The shape of a graph showing a normal distribution. Sometimes also referred to as **normal** curve. It is a bell-shaped curve which occurs for a graph showing how many people obtain each possible score on a measured variable such as height. Psychologists also assume that intelligence falls into a normal distribution, and therefore express **IQ** (intelligence quotient) scores in terms of the Gaussian curve showing very few people as extremely intelligent and very few as extremely dull, with the curve rising to a hump around the average score (in terms of IQ, the score of 100). Opponents of IQ testing frequently complain that it is simply an assumption not an established fact to suppose that intelligence falls into the same kind of curve as height. (*see also* **intelligence test, parametric statistics**)

General Certificate of Education (GCE) The GCE 'O' (ordinary) and 'A' (advanced) level examinations were introduced in 1951 replacing the **School Certificate** and **Higher School Certificate** examinations. GCE 'O' level remained as a school leaving examination for 16-year-old pupils until it was replaced by the **General Certificate of Secondary Education** (GCSE) in 1988. GCE 'A' level, although much criticised, is still the main leaving examination for academic 18-year-old school leavers, and is the normal entrance requirement for higher education. (*see* Section 1, Essay 5)

General Certificate of Secondary Education (GCSE) An examination for 16-year-olds formed from a combination of **General Certificate of Education 'O' Level** and **Certificate of Secondary Education** (CSE). First awards were made in 1988. (*see* Section 1, Essay 5)

general education Perhaps best described as the opposite of 'specialised' or 'specialist' education. Many educationists believe that before embarking upon a specialist course of study it is important to have covered a wide range of subjects and subject matter. This would apply particularly to **primary schools** and the first three or four years in **secondary schools** in the UK. In some **universities** a general **foundation** course is provided in the first year rather than specialist courses. (*see also* **liberal education**)

General National Vocational Qualifications See **National Vocational Qualifications**.

General Teaching Council (GTC) Since 1860 attempts have been made to found a General Teaching Council (GTC) for England and Wales, analogous to the General Medical Council (GMC), to govern the profession. The Council would deal with matters such as the training, the supply and qualifications of teachers, the establishment of a code of conduct and the raising of professional standards. A disciplinary committee might be given powers to strike teachers off the register. A Scottish General Teaching Council (SGTC) has existed since 1965, though its achievements have been limited.

Gestalt Gestalt is the German word for 'configuration'. At the beginning of the twentieth century a school of psychology, developed in Germany, was later referred to as 'Gestalt psychology'. Its main assumption was that the human brain has a tendency to organise experience into patterned configurations or wholes. The word 'Gestalt' was used to refer to the whole of a perception or thought process rather than the individual items within it. In education, Gestalt psychologists have been influential in encouraging teachers to concentrate pupils' attention on the whole (the Gestalt) rather than on parts. In **reading,** this has tended to support 'look and say' or looking at the whole sentence rather than phonic methods of reading. (*see also* **flashcard, learning theory, reading age, reductionism**)

giftedness An ambiguous term, sometimes referring to children of supposed high **IQ** (intelligence quotient) for whom schools should make special provision; sometimes used to identify children with specific talents in fields such as music or dancing. The 'gifted' are also sometimes included in the generic term **'exceptional children'** or **'children with special needs'**. (*see also* **National Association for Gifted Children**)

girls' education Views differ on the benefits of single-sex or mixed schools for girls' education. A 1992 survey by Her Majesty's Inspectorate entitled *The Preparation of Girls for Adult and Working Life* claims that girls are more likely to develop high aspirations in the best single-sex schools. Self-confidence is created in all-girls schools, partly because 'teachers in mixed schools paid insufficient attention to the ways in which boys sometimes dominate work in classrooms and and other key areas of school life.' It is for this reason that in mixed schools classroom management, curriculum policy and pupil counselling all need careful monitoring. (*see also* **Equal Opportunities Commission, Girls' Public Day School Trust, Girls' School Association**)

Girls' Public Day School Trust (GPDST) This Trust was established in 1872 to promote a scheme for a public day school for girls at Chelsea. The Taunton Report of 1868 had disclosed the grave shortage of suitable educational institutions for girls of middle-class families.

governors All maintained schools are required by law to have a board of governors. In recent years the powers and responsibilities of governors has steadily increased. The 1944 Education Act required the duties of governors to be set out in an **instrument of government** and the functions of governors in relation to headteachers and local education authorities set out in **articles of government**.

The 1980 Education Act extended the responsibilities of governors (following the recommendation of the Taylor Report, 1977) and stipulated that elected representation of teachers and parents should be included in the board of governors.

The 1988 Education Reform Act added to governors' responsibilities (*see* **local management of schools** (LMS)). And in the case of those schools which 'opted out' of local authority control (see **grant-maintained schools** (GMS)) the powers of governors appeared to be very great indeed and gave rise to celebrated disputes. (*see also* **manager**)

grade A mark given to students to denote their achievement *either* in a specific test for a specific assignment, *or* to indicate the level of achievement at the end of a year or course. Grades or **levels** of achievement may be in literal (i.e. alphabetical) or numerical form.

grade criteria In **criterion-referenced** assessment each level of achievement or grade should be indentifiable by strictly defined criteria (**standards**).

grade descriptions In order to assist examiners and assessors award appropriate grades, it is sometimes the practice to describe the kind of answer or quality of work expected for grade A, B etc. Grade descriptions are a weaker version of **criterion referencing** than **grade criteria**.

graded assessment (GA) Schemes of graded assessment have been developed as an alternative to **GCE** 'O'level, **CSE** and – more recently – **GCSE** examinations. One purpose is to avoid leaving most assessment until the end of the course; another is to allow pupils to progress at their own individual pace and to be assessed whenever it is most appropriate. It is claimed that graded assessment dramatically enhances student motivation and performance. (*see* **examinations**, and Section 1, Essay 5)

graded reader A reader in this context refers to a book rather than a person. A graded reader is a book which is graded in terms of reading difficulty. Such books are usually produced as a **series** so that a pupil systematically progresses from one level of difficulty to the next. The pupil is gradually stretched, but does not encounter too many difficulties in the same page or chapter of the book. Some teachers and reading specialists, however, dislike this kind of mechanical approach and prefer to use 'real books'. (*see also* reading)

graded test   Graded tests are to be distinguished from graded assessment. Graded tests have been designed to indicate levels of achievement in subjects where progress in specific skills can be measured in a standard way – especially in modern languages and numeracy skills.

graduate   (1) In Great Britain, the term graduate is normally used for a person who has successfully completed an undergraduate or degree course at a university or higher education institution and has been awarded a degree. (2) An honorary graduate is a person awarded a degree (usually a masters degree or doctorate) without taking a course, as a means of publicly recognising distinction of some kind. (3) In the USA (and some other systems) to graduate means to complete any course – hence the term 'high school graduate'.

Graduate Teacher Training Registry (GTTR)   The Graduate Teacher Training Registry is a clearing house for courses of initial teacher education. Graduates, or undergraduates, in the final year of their degree courses, wishing to take a Postgraduate Certificate in Education (PGCE) qualification register with the GTTR. Candidates list the PGCE institutions in order of priority, rather than making separate applications to a number of institutions.

grammar school   The term grammar school was first used in the fourteenth century for a type of school founded to provide free or subsidised education for children (usually boys) in a locality. Latin was always an important part of the curriculum. By the nineteenth century many grammar schools had deteriorated, and were reformed by the Grammar School Act (1840). The 1902 Education Act gave the newly created local education authorities (LEAs) power to provide secondary schools on grammar school lines. The 1944 Education Act stipulated that secondary education should be free and compulsory. Some local education authorities interpreted the Act to mean that three different types of secondary school should be available for three supposed kinds of ability: secondary grammar schools, secondary technical and secondary modern. By 1990 only about 7 per cent of local authorities had retained any grammar schools.

grant-maintained school (GMS)   A school which has chosen to 'opt out' of local education authority control and receive finance direct from the Department for Education. (*see* Education Reform Act (1988), and Section 1, Essay 7)

graphicacy   A term invented as a parallel to literacy, numeracy and oracy. Graphicacy covers the ability to think visually and spatially as well as the mastery of certain basic skills.

'Great Debate'   On 18 October 1976, the Labour Party Prime Minister, James Callaghan, made a speech at Ruskin College, Oxford, calling for a public debate on education. The Ruskin speech was followed by eight one-day regional conferences in February and March 1977. As a result, in July 1977, a **Green Paper**, *Education in Schools: A Consultative Document* was issued. (*see also* **Yellow Book**)

Greats The name given to an undergraduate course at the University of Oxford devoted to classical languages, history and philosophy. Its correct title is *Literae Humaniories*.

Green Paper A government may choose to set out proposals for future policy in the form of a consultative or discussion document. This is known as a Green Paper. (*see also* **Parliamentary Papers**)

Grubb Institute Named after its funding president, the late Sir Kenneth Grubb, the Grubb Institute is a group of consultants who work with clients to develop or improve their own management systems. The Grubb Institute has worked successfully with local education authorities (especially the Inner London Education Authority before its abolition in 1988) as well as with individual schools or groups of schools. The Grubb 'style' is to try to enable schools (as well as other kinds of organisations) to develop their own management system rather than to impose a package or a formula.

h

half-term A short holiday given by schools in the middle of each term. (*see also* **academic year**, **semester**, **vacation**)

hall, university (1) A building, either on or away from the **campus**, for students' residence. (2) At Oxford and Cambridge, formerly a place, not a college, where students lived under the supervision of a Master of Arts. The title still exists in the name of some of the present colleges, such as Trinity Hall and St Edmund Hall.

halo effect The psychologist, R. L. Thorndike, observed that in the process of various kinds of **assessment** the judgements of an assessor tend to be biased by a previous assessment (even if the assessment was of a totally unconnected ability). The halo effect can thus be either negative or positive.

Handbook of Suggestions for Teachers The ending of 'payment by results' at the end of the nineteenth century, left the elementary school teacher free to pursue her/his work without central regulation. The first *Handbook of Suggestions for Teachers* was issued by the Board of Education in 1905 to inform teachers of good practice. All aspects of the elementary curriculum were dealt with, whole chapters being devoted to individual subjects. The 'Handbook' was frequently revised, the last one appearing in 1937.

handwriting The importance of handwriting in schools is becoming increasingly recognised. Studies have shown that pupils with bad handwriting will often disrupt lessons rather than have their lack of skill exposed, and it also tends to lower self-esteem. Many schools, particularly first and middle, have promoted common practices with handwriting development programmes and liaise with parents of pre-school age. Since 1988, it has been part of the English **National Curriculum**. A survey by the **National Foundation for Educational Research** (NFER) in 1992 showed that more 7-year-olds needed a 'writing rescue' programme than special help with reading.

Hansard Verbatim reports on the debates in both Houses of Parliament which are published by Her Majesty's Stationery Office (HMSO). Since 1943, the parliamentary debates, and official reports, have had the name *Hansard* on their covers. This is a reference to the printer, Luke Hansard, who printed the journals of the House of Commons from 1774. *Hansard* is a very useful reference source for researchers on many aspects of education. (*see also* **Hansard Society**)

Hansard Society The Hansard Society for parliamentary government is a non-party organisation, founded by an Independent MP, Commander (later Lord) King-Hall in 1944. The Society's original aim was to encourage people to read the daily *Hansard* reports of parliamentary debates. It now has wider aims, and provides information on the workings of British democracy and assessing how well the system continues to serve today's needs. The Society played a part in promoting political education in schools, and it has a Curriculum Review Unit to monitor trends in teaching politics. (*see also* **Hansard**)

Hawthorne effect In the early days of industrial psychology it was observed in a study by Elton Mayo of the Hawthorne works near Chicago, that when individuals are being observed, they tend to perform better. This is important in educational studies because if a new teaching method or a new curriculum project is introduced into a classroom and the pupils improve their performance, this may be caused not by the value of the new approach but simply because the pupils are receiving extra attention. Hawthorne effect is sometimes extended to mean simply 'the effect of the novelty of a new set of materials which eventually wears off.'

head boy/girl A pupil, elected or appointed as leader of **prefects** in a school. His or her duties are often concerned with maintaining discipline and the orderly running of the school.

head of department or faculty Heads of departments or faculties in schools and colleges are persons who are in charge of their subject or a range of subjects at all levels, and coordinate the work of the department's staff. They are responsible for helping to formulate academic policy in relation to the overall school policy, encouraging curriculum development and often assist the head or principal in deciding on matters affecting the whole institution. A head of department normally holds departmental staff meetings to discuss matters of common concern to teachers working in the department. A **National Foundation for Educational Research** (NFER) survey published in 1989 showed that headteachers all expected their middle managers to be pro-active rather than re-active. The provision of middle management training by schools and authorities varies considerably over the country.

head of house, head of year See **pastoral system**.

Head Start A nationally funded programme started in the USA in 1964 which provided **disadvantaged** pre-school children with educational and social services. In its early years, notably through a study undertaken by Ohio University and the Westinghouse Learning Corporation, it was believed that **compensatory education** programmes had little effect. However, follow-up studies since 1975 have revealed the long-term benefits of Head Start in achievement in primary and secondary schools as well as in out-of-school behaviour. (*see also* **enrichment programme**)

Headmasters' Conference (HMC) Originally set up in 1869 to oppose the investigations of the Endowed Schools Commission into grammar and endowed schools, the Conference consists of headteachers of about 240 boys' and coeducational schools. The main mover of the Conference was Edward Thring of Uppingham, and the first gathering took place in his school. Annual meetings are still held. Membership of the Conference has been the hallmark of a **public school**. (*see also* **Headmasters' Association, headteacher, independent school**)

headteacher The term headteacher covers both headmaster and headmistress and applies to those in primary as well as in secondary schools. The head is expected to provide effective leadership, though systematic training for this role is by no means universal. Research also shows that heads differ widely in their conception of the relative importance of the different aspects of their work. It is now generally agreed that training in the skills of headship is needed in such areas as interpersonal and management skills, and knowledge of how to evaluate a school's performance and the ability to work closely with governors. The majority of heads are men: in 1992 53 per cent of primary school heads were men and 83 per cent of secondary schools. Since the **Education Reform Act (1988)** when the majority of schools were given control of their budgets and **open enrolment** was introduced, heads have had greater responsibilities for promoting the school and ensuring financial viability.

Health Education Authority (HEA) Formerly the Health Education Council, the HEA is a special health authority within the National Health Service. Its task is to provide information and advice about health directly to the public, to support other organisations who provide health education and to advise the Secretary of State on this subject. Health education for young people between the ages of 5 and 19 is an important aspect of the Authority's work. They provide information and encourage skills to enable children to make healthy choices about their lives. Recent work includes the launch of the 'Promoting Health in Primary Schools' project: the training of teachers to use material in connection with the 'My Body' project; the expansion of the 'Happy Heart' project which develops health education through physical activity in primary schools; and the development of the 'Health in Clubs' project by the training of youth workers in respect of health education.

Her Majesty's Inspectorate (HMI)   Her Majesty's Inspectorate dates back to 1839, when inspectors were appointed to supervise the proper spending of public money for the education of the poor. From the passing of the 1944 Education Act, the Inspectorate's responsibilities were widened, with all schools and colleges maintained from public funds open to inspection. From the beginning, HMIs have been called 'the eyes and ears of the Department' and an important function was to give advice to the Secretary of State and officials of the Department of Education and Science. As HMIs are appointed by **Order in Council**, they are not civil servants and are thus able to form independent judgements on educational issues. Until recently, there was a senior chief inspector, six chief inspectors with overall responsibility for the Inspectorate's work and about sixty staff inspectors who had national responsibility for a particular phase or subject.

Although by the 1990s the Inspectorate had only about 500 members, their work included providing **in-service training** courses for teachers, carrying out inspections of institutions, preparing reports and discussion documents for publication, liaising with local education authorities, and serving as observers on many bodies. HMIs were essentially concerned with national developments, and their work differed in many respects from local advisers. Examples of this were the two national surveys undertaken in 1978–9 by HMI of primary and secondary schools, where 10 per cent of each type of school were inspected. In this way, it was possible to form opinions on national **standards**.

A scrutiny of the work of the Inspectorate by Lord Rayner in 1983 agreed with the Inspectorate's policy of carrying out general surveys in order to render advice to ministers rather than conducting inspections of individual institutions. Rayner also suggested that HMI reports on schools and colleges should be published, though in fact this had already been done since January 1983.

The Education (Schools) Act 1992 introduced a new system of privatised inspection. An independent office of Her Majesty's Chief Inspector of Schools was established in September 1992 in place of the Senior Chief Inspector. The name of the department is the **Office for Standards in Education** (OFSTED). The new inspection teams, consisting of registered inspectors, who may be full- or part-time, carry out a programme of four-year inspections of all schools. Recruitment of new inspectors to form the teams was by national advertisement. HMI numbers were reduced and their functions limited mainly to the training and monitoring of the quality of the new inspectors. (*see* **local education authority inspectors**, and Section 1, Essay 4)

hidden curriculum See **curriculum**.

high flier Term used for a very able pupil with high attainments. (*see also* **giftedness, exceptional children**)

high school A term formerly used widely by **grammar** and **independent schools**. It now more commonly describes junior secondary schools, catering for 11- to 14-year-olds.

higher degree A **postgraduate** degree obtained, either by research or by following a taught course, at the Masters' or doctoral levels. (*see also* **dissertation, graduate, university department of education, viva**)

higher education (HE) This term is usually used to distinguish courses of study which result in the award of a degree, diploma or similar advanced qualification, from various kinds of **further education** (FE). So far such work has been conducted in universities, which awarded their own degrees, and polytechnics which offered them in the name of the Council for National Academic Awards (CNAA). **The Further and Higher Education Act** (1992) removed this distinction and replaced it with a single higher education system embodying both institutions.

Higher Education Funding Council (HEFC) Established in January 1992, this Council deals with the funding of the single higher education sector resulting from the **Further and Higher Education Act** (1992). It encourages neighbouring institutions, for example a university and a former polytechnic, to share staff, students and resources whilst remaining competitive. Amongst its tasks is the determination of funding methodology for research and teaching. The Council attempts to measure how well institutions succeed in these functions and awards funds accordingly.

Higher National Diploma (HND) A post-school vocational award of more advanced nature than the **Ordinary National Diploma**. It was usually regarded as roughly equal to the standard of a university pass degree and required the equivalent of two years' full-time study. It was replaced by the **Business and Technical Education Council** qualifications and since 1986, is coordinated by the **National Council for Vocational Qualifications**.

HMI See **Her Majesty's Inspectorate**.

Home and School Council A partnership of four pressure groups, the **Advisory Centre for Education** (ACE), the **National Confederation of Parent-Teacher Associations** (NCPTA), the **Campaign for State Education** (CASE) and the **National Association for Primary Education** (NAPE). The Council, formed in 1967, produces a number of practical guides for parents, teachers, governors and those involved in home-school matters.

home education Section 36 of the 1944 Education Act stated that 'it shall be the duty of the parent of every child of compulsory school age to cause him to receive efficient, full-time education suitable to his age, ability and aptitude, either by regular attendance at school or otherwise.' The final two words give parents the opportunity to educate their children at home in accordance with their own principles. Local education authorities differ in their attitude towards home education; some request detailed curriculum, others are content with a statement of broad aims, and some take parents to court. An organisation for like-minded parents on this issue was formed in 1977 with the title of **Education Otherwise** and has a thriving membership. However, it has been argued that if a child is over-involved with her/his parents, this may lead to difficulties later when the child wishes to establish an independent life. (*see also* **compulsory education, home tuition**)

home-school partnership The **Education Reform Act** 1988 increased the powers of parents as governors, but did little to involve the majority in the day-to-day education of their children. There is increasing opportunity, based on European precedents, for this situation to be changed. A number of schools, in conjunction with parents, have drawn up contracts which are agreements for shared responsibility, with a review each year involving the teacher, parent and child. One example is that parents undertake to attend a workshop where an area of the curriculum is explained in order that they can help their child. The **Plowden Report** (1967) had identified the need for a closer home school-relationship.

home tutor A teacher employed by a local education authority to give lessons to children who are unable for various reasons to attend school. The work may be done in either the tutor's or the child's home. (*see also* **home tuition**)

home tuition Often used by parents whose children need extra coaching in a subject or subjects in order to pass an examination. Home tutors who may or may not be qualified teachers, often advertise locally and visit homes after the school day is ended. Problems may arise with the **General Certificate of Secondary Education** (GCSE), where there is a proportion of course assessment, when the tutor may unduly and unfairly aid the pupil. (*see also* **home education, Education Otherwise**)

homework Originally called 'home lessons', the practice of setting extra work out of school began in the early nineteenth century. After the system of '**payment by results**' had been instituted in 1862, the volume of homework increased in elementary schools: the establishment of the Oxford and Cambridge 'Local' examinations from 1857 had a similar effect on secondary schools. By the 1880s, medical reasons were being advanced against the imposition of homework, but with little effect. In the present century, several government reports dealing with aspects of education have commented on the effects of homework on children's out-of-school life, but no action has followed. Many schools now have homework policies and monitor them to ensure that there is a balance between subjects and types of work. At its best, homework can help pupils to acquire self-discipline, and if used diagnostically, to do better in their work. In 1985, a discussion document by the Department of Education and Science stated that the relationship between homework and the curriculum should be carefully scrutinised as well as the quality and quantity of homework demanded from pupils.

honorary degree A **degree** awarded by a higher education institution to persons distinguished in their own field. The degree is conferred at a public ceremony, usually by the **chancellor** or head of the institution.

honours degree An examination of a higher standard than a pass degree and one which may have a different syllabus. Honours degrees are usually divided into different **classes**, the first being the highest, second (often sub-divided into upper and lower) and third. (*see also* **class**)

house system Originally an essentially **public school** phenomenon, where pupils are allocated to boarding houses under the supervision of a housemaster/ mistress. The house system is now found in the great majority of **comprehensive** schools. These schools may be divided into a number of houses, either located in individual buildings or not, for social and academic activities. All members of staff are attached to houses and most of them look after a tutor group of up to thirty children for the rest of their school lives. **Tutor groups** may consist of pupils of the same age group or of a large age range. (*see also* **boarding school**)

humanities A term usually employed to group a number of disciplines or subjects together, all of which are concerned with some aspect of human life. History, human geography, literature and philosophy, and sometimes the social sciences are included in the term humanities. In schools, under a humanities umbrella, a number of subjects are drawn upon to provide pupils with a coherent approach to understanding major human and social issues.

hurdle Refers to a given level of performance which candidates must reach on an examination component in order to succeed. There are a number of factors which govern the level of the hurdle, the most important of which is a consideration of all the candidates' performances.

i

iconic See **enactive**.

impression marking In the marking of essays there are broadly two approaches. The first is to mark the essay as a whole and to give an overall (or impression) mark for style, content and presentation. The alternative is a more analytic approach which sets down beforehand what kind of points a candidate should make, and then marks are awarded for each of those points made, possibly with marks being added or deducted for style, spelling and other 'automatic errors'. The fairest or most accurate method is said to be a combination of both ways of marking, namely a group of examiners some of whom use the analytic style and some the impression marking, and then averaging the marks for each candidate. This is, however, a very expensive way of treating scripts and is rarely used.

inaugural lecture A lecture given by a new **professor** on aspects of his or her **discipline**.

incentive allowances See **teachers' salaries**.

Incorporated Association of Preparatory Schools (IAPS) The Association consists of over 500 headteachers of **preparatory** schools, and since January 1981 represents girls' as well as boys' schools. It keeps heads informed of developments in education. (*see also* **preparatory school, registration of independent schools**)

independent learning See **individual learning**.

independent schools **Public schools** and other kinds of **private schools** increasingly prefer to be known as independent schools. Many private schools are now members of the Independent Schools Information Service (ISIS) which acts as a pressure group on government. (*see also* **registration of independent schools**)

Independent Schools Information Service (ISIS) This organisation, founded in 1965 and which became a national body in 1972, provides an information service for parents and others interested in independent education. It receives its funds from the Governing Bodies Association (GBA) which also represents schools in the Headmasters' Conference (HMC), the Governing Bodies of Girls' Schools Association (GBGSA), the Incorporated Association of Preparatory Schools (IAPS) and the Independent Schools Association (ISA). There are eight ISIS regional offices which answer more than 100,000 enquiries annually. The National ISIS Commission encourages research about independent schools and undertakes a detailed annual statistical census of all these schools.

individual learning There are at least two somewhat different meanings to this term. (1) The first focuses on pupils working on their own, perhaps by means of worksheets, perhaps by programmed materials of some kind. (2) The second meaning refers to the need to allow children to learn not only at an individual pace, but also to make use of different approaches, styles of learning and personality differences. The latter is much less common than the former. The first of the two meanings is sometimes also referred to as independent learning. (*see also* **mastery learning, programmed learning**)

induction scheme In the past, some local education authorities held short induction courses for newly qualified teachers (and newly appointed **head-teachers** or **deputy heads**). The **James Report** (1972) recommended that all newly qualified teachers should, in the first year at school, be given a light timetable which would enable them to spend one-fifth of the teaching week in some kind of further training. The James Report also recommended that teachers undergoing this induction year should be supported by specially appointed **professional tutors** in the school, possibly one of the deputy headteachers. This aspect of the James Report was never completely implemented, but a few pilot schemes of induction were tried out with varying degrees of success. Many schemes suffered from the financial problems faced by local education authorities in the late-1970s and early-1980s. The emphasis on school-based initial **teacher training** has increased the importance of induction with the virtual abolition of a formal period of probation. (*see also* **probation**, **teacher tutor**)

industrial training The training of employees in industry either at their place of work or in vocationally oriented courses in **further education**. The **Industrial Training Act** (1964) was intended to increase the amount of industrial training as well as its quality. **Industrial training boards** (ITBs) were set up to organise training and to share the cost of training more fairly. Over thirteen million workers were covered by the scheme. The Act was regarded as only partially successful and was modified by the **Employment and Training Act** (1973). ITBs were threatened by the general attack on quangos in 1980 to 1981, and in 1982 the Government decided to wind up the majority of the boards, replacing them with 'voluntary arrangements'. The current arrangement is the network of **training and enterprise councils** which is coordinated by the Department of Employment.

industry, links with schools Throughout the twentieth century and particularly since the 1944 Education Act, schools frequently made a distinction between education, which was the concern of schools, and training which was the concern of industry itself. Any kind of vocational training within schools was particularly offensive to many teachers and their professional organisations. One of the features of James Callaghan's **Ruskin College** speech of 1976 was the insufficient regard by schools for the adult world, particularly the world of work. From this time onwards, Department of Education and Science documents emphasised the need for schools to be concerned with the world of work. At the same time, the **Manpower Services Commission** (MSC) and its various training programmes seemed to be preserving the barrier between school and training for work. This continued until 1982 when a proposal was made, financed by the MSC, to introduce technical education into schools as well as **colleges of further education** starting with the 14-year-old pupils in some selected schools. This was known as the **Technical and Vocational Education Initiative** (TVEI). Links between schools and industry were further encouraged by various aspects of the **Education Reform Act** (1988). (*see also* '**Great Debate**', **industrial training**)

infant school A school catering for children between the ages of 5 and 7. Most now form part of a **primary school** with a **junior** department and perhaps a nursery.

information technology (IT) Information technology draws heavily on three complex technologies which have converged: computing, micro-electronics and telecommunications. Many schools now make considerable use of this technology, for example, personal computers (PCs), videotex such as Prestel and CD ROM, and calculators. (*see also* **computer assisted learning** (CAL))

Inner London Education Authority (ILEA) The Inner London Education Authority (ILEA) was established in 1964 when the London County Council merged into the Greater London Council as a result of the London Government Act (1963). It was the largest local education authority, and was Labour controlled for most of its existence. It was abolished by the **Education Reform Act** (1988) and its responsibilities shared among the thirteen inner London boroughs, each of which became a new local education authority.

in-service education of teachers (INSET) For many years one of the constant complaints about the teaching service has been the lack of provision of **continuing education** and training for teachers. It was alleged that many teachers took no courses after their initial qualification to update their professional skills or to broaden their educational horizons. The **James Report** (1972) was particularly concerned with the provision of professional courses for teachers throughout their careers. INSET is generally taken to include short courses run by the Department for Education or the local authority; short courses or day conferences at **teachers centres** and secondment to study for diploma and higher degrees in education either on a full-time or a part-time basis.

inspection and inspectors See **Her Majesty's Inspectorate**, **local education authority inspectors**.

instruction A term sometimes used to indicate the same kind of process as 'teaching', but generally in a more limited and less ambitious sense. Thus, in English educational terminology, instruction is to training as teaching is to education. (*see* Section 1, Essay 1)

instructor A term for those not holding recognised teacher qualifications. The majority of these teach commercial studies, though there are instructors on **technology**.

instrument of government The 1944 Education Act (Section 17) laid down that every primary school should have an instrument of management and every secondary school an instrument of government, which set out the constitution for bodies of **managers** and **governors**. The 1980 Education Act made a number of changes in nomenclature. The term 'managers' was abolished and now both primary and secondary schools have governors. Similarly, both types of schools now have instruments of government and articles of government.

instrumental enrichment (IE) Instrumental enrichment has nothing to do with music education. It is a set of techniques, based on the ideas of Feuerstein, to help children improve their thinking ability. In the USA materials have been developed by Curriculum Development Associates Inc. to stimulate problem-solving skills in the classroom. They were originally designed for educationally retarded children in order to accelerate their learning and to enable them to be integrated into normal classes; but they have since been found useful for all kinds of children – usually high school students aged between 12 and 14 years. The materials have been used experimentally in the UK.

instrumental learning Instrumental in this sense implies not for its own sake but to achieve some other goal. An example of instrumental learning might be for an individual to learn a foreign language not because he or she found any pleasure in that learning, but because it might be useful for travelling abroad. Most educationists would prefer **expressive** learning, that is, the kind of learning where no external reward or motivation is needed, but where the learning process is valuable and satisfying in its own right. There would be a connection, therefore, between instrumental learning and extrinsic motivation; expressive learning and intrinsic motivation. (*see also* **intrinsic/extrinsic**)

integrated day The conventional school timetable is replaced, under an integrated day system, by a more flexible approach which enables pupils to explore resources and to work at their own pace. This approach is found mainly in **primary schools**.

integrated studies During the 1950s and 1960s various attempts were made, especially in **secondary modern** schools and **comprehensive** schools, to break down the existing subject barriers by planning courses across a wider range. In the primary school there had been a longer tradition of approaching teaching by way of projects rather than through subjects. One such approach was described as the 'integrated day' which virtually abolished the formal timetable and emphasised **topics**, **projects** and interest-based learning. (*see also* **interdisciplinary studies**)

integration Integration can be perceived as a slogan description of various educational procedures, ranging from social functions where children with special needs and 'normal' children are brought together from time to time, to the complete assimilation of disabled pupils into an ordinary school. Integration is seen as one aspect of the moves to 'de-institutionalise' handicapped persons; it has an even closer affinity with the USA concept of 'mainstreaming' children with special educational needs into ordinary classes and schools. Integration thus attempts to shift the emphasis of special services from handicapping conditions and problems to children's learning needs. (*see also* **special educational needs**)

intelligence A term which is widely used but often with insufficient clarity. It has been defined as 'general mental ability' or 'the ability to see relationships' or even 'what **intelligence tests** measure'. It may be useful to use the distinction between intelligence A, B and C. Intelligence A is an individual's innate, genetic potentiality (which must exist but can never be measured). Intelligence B is the result of the interaction of an individual's intelligence A and his environmental experiences; it is what is often described in common-sense terms as intelligent behaviour. Finally, intelligence C is what intelligence tests measure. If it is a good test, then C will be close to B, but it may be a long way from A. (*see also* **age: chronological and mental, Gaussian curve, IQ, memory, normal curve, spatial ability, underachiever, verbal reasoning**)

intelligence test Intelligence tests were first constructed in France by Alfred Binet (1857–1911) to assess children's educability in schools. Binet's intention was more specific than many later psychologists; he was also much more optimistic about the chances of 'teaching **intelligence**'. An intelligence test is **standardised** and a score given as an **IQ** or intelligence quotient. Intelligence tests have sometimes been criticised because they appear to favour certain social groups such as whites in the USA and middle-class children in the UK. (*see also* **Gaussian curve, Koh's blocks, meritocratic education, nature-nurture controversy, reliability, spatial ability, underachiever, validity, verbal reasoning**)

interdisciplinary studies Studies in which two or more disciplines are studied together focusing upon common topics: for example, politics and science (perhaps looking at problems of conservation or pollution of the environment). The essential aspect of an interdisciplinary study is that the disciplines are studied in such a way as to produce planned interaction. It is quite different from a multi-disciplinary approach in which several disciplines are employed to examine the same topic from their own separate perspectives. (*see* **integrated studies**)

internal degree A degree for which the student follows the formal course of instruction at an institution of **higher education** and takes the prescribed **examinations**.

internal examiner *see* **examiner, internal**.

international baccalaureate (IB) An examination designed for students in their last two or three years at secondary school in the UK and in international schools abroad, and intended to qualify them for entry to undergraduate courses not confined to British universities. Six academic subjects are covered in the course: two languages, mathematics, an exact or experimental science, a human science and a subject of the student's choice. Three of these are examined at a higher level and three at subsidiary level. (*see also* **baccalauréat, technological baccalaureate**)

International Institute for Educational Planning (IIEP) Established by **UNESCO** (the United Nations Educational, Scientific and Cultural Organisation) in 1963 in Paris to act as an international centre for advanced training and research in the field of educational planning. It cooperates with training and research organisations all over the world and publishes reports.

intrinsic/extrinsic   Some theories of human motivation make a distinction between **motivation** to perform well or to engage in an activity for its own sake (intrinsic motivation), and the kind of motivation which operates for the sake of some external reward (extrinsic motivation). Most educators prefer students to be stimulated by intrinsic motivation, but on the way to that long-term goal various kinds of extrinsic motivation (for example, a desire to please the teacher or to get good marks) may be employed.

invigilator   An official who supervises students whilst they are answering examination papers.

ipsative assessment   A system by which a student's performance *now* is compared with his/her earlier achievement, not with other members of a class or group.

IQ (intelligence quotient)   A measure of an individual's performance on a standardised intelligence test. Since tests were originally developed mainly for children it was convenient to express a child's score in terms of mental age (MA) rather than chronological age (CA); the score can be converted into a percentage using the following formula:

$$IQ = \frac{MA}{CA} \times 100$$

Thus a child with an average score will have an IQ of 100; a child above average will score more than 100. Tests are usually **standardised** so that two-thirds of the normal population will score between 85 and 115. (*see also* **age: chronological and mental, Gaussian curve, meritocratic education, normal curve, underachiever**)

item   A question or problem designed to be part of an item bank. An item bank is a collection of test questions. New tests can be composed not by creating new items, but by making a new selection from the item bank. Item analysis is the process of studying students' responses to each item in order to improve the test, and then removing items that are seen as too difficult or too easy.

item bank   See **item**.

j

James Report (1972) The Committee of Enquiry into Teacher Education and Training under the chairmanship of Lord James of Rusholme reported in 1972. The Report outlined a completely new system of teacher education. It envisaged three cycles:

First cycle A Students were given the choice of taking a degree at a college or university or a diploma in higher education; the latter course lasting two years and located within the further education system.

Second cycle A one-year course of professional studies and training. Successful candidates would become licensed teachers for the second year, and would be monitored by a professional tutor. After the second year of this cycle, teachers would be awarded a Bachelor of Arts (BA) (Education) degree.

Third cycle Paid in-service training, consisting of one term every seven years, was an essential aspect of the scheme.

There was opposition to the concept of consecutive rather than current training which was clearly spelt out in the scheme. Teachers questioned the status of the proposed new degree and the **Diploma in Higher Education**. The suggested adminstrative structure of teacher education was also criticised. (*see also* **induction schemes**)

junior school Traditionally, a school catering for pupils between the ages of 7 and 11. From the time of the Hadow Report on the Primary School (1931), a distinctive educational philosophy based on enlightened approaches was advocated. The **Plowden Report** *Children and their Primary Schools* (1967) for the most part adapted a similar stance. Many junior schools have now combined with infant schools under one head. Where middle schools exist, the former junior school age range spans both the **first school** and the **middle school** itself.

k

Key Stage (KS) The knowledge and skills pupils are expected to acquire in the **National Curriculum** are sub-divided into four Key Stages. Key Stage 1 (5 to 7); Key Stage 2 (8 to 11); Key Stage 3 (11 to 14); Key Stage 4 (14 to 16). At the end of each Key Stage pupils are assessed for each **Attainment Target** and placed in one of ten **levels**. (*see* Section 1, Essay 7)

kindergarten A system of education for infants based on the ideas of Froebel. Play is regarded as a natural means of children learning, and games are used to develop body, mind and spirit. It has sometimes been pointed out that the 'kindergarten' (children's garden) metaphor is misleading, especially if applied to older children. Whereas plants may grow naturally in a garden, the processes of children's cognitive, social and moral development are much more complex than automatic 'growth'.

knowledge Knowledge is often contrasted with **skills** and with **attitudes** and values, but this is sometimes unhelpful because knowledge overlaps with both those categories. Another distinction is between 'knowing how' and 'knowing that', the former being more closely connected with skills. A related issue is how human beings acquire knowledge. This was Piaget's major interest and formed the basis of his work on stages of development. The conventional pre-Enlightenment view of knowledge was that all knowledge was created by God and only discovered by human beings through the use of their reason. Traces of that view survive in some popular attitudes to education which tend to regard knowledge as a commodity to be collected by a pupil. Post-Reformation science encouraged a move away from a unified view of knowledge to a sub-division of knowledge into science, theology, law and so on.

In the twentieth century the educational argument about knowledge has frequently centred on the relation between the structure of knowledge and the content of the curriculum, particularly subjects. In the USA, Phenix has worked on 'realms of meaning' which has been influential; in the UK, Hirst's seven forms of knowledge approach has been much discussed. The sociology of knowledge is concerned with the idea that the perception of reality is filtered through cultural constraints which differ from one society to another; and also that within any society an individual's view of knowledge and reality is related to his/her own social position. These ideas have generated a good deal of productive criticism, but they can also lead to an extreme form of relativism – the idea that one view of reality is as good as any other. In education, particularly in studies of the curriculum, the danger exists of moving from the recognition of class-based tastes and prejudices to statements that the whole of school knowledge is merely 'bourgeois'. Some Marxist writers such as Gramsci, however, saw that the future of education had to be concerned with making available to everyone those kinds of essential knowledge which had been part of elite education in the past. (*see also* **academic, culture, disciplines, encyclopaedism, essentialism**)

Koh's blocks A non-verbal **intelligence test** in which an individual has to construct from a number of coloured blocks certain patterns presented to him/her from a booklet.

l

labelling A term much used in the sociology of education to indicate the tendency to classify an individual as a member of a category, and then treat him/her as a type rather than a person. The **stereotypes** which are particularly mentioned in this respect are 'slow learning child', 'culturally deprived child' or 'linguistically deprived child', and 'delinquent'. The obvious danger of teachers treating children in this way is that of **self-fulfilling prophecy**. (*see also* **mixed ability grouping, setting, streaming, Pygmalion**)

ladder of opportunity A term associated with the meritocratic view of schooling and with selection in education. Use of the metaphor 'ladder of opportunity' assumes the existence of different levels of school so that an individual child can climb from one level (e.g. the pre-1944 **elementary school**) to a higher level (the **grammar school**). This view of education is objected to by many educationists since it appears to regard the majority level as inferior. Thus, in the early twentieth century many Labour Party educationists as well as those in the Trades Union Congress proposed instead the 'broad highway' approach to education for all. (*see also* **Bryce Report, 'eleven plus' examination, secondary education for all**)

laissez-faire (1) The policy of non-interference by government in the activities of business and industry. It was particularly important in the history of elementary education in the UK, since advocates of *laissez-faire* did not believe that the State should provide or interfere in education. Although the doctrine of *laissez-faire* in education was apparently overcome by the middle of the nineteenth century, the attitude still survives, particularly in England where many parents who can afford to do so choose to send their children to fee paying schools. Many politicians of the Right believe this to be a much healthier attitude to education than State provision. (2) The teaching style which allowed pupils to work according to their own interests, with a minimum of direction and control. (*see* Section 1, Essay 8)

language across the curriculum See **Bullock Report**.

language deficit The theory that some children underachieve at school because their language skills are inadequate. The theory is related to a view of society which suggests that certain kinds of homes – working-class and some ethnic minorities – do not equip children with adequate language skills to cope with the curriculum and other demands of the classroom. (*see also* **Bullock Report, compensatory education, disadvantage**)

language laboratory A specifically designed room equipped with electronic equipment for the teaching of languages. The laboratory consists of booths for the students and a console, a large control desk, for the instructor who communicates through a microphone with one or more students at a time.

In more sophisticated installations tape-recorders (previously, record players) carrying programmes enable individuals to proceed at their own pace. Language laboratories became popular in the 1960s; but though common enough in higher education, they have almost disappeared from maintained secondary schools. (*see also* **direct method**)

language schools Schools mostly aimed at overseas students who wish to learn **English as a second language**. A number of examinations which test efficiency at the end of the course are available. Many schools, which are privately owned, seek accreditation by becoming accepted as members of the Association of Recognised English Language Schools (ARELS).

late developer Children develop physically, emotionally and intellectually at different rates. Late developers are those who realise their potential in some or all aspects of school work after the majority of their contemporaries. (*see also* **intelligence, intelligence test**)

lateral thinking A technique of looking at a problem from many different points of view instead of following the one which is most obvious. In some respects, lateral thinking is related to **divergent** thinking. Lateral thinking is particularly associated with the work of Edward de Bono.

law of education The law of education is enshrined in Education Acts such as that of 1944 which stated that education was to be organised in three successive phases: primary, secondary and further. Statutory law is complemented by common law; for example, the teacher is said to be *in loco parentis* and is accountable to the Courts if there is a failure to fulfil this responsibility. Recent sweeping changes in education have been brought about by legislation. For instance, the Education Reform Act (1988) introduced the **National Curriculum** in schools; the Children Act (1989) established a comprehensive legal framework for the care and upbringing of children which has extensive implications for education; the Further and Higher Education Act (1992) abolished the binary line and established a single framework for higher education; and the Education (Schools) Act (1992) provided for a new system of inspection which greatly reduced the role of Her Majesty's Inspectorate in this work. (*see also* **Education Acts**, **Local Government Acts**)

league tables *The Parent's Charter* issued by the Government in 1991 stipulated that parents should in future receive an annual written report which gives information about their children's performance in examinations and **National Curriculum** tests. In addition, the report will include a comparison with those of children of the same age, and the Department for Education will publish performance or league tables of examination results, National Curriculum tests, **truancy** rates of pupils' destinations and other **performance indicators** of all schools.

Most local authorities already devise school examination league tables but do not publish them. It is claimed that such raw material needs careful interpretation, for example, the school's intake and social background are important determining factors. Another possible outcome of publishing league tables is that schools may concentrate on producing good examination results at the expense of a balanced education, and may exclude children with special needs for this reason. (*see* Section 1, Essay 4)

learned journal A publication in an academic discipline or field of study normally consisting of a collection of articles, written by authoritative figures. In education, for example, all the foundation disciplines have such journals, e.g. *British Journal of Educational Psychology, Journal of Philosophy of Education*. Frequency of publication may vary from journal to journal.

learning A permanent or lasting change in knowledge, skill or attitude which is the result of experience rather than maturation. (*see also* **active learning, computer assisted learning, conditioning, distance learning, individual learning, instrumental enrichment, learning theory, over-learning, passive learning, precision learning, programmed learning, rote learning**.)

learning difficulty Where a child has significantly greater difficulty in learning than most pupils of his/her age or where there are disabilities which prevent using the normal education facilities which are available. (*see also* **special educational needs**)

Learning Support Service A system operated by many **local education authorities** which provides a central team of special needs teachers to help and advise schools on children with **learning difficulties**.

learning theory Different schools of psychology explain learning in different ways. There are, therefore, many learning theories rather than a single learning theory. Behaviourist psychology explains learning in one way, **Gestalt** psychology quite differently, and there are also different kinds of developmental theories which include learning.

lecture Presentation of a topic in oral form by a lecturer to students, who may take notes. It may be accompanied by visual aids and followed up with a **seminar**. The original meaning of 'lecture' was a reading of a text: before the invention of printing this was a useful practice. Some lecturers still read texts to students. (*see also* **tutorial**)

lecturer (1) A post associated with **higher education** institutions. Above this position is senior and principal lecturer and **Reader**. (2) A person who delivers a lecture.

left-handedness In a predominantly right-handed environment, teachers tend to be less aware of the problems of left-handed children. Awkwardness in writing postures and in practical work are examples. To counter this, some schools successfully run clubs to give left-handed pupils a positive image and to act as a support group.

lesson (1) A period of time, usually between thirty-five and fifty minutes, into which the timetable is divided for teaching purposes. Traditionally at secondary school level, some subjects are allocated double periods or more of lesson time, for example home economics and technology. (2) The smallest unit of **curriculum** planning, that is a single planned learning episode which would normally form part of a sequential scheme of work. (*see also* **syllabus**, **timetabling**)

levels Increasingly the word 'level' is used to refer to the **standard** of achievement within a pre-specified **curriculum** and assessment system. For example:
(1) reaching one of the ten levels within an **Attainment Target** in the **National Curriculum**;
(2) **national vocational qualifications (NVQs)** are awarded at five levels:
　Level 1 overlaps the National Curriculum; (foundation level)
　Level 2 GCSE; (intermediate level)
　Level 3 'A' level; (advanced GNVQs or vocational 'A' level)
　Level 4 first degree;
　Level 5 post-graduate.
(*see* Section 1, Essay 7)

levels of attainment Under the National Curriculum, pupils are measured on a ten point scale from the age of 5 to 16. It is assumed that they will progress through the ten levels at different rates. An average child should reach Level 2 at 7 years, Level 4 by 11 years, Levels 5 or 6 by 14 and Levels 6 or 7 by 16. (*see* **National Curriculum**)

liberal education The meaning of 'liberal' in this connection is associated with freedom. Liberal education is that kind of education which broadens and therefore frees the mind from narrow prejudices and preconceptions. Liberal education avoids premature specialisation. In England, sixth-form studies have attempted to be both specialised and 'liberal' by the strategy of '**general studies**'. Liberal education is frequently contrasted with **vocational** training by association with a nineteenth-century upper-class view of the correct form of education for Christian gentlemen. In the nineteenth century, the upper classes were regarded as needing liberal education whereas vocational training was more appropriate for the lower classes. (*see also* **general education**, **liberal studies**)

liberal studies The curriculum followed by many students in **further education** is narrow and vocational. It was frequently thought that such students needed a liberalising element in their programme and the teaching of liberal studies became a compulsory part of many further education programmes. Liberal studies is derived from the medieval idea of liberal arts which consisted of the trivium (grammar, logic and rhetoric) and the quadrivium (arithmetic, geometry, music and astronomy). Modern liberal studies is, however, much more likely to be concerned with literature, social studies and possibly appreciation of film and television. (*see also* **liberal education**)

Library Association The Association was founded in 1876 and received a Royal

Charter in 1898. It is concerned with the professional education and raising the standards and working conditions of it members. The Association actively promotes the improvement of library services. The importance of the links between schools and the library service have long been recognised by the Association and Heads of Library and Information Services within schools. Chartered librarians have expertise in matters relating to information and information handling, learning resources and the library process. (*see also* **School Library Association**)

licensed teacher The Licensed Teacher Scheme was introduced in 1991, together with the **Articled Teacher Scheme**, to offer an alternative to the two established routes (**Bachelor of Education** (BEd) and Postgraduate Certificate of Education (PGCE). The Scheme is available to suitably qualified applicants, including teachers with overseas qualifications not fully recognised by the Department of Education and Science. The school in which a licensed teacher is employed is responsible, in consultation with the local education authority, for prescribing a course of study to complement the teaching experience being gained at the school; the school and local authority are also responsible for deciding whether the licensed teacher has satisfactorily completed such a course of study, in an institute of higher education or elsewhere. If the licensed teacher's performance is in all respects satisfactory, he or she becomes a qualified teacher after one year or whatever longer period might be specified. The **Open University** was involved in preparing study materials for licensed (and articled) teachers. (*see also* **teacher training**)

limited grade examination An examination, or a section of an examination, for which the range of grades or marks that may be awarded, is restricted. This may be achieved by insisting that candidates enter for a paper which only gives scores for the lower range, or, at the other extreme confines scoring possibilities to the highest grades. For example, in some GCSE subjects candidates enter for one of three papers: the easiest paper would give access to grades E to G; the 'middle' paper to grade C to F; the difficult paper A to D. An objection to this procedure is that if a candidate is entered for the difficult paper but fails to reach grade D, then no lower grade is possible.

limited-range syllabus A syllabus where the entire range of content or skills is not covered in the syllabus. In the case of the **National Curriculum** it would refer to a syllabus where the range of possible awards covers only some of the ten levels of **attainment**.

link course A course run cooperatively by two or more institutions. Some courses, mainly vocational in character, for the 16 to 19 age group are run jointly by secondary schools and by local colleges of further education.

literacy The ability to read and write at a conventionally accepted level. There is no universal standard of literacy, but within any given society it is possible to define **'functional literacy'** and then to arrive at figures for the number of illiterates in that particular society. (*see also* **graphicacy**, **numeracy**, **oracy**)

loans By the Education Students Loans Act (1990), the Government introduced a top-up loans scheme for full-time home students, except postgraduates, up to the age of 50, in higher education. The stated objective was to identify a cost-effective scheme which would be reasonably economical to administer. Students are offered the loans for a three-year course at a 'real interest rate of zero'. It was envisaged that repayments were to be tailored to individuals' economic circumstances. Students are no longer eligible for social security benefits, whether or not they qualify for top-up loans. Opponents of the scheme claim that it will deter working-class youngsters from going on to **higher education**.

local education authority (LEA) Local education authorities came into existence with the 1902 Education Act, replacing the school boards. Unlike the latter, the new education authorities were also responsible for voluntary schools; the county and borough councils were also given responsibility for secondary and technical education. One important feature of the system was that each local education authority had to appoint an education committee (Section 101, Local Government Act 1972) consisting of elected councillors and co-opted members. The political party gaining a majority at a local election elects from its members a chairman of this committee.

Traditionally, education accounted for a large part of a local authority's budget. This has been eroded by the introduction of education support grants in 1984, when grants were earmarked for specific education policies and the Interim Advisory Committee in 1987 which gave Secretaries of State for Education control over teachers' pay and conditions of service. Successive changes in methods of raising local authority finances and rate capping have also had serious consequences. The **Education Reform Act** (1988) which introduced local management of schools and grant-maintained schools has further undermined the role of local education authorities. This has continued with the loss of **polytechnics** from local authority control and the independence granted to **further education**, tertiary and sixth-form colleges under the **Further and Higher Education Act** (1992). (*see also* **local education inspectors**, **Local Government Acts**)

local education authority inspectors Employed by **local education authorities** to ensure that standards are being maintained. Until recently, the term '**adviser**' was commonly used, but the change of name to 'inspector' indicates an important change in their functions. Under the **local management of schools**, their role has been further modified. In some authorities, the entire advisory budget has been given to schools, which will be able to buy in advice either locally or elsewhere. The Education (Schools) Act 1992, setting up a system of four-year inspections, obliged governing bodies to consider two tenders for each inspection. With the appointment of 5000 lay inspectors under the Act, local authority inspectors still have the task of monitoring the implementation of the National Curriculum but have lost the right to inspect. Governing bodies receive £70 million from funds formerly allocated to local education authorities. Under Section 14 of the Education (Schools) Act, local education authority inspectors are able to tender for inspection of grant-maintained and independent schools, as well as schools in neighbouring authorities. (*see also* **Her Majesty's Inspectorate**, **Local Government Acts**, and Section 1, Essay 4)

Local Government Acts Local government legislation from the last quarter of the nineteenth century has had a direct effect on the development of the education service in England. The 1888 Local Government Act set up county and borough councils and provided the administrative unit for education – entitled the **local education authority** – under the 1902 Education Act; local education authorities received greater powers under the 1944 Act. The system of percentage grants was swept away by the 1958 Local Government Act, to be replaced by a rate support grant.

There was a shake-up of local educational administration following the 1963 Government Act, which abolished the London and Middlesex County Councils; these were replaced by the Greater London Council, with education powers exercised by an **Inner London Education Authority** (ILEA) and twenty separate outer London boroughs. The 1972 Local Government Act, which came into effect on 1 April 1974, dealt with the remainder of the country, and reduced the number of local education authorities. Larger conurbations were divided into metropolitan districts and some county authorities disappeared, leaving shire counties responsible for education.

Traditionally, the cost of education was shared between central and local government. Since the 1980s there has been a significant shift towards governmental control of local government finance. The Local Government Finance Act (1988) replaced domestic rates by the Community Charge, widely known as the Poll Tax, and another Act of 1992 again changed the system with the introduction of the Council Tax. The Local Government (Access to Information) Act (1985) gave the public the right to inspect the agendas, reports and minutes of council meetings and sub-committees. Four years later the Local Government and Housing Act (1989) removed the voting rights of non-elected education committee members including teachers' representatives. Compulsory competitive tendering for local authority services was introduced by the Local Government Act of 1988: this applied to aspects of education such as catering and the maintenance of school playing fields. The scope of competitive tendering was widened by the 1992 Local Government Act to include legal services, information technology and pay rolls. The Act also included provision for the **Audit Commission** to devise **performance indicators** for local government services, including education. (*see also* **law of education**, **revenue support grant**, **standard spending assessment**)

local management of schools (LMS) In 1987, when the Government was preparing the Education Reform Bill, it commissioned the management consultants, Coopers & Lybrand Deloite, to produce a study of the implication of the financial delegation aspects of the Bill. The report stated, 'The changes require a new culture and philosophy of the organisation of education at the school level. They are more than just financial; they need a general shift in management. We use the term *local management of schools (LMS).'*

The financial basis for LMS is determined by **local education authorities** in England and Wales setting funding levels for each school according to a strict formula, mainly based on the number of pupils. Each local authority's formula must be approved by the Secretary of State for Education. The money is then delegated to the school which is responsible for the budget. This is carried out by the governors and the head. Schools must work out their priorities and operate within their budgets.

Governors play a much greater part than formerly under LMS. Apart from deciding how the budget is spent, they decide on staffing levels and can require dismissal where necessary. They are also concerned with curriculum policy and consider complaints from parents. Under LMS the head, who may be a governor, carries out the day-to-day running of the school in consultation with the governing body.

One of the stated aims of the Government in introducing LMS was that, by lessening the role of local education authorities in school administration, parents would have a greater say, through an elected and accessible governing body, in their children's education. (*see* Section 1, Essay 7)

London allowance An extra sum of money paid to teachers and others, working within the defined London area, to compensate for the higher cost of living – especially in housing and travel.

London Chamber of Commerce and Industry (LCCI) The LCCI was founded over a century ago with the aim of providing a unified representational voice for business that would enable commercial interests to influence government policy. The Chamber's role has expanded in recent years and it now offers its members practical assistance in the form of business services and information facilities. The LCCI Examination Board is one of the oldest and largest examining bodies in the field of business. It prepares for a broad range of business careers both in the UK and abroad. Examinations are offered at Certificate and Diploma levels in a wide range of managerial, secretarial and technological subjects. The Board may also approve the use of designatory letters, Associate Licentiate and Diplomate. The LCCI is accredited by the **National Council for Vocational Qualifications** (NCVQ) in business administration and retailing (*see also* **business education**)

longitudinal study A study over a period of time which is concerned with following through changes in an individual or a group of individuals, with reference, for example, to health and educational achievement. (*see also* **National Children's Bureau**)

lower school Formerly a term used to refer to the first two or three forms of a

public or **grammar school**, but now more commonly to **comprehensive schools** where, for organisational purposes, there is a lower, followed by a middle and upper school.

m

magnet schools Since their election in 1979, Conservative politicians have been looking for alternatives to the alleged uniformity of comprehensive secondary schools. **City technology colleges** (CTCs) and **grant-maintained schools** have emerged from this search, but when Kenneth Baker, then Secretary of State, visited the USA in 1987 he was impressed by some of the magnet schools he saw.

The idea behind magnet schools is that they should specialise in some way: one well known New York magnet school specialises, for example, in the performing arts; others are concerned with science or technology. In addition to catering for special interests, magnet schools also provide a broad curriculum. Some magnet schools in New York and Washington are very popular, but their critics complain that they succeed by attracting the most motivated parents in a district, thus making the problems for other schools more severe. There have been some attempts to evaluate magnet schools in the USA, but without conclusive results. Nevertheless, the idea has spread rapidly to many parts of the USA. In England, Wandsworth and Bradford have expressed considerable interest.

maintained school The correct term for what are generally known as 'state' schools – that is schools that are maintained from public funds. Since the **Education Reform Act** (1988) there are three types of maintained schools:

(1) schools which are the responsibility of **local education authorities**;
(2) schools which, although in receipt of public funds, are the responsibility of voluntary bodies (such as the Church of England); and
(3) **grant-maintained schools** (GMS) which receive their funding direct from the Department for Education. These are schools which decided to 'opt out' of local authority control under arrangements specified in the Education Reform Act (1988). (*see also* **voluntary school**)

maintenance grant A sum of money awarded to students to meet day-to-day living and accommodation costs, as distinct from fees, for college courses. Many local education authorities have **discretionary** schemes for educational maintenance allowances to enable children to stay on at school or college after age 16. (*see also* **discretionary award, Educational Welfare Service, entrance award, mandatory award**)

Man – A Course of Study (MACOS) A **curriculum development project** based on the work of Jerome Bruner and developed by Peter Dow. The project included film and course materials for which teachers needed a course of training. It has been used to a limited extent in the UK as a social studies teaching kit. In some parts of Australia and the USA it was thought highly controversial and sometimes banned.

manager Historically associated with nineteenth-century **voluntary elementary** education, school managers were responsible for the control and supervision of school personnel and organisation as well as raising funds. After the 1870 Education Act, school boards appointed managers to their schools. The 1902 Act took away many powers from voluntary school managers: at the same time all county council schools were in future to have managers, though this was left optional for borough councils. It was not until the 1944 Education Act that it was made a requirement for all primary schools to have managers, whose powers and terms of office were stated in an instrument of management. Since the 1980 Education Act came into force, the use of the term 'manager' has disappeared, with all schools now having **governors**. (*see also* **instrument of government**)

mandatory award Local education authorities have a duty under law to make grants to full-time students taking advanced courses if they are eligible under national regulations. For example, first degree courses and those for initial teacher training fall into this category. The award, covering fees and maintenance during term time, is means tested. (*see also* **discretionary award**, **entrance award**, **maintenance grant**)

Manpower Services Commission (MSC) A national training agency set up in 1974 to coordinate the work of statutory training boards and to take over and expand the Government's own vocational training schemes. Later these included **Training Opportunities Scheme** (TOPS), **Youth Training Scheme** (YTS), the **Community Programme** and the introduction of the **Technical and Vocational Education Initiative** (TVEI). In 1988, the MSC became the Training Agency, which in turn has been superseded by **Training and Enterprise Councils** (TECs).

mastery learning A theory put forward originally by Benjamin Bloom and some of his colleagues that mastery of any kind of knowledge is theoretically possible for any learner given sufficient time and appropriate teaching. Part of the theory is that pupils differ not only in their pace of learning, but also in learning styles. Mastery learning is closely associated with **individualised learning**.

matching A type of item in an **objective test** where the student has to choose from a set of pictures the one that matches a corresponding word (or vice versa).

matriculation Candidates who achieved credit grades in five subjects including one at least from each of three groups – humanities, foreign languages, mathematics and science – at the **School Certificate** examination were given matriculation exemption by the majority of universities. The University of London, as early as 1858, offered a matriculation examination which could be taken by external candidates wishing to go on to **higher education**. The term originated with the ceremony of signing the roll (matricula) on being admitted to a university. From 1951, matriculation come to depend on the passing of two **'A' levels**.

maturation The physical, mental or moral changes that occur as part of an individual's 'natural' development: maturation is by definition the result of innate factors, not environmental ones. The work of Piaget is much concerned with the development, and thus the maturation of, certain innate abilities. (*see also* **Piagetian**)

mature students Universities and colleges differ in the age they regard students as 'mature'; 25 used to be the norm but some now accept a lower age of 21 or 23. Mature students are often exempt from normal **entry requirements**. (*see also* **entry qualification, Open Tech, Open University, university entrance requirements**)

memory An individual's inner record of his past mental and sensory experience. Memory may be made evident by the individual's ability to recall or recognise. Memory span is the technical term indicating the amount of information a person can remember either immediately after, or within a specified time, of having data presented. Some **intelligence tests** involve, for example, the memorisation of unrelated digits. Certain psychologists have claimed that the ability to memorise a long series of unrelated digits is a good indication of general intelligence.

mental age See **age: chronological and mental**.

mentor A trusted adviser – in education there are specific meanings according to context. For example, a newly recruited inspector of **Her Majesty's Inspectorate** has, as a mentor, an experienced inspector who will guide him or her for the first year of service; a **tutor** in a school who supervises student teachers on teaching practice is sometimes called a mentor; in the field of nursing education, nurses supervising the work of student nurses are sometimes given the title of mentor.

meritocratic education Meritocracy was a word invented by Michael Young in *The Rise of the Meritocracy 1870–2033: an essay on education and equality* (1961). This book satirised a society in which the status of a person is determined by 'merit' which is determined by the simple formula 'IQ plus effort equals merit'. Meritocratic education is that kind of education which concentrates on the identification of talent, preferably by means of **intelligence tests**, and then separating the talented from the less talented into different schools and curricula. Meritocratic education is different from elitist education inasmuch as elitist education depends upon social selection, whereas meritocratic education depends on selection by '**ability**'. Michael Young's book demonstrated the folly of such a system very convincingly. (*see also* **ladder of opportunity**)

microteaching A system used in some colleges and departments of education for developing specific teaching skills. Normally, the student teacher would teach a small group for a limited amount of time, perhaps only ten minutes, concentrating on a specific objective. The lesson is then analysed with the help of the tutor and other students from a film or video tape recording. It is a technique which is usually regarded as having some value in **teacher training**, but is rarely used with all students. It is increasingly likely that its use is confined to those with particular problems or difficulties. (*see also* **competency based teaching**)

middle school The shift to a comprehensive school system in the early 1960s without a stock of adequate buildings gave rise to the setting up of middle schools. In 1963 the West Riding of Yorkshire submitted plans to introduce schools for the 9 to 13 age range and in the following year the law was amended to allow **transfer** ages other than 11. A further impetus to the spread of middle schools followed with Department of Education and Science Circular 10/65 which suggested middle schools as one way of establishing **comprehensives**. The **Plowden Report** also recommended an extension of the primary mode until age 12 or 13. The starting and leaving ages of pupils differ depending on the individual local education authority, with patterns such as 8 to 12, 9 to 13 and 9 to 14. There were some 1400 middle schools in England and Wales in 1981. However, falling rolls and the changing pattern of sixth-form education has resulted in local education authority returning to schools for the 11 to 16 age range, at the expense of middle schools. (*see also* **junior school**)

Ministry of Education The 1944 Education Act provided for a minister of education in place of a president and a corresponding change in the title of the department from **Board of Education** to Ministry of Education. In 1964 the Ministry was replaced by the **Department of Education and Science** which has now become the **Department for Education**.

minor authority A parish, district or urban council with authority to appoint a governor to local **primary schools**.

minority group Refers to a group in any society which can be identified usually by reason of religion, race, nationality or special needs. (*see also* **sub-culture**)

mission Part of the **accountability** language of the 1980s and 1990s. Every educational institution should have a mission – that is a list of **aims** and strategies for achieving them which could be expressed as a 'mission statement'. (*see* Section 1, Essay 4)

mixed-ability grouping The grouping of pupils in such a way that each class in a year group has a roughly equal range of attainment. A survey undertaken by Her Majesty's Inspectorate and published in a report entitled *Mixed Ability*

Work in Comprehensive Schools (1978) stated that only in a very small number of the schools visited were pupils learning at an appropriate level and pace in classes organised in this way. Other criticisms made were that bright pupils were not being extended and that too much emphasis was put upon social **objectives**. A third of all comprehensive schools in the sample were undertaking some mixed-ability work which was found largely in the first three years of school. Since this survey there has been a decline in mixed-ability grouping. (*see also* **labelling, setting, streaming, unstreaming, workcards**)

mock examination An internal examination taken by candidates preparing for a public examination such as the **General Certificate of Secondary Education** (GCSE) or 'A' level. It is designed to give candidates 'examination experience' some months before taking the final exam; it may also be used to judge whether candidates are likely to be successful and to estimate the final **grade**.

moderation The process of aligning standards – often between teachers responsible for the assessment of their own candidates. The methods of moderation fall into two broad categories: (1) Statistical moderation which involves some form of **scaling** or alignment against performance in an externally assessed component. (2) Moderation by inspection which involves candidates' work being inspected by an external moderator, or by peer group moderation through an agreement trial.

The most appropriate form of moderation will depend on the nature of the assessment being moderated.

'Modern Greats' The final honours degree course at Oxford University in philosophy, politics and economics (PPE). (*see also* **Greats**)

modular course When the normal Bachelor's degree course consisted of the study of one subject or discipline, the mode of assessment tended to be a series of 'final examination papers' taken at the end of the course. During the last twenty years or so several developments have taken place: more and more courses consisted of a mixture of subjects organised in units or **modules** (some or all which would be 'chosen'); and it became convenient to examine each module or group of modules year by year rather than waiting for the end of the whole course. The trend has now spread into the school system so that **General Certificate of Secondary Education** (GCSE) and 'A' and 'AS' level courses can be 'modularised'.

mongol, education of See **Down's syndrome**.

monitoring Systematically studying the work of pupils, teachers, schools or even **local education authorities** in order to assess levels of performance. During the 1970s, the phrase 'monitoring standards' became commonly used especially in connection with the work of the **Assessment of Performance Unit** (APU). (*see* Section 1, Essay 4)

moral development, moral education Moral development is sometimes confined to **maturation** or the innate development of a child's moral thinking; more commonly, it is used to refer to the combination of maturation and experience including moral education. Moral education is the conscious attempt to contribute to a child's moral development. In the UK, various attempts have been made to base moral education on sound psychological and philosophical criteria, and to distinguish moral education from religious education.

multicultural education England and Wales, like many other modern industrial societies, are now multicultural societies. It is usually accepted that even if children live in an area where there are no ethnic **minorities**, schools still have a duty to include in the curriculum topics which will help pupils to understand the concept of **culture** and to appreciate the variety of cultures which now exist in the UK, not least to promote better race relations. (*see also* **Rampton Report**)

multidisciplinary studies See **interdisciplinary studies**.

multilateral school A school which catered for all the **secondary education** of children in a given area and included provision for **grammar**, **technical** and modern courses on one site. Unlike children in **comprehensive** schools, those in multilateral schools remained in separate courses during their secondary school life. This type of school was advocated by the Trades Union Congress (TUC) from the 1920s as a first step to breaking down class distinctions in education. (*see also* **secondary education for all, tripartite system**)

multiple choice test A form of **assessement** where the candidate is presented with a number of alternative answers to questions posed. Responses are usually denoted by ticks. Multiple choice tests are now common in many public examination papers in addition to essay type questions. (*see also* **open-ended**, and Section 1, Essay 5)

Munn Report (1977) A Scottish Committee under the chairmanship of Dr James Munn considered the appropriate curriculum for third- and fourth-year secondary school pupils. A **core curriculum** was favoured, based on a forty-period week; and fourteen 'non-core' periods were recommended for two additional optional activities which were available. An important point made by the Committee was that assessment should be geared to educational **objectives** in the curriculum, rather than the curriculum being controlled by the assessment system. This might be achieved by schools making their own assessment on a range of subjects. Further consideration of assessment procedures was undertaken at this time by the **Dunning Committee**. (*see also* **Scottish Education Department**)

museum education The educational value of museums has long been recognised. The appointment of education officers in national and some local museums to liaise with schools is now quite usual. Museums cater for groups of pupils who may be preparing for examinations, engaged on topic work or making a visit in connection with some aspect of the school **curriculum**.

n

National Advisory Body (NAB) The National Advisory Body for local authority higher education was formed by the Government in December 1981. Its main task was to advise on the present and future provision of higher education in the non-university sector at a time when available resources were shrinking. The Board was replaced by the Polytechnics and Colleges Funding Council (PCFC) in 1988, which in turn was disbanded and became the **Higher Education Funding Council** (HEFC) in 1992. (*see also* **polytechnics**)

National Advisory Council on Education for Industry and Commerce (NACEIC) The NACEIC was established in 1948 following the recommendations of the *Percy Report*. During its twenty-nine years, it issued a series of important reports. The first, *The Future Development of Higher Technological Education* (1950), led to the setting up of the National Council of Technological Awards, later the **Council for National Academic Awards**, and others dealt with such areas as **business studies, sandwich courses** and **day release**. The Council was disbanded in 1977. (*see also* **business education**)

National Association for Gifted Children (NAGC) The aim of the Association, which was founded in 1966, is to enable gifted children to achieve their full potential both at home and at school. Membership comprises parents, teachers and other interested adults. Local support groups for parents have been set up, research is carried out, INSET courses are offered and there are a number of resource centres for teachers. In 1990 the NAGC, together with the teacher organisation, the National Association for Curriculum Enrichment, set up the National Centre for Able and Talented Children (NCATC) at Northampton. (*see also* **giftedness**)

National Association of Governors and Managers (NAGM) Launched in 1970, this pressure group was constituted for the purpose of reforming governing bodies by involving parents, pupils, teachers, the local community and the local authority. This philosophy was later endorsed by the Taylor Committee in its report. The Association, which is non-political, has played a leading part in the debate on the duties and responsibilities of **governors** and governing bodies since the **Education Reform Act** (1988). It has also set up training courses for governors.

National Association of Headteachers (NAHT) Established in 1897, it now has a membership of over 30,000 which represents the interests of **heads** and **deputy heads** in both primary and secondary sectors in England and Wales. More than 75 per cent of primary heads and over 60 per cent of secondary heads are members. (*see also* **headteacher, teachers' unions, Secondary Heads Association**)

National Association of Schoolmasters/Union of Women Teachers (NAS/UWT) The second largest teachers' union since the amalgamation of the two separate bodies in 1976. At the present time there are more than 120 000 members, with twice the number of men to women. It is now the largest teachers' union in Northern Ireland and is the only English union represented on the Scottish national negotiating body. (see also **teachers' unions**)

National Association of Teachers in Further and Higher Education (NATFHE)
Formed in 1975 from the Association of Teachers in Colleges and Departments of Education (ATCDE) and the Association of Teachers in Technical Institutions (ATTI), this body represents the majority of teachers working in this sector. About a quarter of the 70 000 members work in **higher education**. With the removal of **polytechnics** from local authority control and the granting of university status to these institutions in 1992, new divisions within the Union may be created.

National Children's Bureau Founded in 1962 as the National Bureau for Co-operation in Child Care, with Dr Mia Kellmer Pringle as its director, it has addressed itself to research into the care, development and education of children. Its purpose is to identify and promote the interests of all young people and to improve their status in a diverse and multicultural society. The Bureau membership ranges from local and health authorities to professional and voluntary organisations to universities and other teaching bodies. It is perhaps best known for The National Child Development Study, a **longitudinal** study based on subjects born in one week in March, 1958, and followed up by the Bureau when they were aged 7, 11, and 16 years. Since its inception, the Bureau has undertaken many research projects. Present ones include evaluating a curriculum for pre-school children and examining the services offered by three multi-racial nurseries in London.

National Commission on Education (NCE) The refusal of the Government to set up a Royal Commission on education led to the establishment by the **British Association for the Advancement of Science**, with the active support of the Royal Society, the British Academy and the Fellowship of Engineering, of a National Commission on Education in May 1991. Sir Claus Moser was a prime mover in the matter. The terms of reference are to consider educational goals, policies and practice to meet both the country's needs and those of individuals throughout their lives in the light of the opportunities and challenges that will face the UK over the next twenty-five years.

National Confederation of Parent-Teacher Associations (NCPTA) **Parent-teacher associations** (PTAs) exist in many schools and are mainly concerned with local issues. The NCPTA, formed in 1954, provides a national organisation to which PTAs can affiliate. A non-political body, it holds annual conferences and raises issues of concern with government departments. At one stage it was dominated by teachers, but at its 1987 conference, the constitution was changed to give parents a two-thirds majority. (*see also* **parent power**)

National Council for Educational Technology (NCET) A registered charity funded by the government, the Council promotes and develops the use of educational technology in all areas of education and training. For example, it produces resource packs for primary school teachers working on plans to incorporate **information technology** into history and geography at Key Stage 2, as well as for teachers involved in implementing **Attainment Targets** of the technology curriculum.

National Council for Vocational Qualifications (NCVQ) The Council was established in 1986 to monitor vocational awards and qualifications but is not itself an examining body. Certain standards must be met before the NCVQ will grant its approval. It has devised a national framework for awards based on four graded levels that define the skills needed by industry. (*see also* **National Vocational Qualifications**)

national criteria In February 1980 the Government announced its proposal for a single system of examining at 16 plus recommending that national criteria should be established for syllabuses and assessment procedures 'to ensure that all syllabuses with the same subject title have sufficient content in common, and that all Boards apply the same performance standards to the award of grades.' The **General Certificate of Education** (GCE) and **Certificate of Secondary Education** (CSE) examination Boards were invited to draft the criteria for some twenty subjects for the examination later called the **General Certificate of Secondary Education** (GCSE). The Secretary of State for Education provided guidelines for the work.

national curriculum A national curriculum for children aged 5 to 16 in all state schools in England and Wales was introduced by the **Education Reform Act** (1988). The ten subjects which must be studied are: English, mathematics, science, technology (and design), history, geography, art music and physical education, with a modern foreign language for 11- to 16-year-olds. These subjects are called foundation subjects, with English, mathematics and science being also known as 'core' subjects. In Wales the Welsh language is an additional foundation subject either as a first or second language. For each foundation subject there are objectives or goals, **Attainment Targets** (ATs), which are set out, stating what children should know and be able to do at each Key Stage of schooling. There is testing, in the form of **Standard Assessement Tasks** (SATs), at the ages of 7, 11, 14 and 16, in order to check how well children are progressing in terms of the levels of the Attainment Targets. The four stages during a child's compulsory schooling, '**Key Stages**' will assist parents in knowing what their children should be learning at a given age. The first tests for some 600 000 children aged 7 were taken in the summer of 1991, followed by 14-year-olds in 1992. The General Certificate of Secondary Education (GCSE) will be the main form of assessment for Key Stage 4. (*see* Section 1, Essay 7)

National Curriculum Council (NCC) Established in 1988 as part of the **Education Reform Act** (1988), it conducted statutory consulatation on the subjects of the National Curriculum and received remits from the Secretary of State; provided advice to a wide range of interests on the implementation of the National Curriculum; advised the Secretary of State on curriculum research and development and kept the curriculum of maintained schools under review; and disseminated information relevant to the curriculum. The Council consisted of fifteen members and operated thorough a variety of committees which were directly responsible to the Council. It worked in partnership with the **School Examinations and Assessment Council** (SEAC) and the **Curriculum Council for Wales** (CCW). In 1993, the Education Act merged the National Curriculum Council and the School Examinations and Assessment Council to form the **School Curriculum and Assessment Authority** (SCAA).

National Education Trust Founded in 1972 with the title the National Council for Educational Standards because it was felt that rising expenditure on education was not leading to any proportionate improvement in standards. The Trust aims at influencing and alerting public opinion through its conferences and twice-yearly *Bulletin*. Many of the contributors to the latter have also written for the **Black Papers**. (*see also* **pressure groups, standards**)

National Extension College (NEC) Founded in 1962, the College was established in order to give adults a second chance in education. It is an independent organisation and conducts its work by means of correspondence courses, and preparing many of its students for the **Open University**. Of the 10000 students who enrol each year, approximately two-thirds are women.

National Foundation for Educational Research (NFER) Established in 1946 by **local education authorities**, with the cooperation of the **Ministry of Education**. The NFER's task was to investigate 'practical problems arising within the public system of education as are amenable to scientific investigation.' Its research programme ranges from the pre-school stage to higher education. It is an independent body and carries out research projects commisioned by a large range of organisations. Recent work includes a comparative study of the reading performance of 7-year-olds, the development of **Standard Assessment Tasks** in the core subjects for Key Stage 1, patterns of local education authority in-service education of teachers (INSET) organisation, **multicultural education** after the **Education Reform Act** (1988) and local authority support for assessment in schools.

National Institute of Adult Continuing Education (NIACE) A national centre for cooperation, enquiry, information and consultation in the field of continuing education for adults, founded in 1949. It receives support and finance from local education authorities, universities, residential colleges and the Department for Education. The Institute carries out surveys in such areas as mature students, open learning systems and the training of tutors. The **Adult Literacy and Basic Skills Unit** (ALBSU) was an agency of the Institute as well as the Unit for the Development of Adult Continuing Education (UADCE).

National Nursery Examination Board (NNEB) The Board is the main provider of the nationally recognised child-care qualification for **nursery nurses**, the NNEB diploma in Nursery Nursing. The diploma qualifies the holder to work in hospitals, schools and day nurseries, and private homes. The diploma course, run mainly by local **colleges of further education** and **sixth-form colleges**, consists of two years' full-time or five years part-time study. In addition, practical experience is gained in different age groups up to the age of 7. (*see also* **nursery classes**)

National Record of Achievement (NRA) Developed in the 1970s as a result of widely voiced dissatisfaction with the educational examination pattern which did not take into account or encourage the wide range of pupil attainment. It is a record of a young person's achievements which, together with portfolios of evidence, will help that person to decide his/her next steps either in education, training or employment with governmental desire for course skills to be included in both academic and vocational post-16 courses. Records of achievement can play a leading part in recording achievements. In 1990, the Department of Education and Science records of achievement were 'the means by which achievement across the **National Curriculum** and beyond can be most effectively reported to a range of audiences.' From 1993, the scheme was made compulsory. The **National Council for Vocational Qualifications** is responsible for its management. (*see also* **record of achievement, school records**)

National Union of Students (NUS) Founded in 1922, the NUS was initially intended for university students only, but now includes most institutions in further and higher education in the UK. The NUS is a federation of the autonomous students' unions which each send delegates to the twice annual conference. There is an elected executive body which carries out the decisions made at the conferences. The main aim of the union is to promote and maintain the educational, social and general interests of students. Membership consists of one-and-a-half million members at 850 institutions. (*see also* **Students' Union**)

National Union of Teachers (NUT) The largest and oldest of the teachers' associations with a membership of over 200 000. Originally called the National Union of Elementary Teachers when it was founded in 1870, it dropped 'elementary' from its title in 1889. The local associations, of which there are more than 400, elect delegates at the annual conference, where policy matters are debated. (*see also* **teachers' unions**)

National Vocational Qualification (NVQ) The National Council for Vocational Qualifications was established in 1986 to reform and rationalise existing vocational qualifications. The latter are designed to meet the needs of employers and employees and indicate competence at work. There are five levels of NVQ:

Level 1 – competence in a range of work activities;
Level 2 – competence in more complex activities e.g. teamwork;
Level 3 – competence in a broad range of activities including supervisory work;

Level 4 – complex technical or professional work;
Level 5 – similar to vocationally related postgraduate qualification.

The Council envisages that NVQs may eventually be used to grade every occupational postholder. The Council has adapted a **competency-based** model for the specification of the qualification, with 'statements of competence' for each particular vocational area. The task of setting standards has been entrusted to a large number of organisations. NVQs can be gained in a variety of settings – at college, work or home – and comprise a number of units. Each level relates to the other with broad equivalences in academic terms. For instance, Level 1, equates with the **National Curriculum**; Level 2 with four GCSEs, Level 3 with 'A' or 'A/S' levels; Level 4 with a degree; and Level 5 with a postgraduate award. The main awarding bodies in the field are the **Royal Society of Arts, City and Guilds** and the **Business and Technology Educational Council**. They are also piloting bodies for the **General National Vocational Qualification** (GNVQ), introduced in 1992 in an attempt to bridge the academic-vocational divide. The GNVQ is seen as an alternative route through the sixth form or **further education college**. It is a full-time one-year course, which includes skills relating to specific jobs but which also gives a broad preparation for work in five vocational subject areas. Most students will take twelve units, six units being the equivalent of one 'A' level. Grading is in three bands – pass, merit and distinction. (*see also* **Youth Training** and Section 1, Essay 9)

N and F levels   A proposal put forward by the **Schools Council** in 1973 to replace the **General Certificate of Education** (GCE) **'A' level** examination with a two-tier five-subject system entitled 'N' (Normal) and 'F' (Further) levels. Occupying the same amount of time as the present 'A' level course, the two-level course was to be organised in such a way that students would take three 'N' levels each equal to half an 'A' level, and two 'F' levels, each equal to three-quarters of an 'A' level. Although there was widespread agreement in schools and colleges on the need for change, the proposal encountered opposition and has now been dropped. (*see also* **examinations; history of, 'Q' and 'F' levels**)

natural wastage   The process of achieving a smaller teaching staff, either in schools or in universities and other institutions of higher education, by allowing members of staff to leave either on retirement or by resignation without them being replaced. Many institutions have preferred to pursue the policy of 'natural wastage' rather than invoke redundancy. The problem of such policy is, however, that this frequently results in a very unbalanced staffing and a patchy curriculum since retirements and resignations tend to be completely haphazard rather than falling equally across all subject areas. (*see also* **falling rolls**)

nature-nurture controversy   For a number of years psychologists, sociologists and others have debated, sometimes bitterly, about whether aspects of an individual's personality are mainly inherited genetically or are due to environment, in particular, learning. The argument has been pursued on both sides of the

Atlantic. In England, advocates of the genetic point of view have included Sir Cyril Burt (whose work has been partly discredited) and Professor H. Eysenck; in the USA the best known advocate of hereditarianism was Professor Arthur Jensen, who felt that there was evidence to suggest that black children and working-class children were genetically inferior in terms of **intelligence** scores.

neighbourhood school　(1) A school which draws its pupils from a clearly identifiable 'neighbourhood' in the sense of a **catchment area** which is both homeogeneous and compact. (2) The view that schools should identify closely with neighbourhood people and neighbourhood interests. Some comprehensive schools would be classified as neighbourhood schools, whereas **grammar schools** often draw their pupils from a much wider area. (*see also* **community school/college**)

New Education　The name given to reformers active from the end of the last century who were opposed to the traditional, instrumental education of the time. There was no conscious school united under one banner and the views of individual reformers often differed widely. One group, the practical educationists, advocated manual training as a means of promoting educational values. Another, the social reformers, placed more emphasis on ways of improving the physical well being of children. The naturalists expounded the theories of Froebel and Pestalozzi whilst others looked to Herbart's teachings. There were also the scientific educationists who based their work largely on psychological research as well as those who looked to moral education as a replacement for religious instruction. The ideas of the New Educationists helped to provide a basis for the later progressive education movement. (*see also* **progressive education, progressive schools, New Education Fellowship**)

New Education Fellowship (NEF)　An organisation designed to promote various aspects of progressive, non-authoritarian education in schools. It was launched by Mrs Beatrice Ensor at the Calais Conference in 1921. The journal, *The New Era* was part of the early work of the NEF and is still published. In 1966, the NEF became the **World Education Fellowship**. (*see also* **New Education, progressive education, progressive schools**)

normal curve　A bell-shaped curve on a graph that shows the distribution which is expected to occur when the number of people obtaining each score follows the distribution which occurs for height in the adult population. There are very few people who are very tall and very few who are extremely short, but the curve rises to the highest point midway between the two extremes, showing that the majority are around average or medium height (hence the bell-shaped curve). Psychologists involved in constructing **intelligence tests** make the assumption that intelligence follows the normal distribution and therefore construct tests so that a normal population will have the same kind of distribution. Not all social scientists accept this assumption.

norm-referenced testing　Where a pupil's performance is compared with the performance of other pupils; the pupil's grade is therefore dependent on the average performance of the candidates as a whole. Norm-referenced testing is contrasted with **criterion-referenced testing**.

Nuffield Science In 1962 the Nuffield Foundation, a body concerned with making funds a available for research in academic subjects, intended to encourage the development of curricula in school science. Since then, more than twenty projects in science and mathematics have been produced and published. These include secondary-level schemes for children aged 11 to 16 and 16 to 18 in physics, chemistry and biology, in integrated and coordinated science and a primary science scheme. Most of these projects have now been revised and adapted to new and changing conditions. Originally 'O' and 'A' level examinations were provided; currently only the 'A' level examinations remain. (*see also* **curriculum development project**)

numeracy The Crowther Report (1959) first introduced the concept of numeracy, defining a well-educated man as one who was both **literate** and numerate (paragraph 401). Numeracy includes the need to think quantitatively and have an understanding of the scientific approach to the study of phenomena – observation, hypothesis, experiment and verification. Some twenty years later, the Cockroft Report (1982) proposed a more modest approach: that the individual should be sufficiently familiar with mathematical skills to cope with everyday life and that he or she should have some understanding of information presented in mathematical terms, such as graphs, charts or tables (paragraphs 35–9). (*see also* **graphicacy, literacy, oracy**)

nursery classes For children between the ages of 2 and 5, these classes form part of an infant primary school (unlike **nursery schools** which are free-standing institutions). (*see also* **playgroups, pre-school education**)

nursery nurse An asistant to qualified teachers in **nursery schools** and classes who holds the Nursery Nurses' Examination Board Diploma.

nursery school Caters for children of pre-school age, usually between the ages of 2 and 5. There are both State and private schools, though the former invariably have qualified staff. State schools have a recommended staff/child ratio of 1:13. The school day usually begins at about 9.00 a.m. and normally ends at 3.30 p.m. (*see also* **nursery classes, playgroups, Plowden Report, positive discrimination, pre-school education**)

O

'O' level The General Certificate of Education (GCE) Ordinary ('O') level examination was intended, when it replaced the **School Certificate Examination** in 1951, as a test for bright pupils who had completed a secondary school course up to the age of 16. The minimum age limit was abandoned in 1953 and it was clear from the number of candidates who attempted the examination each year that it was not entirely appropriate for many. The pass level was equivalent to the credit grade of the former School Certificate Examination. It was originally designed for potential **higher education** students and those entering the professions and business, though 'O' levels were always more widely demanded by employers. Unlike the School Certificate, it was a single-subject examination and was offered by eight different examining boards.

The introduction of the **Certificate of Secondary Education** (CSE) in 1965 for the ability range below those thought capable of achieving 'O' levels raised questions of comparability between the two examinations – for example, a CSE Grade I was accepted as equivalent to 'O' level grade C or better. It was because of these and other pressures that moves were made to establish a common system of examining at sixteen plus. This was eventually achieved in 1988 when GCE 'O' level and CSE were combined to form the **General Certificate of Secondary Education** (GCSE). (*see* Section 1, Essay 5)

objectives There are a number of different interpretations of this word in an educational context. **Behavioural objectives** are concerned with the desirable changes in behaviour of pupils to be brought about by formulating specific objectives at the beginning of a course. Such an approach is criticised on the grounds that it is too deterministic, the outcomes may be trivial and it is not applicable to the arts and humanities. One writer, Elliot Eisner, therefore, suggested the need for **expressive objectives** as well, where the predicted terminal behaviour is not fixed in advance, in some aspects of the curriculum. It is important, too, for teachers to distinguish between the short-term and the long-term objectives they wish to achieve. (*see also* **aims, objectives teaching**)

objectives teaching The objectives model of teaching seeks to evaluate pupil performance in any **curriculum** area against an agreed list of curriculum objectives. It implies that the teacher has already formulated, clarified and written down objectives which he or she wishes to attain and is the medium through which the recording and evaluation of pupil performance takes place.

objective test A test designed so that all examiners agree on the scores achieved by candidates. There is no room for interpretation on the part of the tester.

Objective tests take several forms: **multiple-choice** questions, or filling a blank with a single word or short phrase. Some objective tests may be marked by computer.

object lessons Stemming from Pestalozzi's teaching that the educator must work in accordance with natural laws which are discoverable by observation, object lessons consisted of lessons where objects were analysed, under such headings as qualities, parts and uses, by first-hand examination. This system was popularised in England by the publication of a series of textbooks in 1830 by a disciple of Pestalozzi, Elizabeth Mayo, entitled *Lessons on Objects*. Object lessons remained popular in elementary schools for the rest of the century and were often badly taught.

OFSTED (Office for Standards in Education) In September 1992 **Her Majesty's Inspectorate** (HMI) was completely reorganised and reduced in size. The grade of Senior Chief Inspector was abolished, the new head of HMI being called Chief Inspector. HMI were to be completely independent of the Department for Education and government, and the inspectors became collectively known as the Office for Standards in Education (OFSTED).

open admission The policy of allowing students into a university (or other institution) irrespective of their possession of normal **entry qualifications**. In the USA, a few universities operate an open admission system (or open access, open enrolment or 'open door' policies). In the UK, the **Open University** is the only institution of **higher education** which operates on this basis, although many other universities have admission systems for **mature students** which are more permissive but not completely open – in other words, access would be by means of alternative methods of assessment such as interview or essay writing rather than 'A' level results. (*see also* **Open College, Open Tech**)

Open College The Open College was set up by Lord Young (then Secretary of State for Trade and Industry) in 1987 to help retrain Britain's workforce for the 1990s. The College's original intention was to attract individual learners through an extensive network of local colleges, but has now been transformed into catering for individual learners via customised contracts with several hundred corporate customers. The College updates employee skills, for example, by running supervisory management courses for the staff of superstores. (*see also* **Open Tech, Manpower Services Commission**)

open day An occasion when a school or college opens its doors for visitors to view aspects of its work. There are usually displays of students' work and demonstrations of activities. (*see also* **parents'evening**)

open-ended An item on a test where the candidate is encouraged to answer the question in his or her own words, and where a variety of responses is possible. This is a very different technique from a **multiple choice** item in which only one of the alternatives is correct. Open-ended questions avoid the danger of guessing and enable candidates to express themselves more fully; marking and scoring are, however, much more complex and less 'objective'. (*see* Section 1, Essay 5)

open-plan school Open planning recognises the link between progressive educational methods and the need to break down the class or form into several working groups. This flexibility is achieved in a number of different ways and there is no one standard pattern. Ten per cent of all **primary schools** are of open-plan design, but this is much less common in the secondary sector. (*see also* **progressive education**)

Open Tech A government-sponsored body, set up in 1981 by the **Manpower Services Commission** and involving both the Department of Employment and the Department of Education and Science. It consisted of fourteen members from industry and education and was charged with the task of creating a system to help people of different ages to learn technology and to enable adults to retrain for different jobs. (*see also* **Open College**)

Open University (OU) A university established in Buckinghamshire in 1966 to provide degree and other courses for students of 21 years and over. The OU is 'open' in the sense that it operates an *open admissions* policy – that is, not insisting on normal entrance qualifications such as two GCE 'A' levels. The University arose out of the idea of a 'university of the air' much favoured by Harold Wilson when he was Prime Minister. However, the courses now provided are more like well-planned **correspondence courses** with supplementary tuition by means of television and radio. Tutorial advice on a local basis is also usually available. Students pursue their courses at home for about twelve to fifteen hours a week, thirty weeks in each year.

Many students follow undergraduate courses; others are involved in MA units, PhD theses and special short courses or various forms of **continuing education**. Each undergraduate course is planned as a year's (part-time) study on this basis, and a degree is awarded after successful completion of six courses (or eight courses of suitable standard for an honours degree). Courses are available in arts (humanities), social sciences, mathematics, science and technology, as well as education. Professional qualifications in law and medicine are not available. (*see also* **academic year, developmental testing, foundation course, PICKUP, universities: history of**)

opting out A decision by parents to convert a maintained school (one under the control of local education authority) into a **grant-maintained school** (GMS) receiving direct funding from the government.

options Many courses at school and university are designed on the 'core plus options' system. This means that a certain amount of the learning required is laid down as a compulsory 'core', but beyond that a student would be free to choose from a number of alternatives. For example, a student involved in a BA in English literature might be required to study a core course of Chaucer, Shakespeare and seventeenth-century literature, but after that would be free to choose from a number of specialist courses.

In English secondary schools most pupils have a core or common course for the first three years, but in the fourth and fifth years, options schemes tend to operate. This system has been much criticised by **Her Majesty's Inspectorate** and others as a poor substitute for **curriculum** planning. When the **National Curriculum** was introduced in 1988, many assumed that this would bring about the end of the options system for pupils aged 14 to 16. However, early modification of the National Curriculum meant that history, geography, art and music, although compulsory up to age 14, effectively became optional for Key Stage 4 (i.e. for pupils aged 14 to 16).

ORACLE (Observational Research and Classroom Learning Evaluation) A project funded by the **Social Science Research Council** and carried out by members of the University of Leicester School of Education on primary school children's behaviour and progress when working with different types of teachers. The conclusion of the ORACLE project was that **teaching styles** had a large effect on achievement.

oracy A term invented to indicate that speech is just as important educationally as reading and writing. Whereas **literacy** is the ability to read and write adequately, oracy is the ability to understand and communicate fluently in speech. In the **National Curriculum** (1988), although the word 'oracy' is not used, its importance is indicated by the fact that 'speaking and listening' is an '**Attainment Target**' alongside reading and writing. (*see also* **graphicacy**, **numeracy**)

oral examination A form of **examination** in which the candidate is assessed on her/his performance in response to an examiner's questioning. Examinations in music and modern languages often contain an oral component. (*see also* **viva**)

Order in Council An Order made by the Queen 'by and with the advice of Her Majesty's Privy Council' for the carrying on of government business. The Order may be either in virtue of the Royal Prerogative, such as declaring war, or under statutory authority. The latter category, often termed subordinate legislation, is widely used by governments to give force to administrative regulations. (*see also* **statutory instrument**)

Ordinary National Certificate (ONC) A post-school vocational award, sponsored by the **Department for Education** and the professional institution concerned. The two-year part-time course, of approximately '**A' level** standard, was offered in a limited range of subjects, but was later replaced by the **Business and Technician Education Council** certificates, and since 1986, coordinated by the **National Council for Vocational Qualifications**. (*see also* **Ordinary National Diploma**)

Ordinary National Diploma (OND) A post-school vocational course, (either two years full-time or on a 'sandwich' basis) sponsored by the **Department for Education** and the professional institution concerned. The Diploma was replaced by **Business and Technician Education Council** qualifications and since

1986 is coordinated by the **National Council for Vocational Qualifications**. (*see also* **Higher National Diploma, Ordinary National Certificate**)

Organisation for Economic Cooperation and Development (OECD) Established in Paris in 1961 as successor to the Organisation for European Economic Cooperation (OEEC), the OECD aims to promote economic and social welfare by assisting its member governments in the formulation of such policies. As a result, coordination of policies might be achieved. There is world wide membership, consisting of twenty-four countries. The Council consists of one representative from each country, and decisions and recommendations are adopted by mutual agreement of all members. There are more than a hundred specialised committees and working parties including one on education. Much of the educational work is carried out by the **Centre for Educational Research and Innovation** (CERI). The OECD publishes reviews of national policies for education of its member countries.

organised games Activities, involving teams or classes, such as rugby, cricket, hockey and netball, which are timetabled as a regular feature of the school **curriculum**.

orienteering An outdoor activity which combines cross-country running, map-reading, and locating check points with the assistance of a map and compass. Orienteering is sometimes (but not always) organised as a race in which contestants follow a pre-planned course in much the same way as drivers in a car rally. The educational merits of orienteering are considered to be the development of map-reading skills, enjoyment of the environment and the practical application of physical fitness.

outreach Originally a USA term, but one which is increasingly being used to describe certain programmes in the UK to describe activities where it is an advantage for staff to go out into the community rather than wait for young people to come into the college or university. In some projects, outreach workers are employed to make contact with the kind of young person not otherwise attracted to further education. Outreach staff are also employed by the **Youth Service** and in **adult education**.

over-learning A technical term in psychology to indicate that learning continues in the process of practising a **skill** or piece of **knowledge** which is already superficially learned. The theory behind over-learning is that short-term retention of knowledge or skills may be possible after a certain period, but if the need to recall the knowledge or recover the skill is required over a longer period, then it will be necessary to continue practising beyond a time when apparently the skill has been acquired.

Oxbridge A colloquial name given to the ancient universities of Oxford and Cambridge, as distinguished from the later nineteenth- and twentieth-century creations. (*see also* **universities, history of**)

pacing It is sometimes suggested that a good teacher carefully matches the rate of material presentation with the pupil's abilities and attention span; he/she paces his/her teaching carefully.

paradigm In 1970 the American writer on the philosophy of science, Thomas Kuhn, wrote a book *The Structure of Scientific Revolutions* which suggested that science did not develop in a linear fashion, but by a series of revolutions in which the dominant paradigm was replaced by a new paradigm. Since then, the word paradigm has been much used in the sociology of knowledge to indicate a set of perspectives or assumptions which may be dominant at one time, but which is eventually replaced suddenly by a new paradigm. In the sociology of education, the traditional paradigm which took for granted official statistics and positivist methodology was replaced by the new wave sociology described by Michael Young in his book *Knowledge and Control* (1971). Kuhn's view of the development of science and the application of that view of social sciences has been challenged a good deal since the 1970s. The use of the word paradigm has been particularly criticised for its ambiguity.

parametric statistics Statistical procedures based on the assumption that a sample is appropriate because the parent population was 'normal,' that is, had a normal distribution. If that assumption cannot be made safely, then non-parametric statistics are recommended. In mathematics, a parameter is a constant occurring in the equation of a curve, by the variation of which the equation can represent a whole family of curves. In other words, some kind of regularity can be assumed from the existence of a curve. Difficulties exist in educational experiments in terms of whether a population can be regarded as falling into a normal curve or not. (*see also* **Gaussian curve, normal curve**)

parent governors By the Education Act of 1986 parents were given equal representation with local education authorities and constitute a quarter of the membership of the governing body of a school. Parent governors are elected for four years by secret ballot, the candidates list being sent by post. Given the wide-ranging nature of the responsibilites of school governors, and expertise needed in curriculum and other matters, parent governors require appropriate training courses. (*see also* **Education Acts**)

parent power The 1944 Education Act stated that pupils were to be educated in accordance with the wishes of their parents, subject to public expenditure and so far as it was compatible with the provision of efficient instruction and training. However, parents had limited rights over involvement in **curriculum** policy-making in schools and the type of school to which their children were sent. An exception to this was the 1981 Education Act which provided for parents being consulted when decisions or the provision for meeting **special educational needs** of their children were being made.

The **Education Reform Act** (1988), according to its architect, Kenneth Baker, then Secretary of State for Education, was designed to give parents unprecedented power. Since then, politicians of each parties have espoused the cause of parent power. *The Parent's Charter* (1991) set out their rights, though it could be argued that the relationship between parents and schools varies from area to area and from school to school. The degree of parental involvement, for example, as helpers in the classroom is often encouraged, but more often at the primary stage. The partnership idea has been developed over such matters as the teaching of reading and writing which used to be seen as the exclusive province of the school. **Parent governors** and **parent-teacher associations** can also be effective channels for raising pertinent issues.

Since the 1988 Act, with its market-orientated philosophy, parents are regarded as consumers with schools seen as offering appropriate services. Marketing the schools by means of glossy brochures in order to attract parents and increasing emphasis on public relations are two examples. However, parent power may in many instances be illusory if seen as a threat to teacher professionalism, or as is more likely, through parental apathy. (*see also* **National Confederation of Parent-Teacher Associations**)

parent-teacher association (PTA) An association, consisting of members of staff and parents of pupils in a particular school, for discussing educational issues, raising funds for the school and organising social functions which lessen the division between home and school. Much depends on the enthusiasm or otherwise of the headteacher for the success of such an association There is a **National Confederation of Parent-Teacher Associations** which puts forward policies reflecting the views of its membership. (*see also* **Home and School Council, parent power, pressure group**)

Parent's Charter The new rights and responsibilities in education for parents in the government's Citizens' Charter were stated in a booklet *The Parent's Charter: You and Your Child's Education* issued in July 1991. The Charter included plans for annual written reports on children's progress; regular reports by independent inspectors on each school's strengths and weaknesses; published league tables which made possible comparison between the performance of local schools; and independent assessors on panels which would hear parents' appeals if they were unable to get the school of their choice for their children. Some of these items were included in the **Education (Schools) Act (1992)**

parents' evening An evening arranged for parents at their children's school in order to discuss progress and other aspects of their children's performance. The frequency of open evenings varies from school to school but they are held at least once a year. (*see also* **open day**)

Parliamentary Papers Documents ordered to be printed by the House of Commons for its own use or delivered to the House for the information of MPs; and listed in the daily Votes and Proceedings of the House. Many are subsequently printed by **Her Majesty's Stationery Office** (HMSO). They include Bills, reports of **Royal Commissions, Select Committees**, and **Departmental Committees, White Papers**, some **Green Papers** as well as about 40 per cent of Statutory Instruments (which can include Orders in Council). Before 1921, virtually all important official reports and documents were issued as Parliamentary Papers. (The nineteenth-century term for Parliamentary Papers was 'Blue Books' but since that date, many have appeared outside the Parliamentary Papers series.) Documents delivered to or printed by the House of Lords are also Parliamentary Papers.

participant observation Research in the field of social psychology in which the researcher takes part as a member of the group being observed and records the behaviour of the group. See, for example, Ervin Goffman's fieldwork on the social world of the hospital inmate, published as *Asylums* (1968). (*see also* **case study, triangulation**)

participation rate See **age participation rate**.

part-time education Refers to courses in further and higher education which students take on a part-time basis. Courses may range from those of a recreational nature to PhDs. Many part-time students combine these courses with other occupations.

passive learning Some educational psychologists and other educationists make a distinction between **active learning** and passive learning. In a passive learning situation, a pupil is given no opportunity to make any contribution and is simply expected to learn pre-digested information which is presented to him/her by the teacher or lecturer. (*see also* **learning**)

passive vocabulary Words which an individual can recognise and understand when used by others, although they may not be part of that individual's **active vocabulary** (i.e. the vocabulary which he actually uses himself). Active and passive vocabulary may be confined to speech or may also be measured in terms of reading and writing.

pass mark The grade or numbered mark fixed by examiners which examinees are required to obtain to be successful.

pass rate The ratio or proportion of candidates who are successful in an examination or assignment.

pastoral system During the 1960s it became common in some local authorities for **comprehensive schools** to divide the responsibilities of teachers into academic and 'pastoral care'. In such schools there were two hierarchies of teachers and senior staff: one academic and the other pastoral. This system of separating academic from pastoral was sometimes referred to as the 'pastoral system'. Pastoral care is seen to have a dual role: on the one hand it serves as a support system to pupils in academic aspects of the school's work, and on the other, it serves as a 'pastoralising agent' for those pupils who do not appear to benefit from what the school offers. Pastoral systems tend to be structured into Year or House groupings, with **tutors** attached, responsible to a pastoral leader, called head of house or head of year, for the guidance of a number of pupils.

'payment by results' The Newcastle Report, published in 1861, was concerned with the cost of extending sound and cheap instruction to all classes. As a result, Robert Lowe, then Vice-President of the Council, introduced a revised code in the following year. Grants hitherto payable to certificated teachers were abolished. A school's finances were dependent on the annual examination of children in the three Rs, with plain needlework for girls, by **Her Majesty's Inspectorate** (HMI) ('payment by results'), coupled with the fulfilment of a minimum number of attendances. The grant earned by the school was paid direct to the **managers**. Opposition to the revised code delayed its introduction until 1863, but its effects on elementary schools were felt until after the close of the century. More recently, some politicians have revived the notion that teachers' pay should be linked to their pupils' tests and examination results. (*see also* **homework, performance related pay**)

pedagogy Defined by Brian Simon as 'a science of teaching embodying both **curriculum** and methodology'. Unlike their continental counterparts, British schools have tended to shy away from evolving a pedagogical method, focusing instead on the 'needs' of the individual child.

percentile A statistical term used for many educational tests. A percentile indicates the point in a set of scores or marks that exceeds a given percentage. For example, the fortieth percentile is the point below which 40 per cent of all the candidates score. The term percentile rank is used to indicate the relationship to all other scores. Thus a person might score 59 per cent on a test, but if that score was better than 70 per cent of all other candidates, he would be said to have the percentile rank of 70.

performance contracting During the **accountability** debate in the USA in the 1970s, some states employed commercial organisations to provide instructional services to a school district on the basis of a fee being determined by success rates measured by performance of students on criterion tests. Such schemes were closely scrutinised by teachers' professional organisations who were delighted to report those occasions when the organisations failed, or where maladministration amounting to fraud was reported.

performance indicators (PIs) A series of indicators which are postulated in order to judge whether a school or other institution is **effective**. PIs originated from economics, where it was applied to 'value for money' and cost effectiveness. They are seen as a way of monitoring the work of a school. Lists of PIs show differences of approach. *The Parent's Charter* (1991) mentions the construction of performance tables which will include examinations, National Curriculum tests and truancy rates. Others prefer the quality of the teaching/learning experience, good management, the level of care offered by the school and a shared sense of mission by the staff, which would include leadership. Problems arise from the difficulty of collecting different types of indicator, the interpretation of raw data, the effects on school intakes of the publication of the results and the need to differentiate school performances in terms of their physical location.

By the **Education (Schools) Act** (1992), the Department for Education proposed three categories of indicators: **GCSE** and **'A'/'AS'** examination results, **National Curriculum** assessment results, truancy figures and a matrix of destination data for each of the 15, 16, and 17 age groups. (*see also* **league tables**)

performance related pay (PRP) **Governing bodies** determine **headteachers'** salaries by various methods, the most common of which is PRP. This consists of two parts: the basic performance bonus which most people would achieve, and an 'output' bonus based on achieving a specified target or targets. The second is based on an industrial model which arguably is not applicable to teaching. There is little evidence that PRP improves performance. Further, although headteachers are obviously very important in making a good school, the credit attributable to one person as against the whole teaching staff is difficult to extrapolate. The use of **league tables** showing school performance in a number of areas such as examinations and truancy should not be used as a determinant of PRP. Such performance would be difficult to relate to the pay of individual teachers. (*see also* **teachers**)

performance test (1) The kind of test in which the candidate is required to demonstrate a practical **skill** rather than write about it. (2) A test which requires a candidate to perform certain tasks specified as a means of **selection**. (3) A test of actual ability and/or attainment rather than an indication of possible future potential. (*see also* **aptitude test, attainment test**)

peripatetic teacher A teacher, usually in subjects such as languages and music, who is not attached to any one particular school, but visits various schools in a **local education authority** for a number of sessions with pupils.

permanent education (l'education permanente) A term more frequently used in Europe than in England, but one which is gaining ground. Permanent education is an ideal which aims for the availability of education throughout an individual's life, not ending with the completion of **compulsory schooling** or a further period of **higher education** or **further education**. The **Council of Europe** has committed itself to the ideal of permanent education and has produced a large number of reports on this subject. Permanent education overlaps but is not identical with either **recurrent education** or **continuing education**. (*see also* **adult education**)

personal and social education (PSE); personal, social and health education (PSHE) One of the problems of the **National Curriculum** (1988) like the typical secondary curriculum before 1988 was that it is essentially a list of subjects. Yet some of the most important aspects of adolescent development do not fall neatly into any one subject area. One of these areas is the whole question of personal and social education (PSE) – how to come to terms with the individual 'self' and with other individuals in society. This kind of development, together with **moral education** and **health education**, is recognised to be important, but in the past, little systematic attention has been paid to it. The **National Curriculum Council** (NCC) has acknowledged that the National Curriculum is not the whole curriculum, and has urged schools to take seriously the responsibility for organising the whole curriculum in its own way. As a contribution to this debate the NCC has published a number of booklets on 'cross-curricular themes', including one on personal and social education. In some schools, coordinators have been appointed for PSE; in other schools this work has been combined with some aspects of health education, and coordinators have been appointed for PSHE. (*see also* **social skills**)

phonic method A technique used in the teaching of **reading**. It is based on the sounds of letters rather than the names of letters. Most teachers combine this method with 'looking and saying', that is by reading aloud. (*see also* **Gestalt**)

Piagetian The adjective referring to the work of Piaget, in particular the stages of development approach. Piaget's theory was that children, by a process of maturation, progress through four stages of development: (1) the sensory motor stage; (2) pre-operational; (3) concrete operations; and (4) formal operations. (*see also* **enactive**)

PICKUP Acronym for the Government's scheme announced in 1982 – Professional Industrial and Commercial Updating – an information system initially sponsored by the **Department of Education and Science** (DES) which stored details of courses available at colleges for updating the skills of workers in industry. Colleges are being encouraged to devise short and part-time courses which meet the needs of local industry and which will be self-financing, paid for either by employers or the trainees themselves. Distance learning packages have been developed for the scheme by the **Open University**. The schemes are regionally operated with regional development officers appointed to liaise between education and industry. (*see also* **recurrent education**)

pilot scheme; pilot study Many **curriculum development projects** involve a 'pilot stage'. This usually involves trying out experimental materials in a small number of 'pilot' schools. The object is either to improve the materials at this stage, or possibly to reject them completely as inappropriate. In more general terms, a pilot study is one which precedes a main study. (*see also* **feasibility study**, **induction scheme**)

playcentre Introduced in London in 1898 by Mrs Humphry Ward, playcentres offer a range of leisure activities for children of primary school age after school, in term time, and full time for an extended age range in the school holidays. Playcentres are situated in schools near to the children's homes and may be staffed either by teachers or outside helpers. Since the abolition of the **Inner London Education Authority**, a large number of playcentres have been closed. Similar schemes exist in many local education authorities.

playground An area normally within the precincts of a school where pupils may play either before, during or after school hours. The official morning and afternoon breaks in the **primary school** day are often called 'playtime'. The playground is also frequently used for outdoor physical education and games. It is regarded as much more important in England than elsewhere.

playgroups Introduced in 1960 after the refusal of the **Ministry of Education** to give preference in State **nursery schools** to teachers' own children. A playgroup has a minimum of six children aged between 2½ and 5 supervised by leaders who do not have to hold teaching qualifications. Sessions usually last for a morning or an afternoon in premises which have been passed by the Social Services Department. There is a national body which looks after the interests of its members, the **Pre-School Playgroup Association**. A survey by the Association in March 1992 showed that most of Britain's 15 000 playgroups were being run on a small budget and advocated a comprehensive system for resourcing their work. (*see also* **Children Act** (1989))

playing field An area for school children where sporting or physical activities such as football, rugby and tennis can be carried out. Because of financial constraints, a growing number of local education authorities have been selling off playing fields.

Plowden Report The Report of the **Central Advisory Council** (England) entitled *Children and their primary schools* was published in 1967. The Council's terms of reference were 'to consider primary education in all its aspects, and the transition to secondary education.' This aspect of schooling had not been examined since the two Hadow committees in the 1930s. Under the chairmanship of Lady Plowden, the Council made a number of important recommendations for the amelioration of social disadvantage. **Positive discrimination**, in the form of educational priority areas (EPAs) where extra staffing and resources could be allocated, was suggested. Better nursery education provision was needed nationally, but especially for EPAs. The structure of primary education was to be changed. Instead of the existing pattern of infants (5 to 7) and junior (7 to 11), there should be a first school (5 to 8) and then a middle school (8 to 12). The starting age for children was to be more flexible. Continuity between the stages was recommended, including the secondary stage. The Report also stressed the need for more cooperation between home and school: as the focus of the community, the school should welcome parents to participate in school activities. The Report, the last of those produced by the Central Advisory Council, has recently come under attack from right-wing educationists who attribute to it the decline in educational standards. The statement at the beginning of Chapter 2 'At the heart of the educational process lies the child' has been interpreted as an advocacy of '**progressive education**', encouragement to neglect the three Rs and a deterioration in teaching methods.

polytechnics In 1965, the then Secretary of State for Education, Anthony Crosland, made his famous Woolwich speech calling for a distinct system of higher education with the establishment of polytechnics. The 1966 White Paper *A Plan for the polytechnics and other colleges* (Cmd 3006) described the polytechnics as regional centres which linked with industry and business. University validation was largely replaced by the **Council for National Academic Awards** (CNAA) though institutions would continue to be financed by local authorities. In 1969, eight polytechnics were created in England and Wales and the number expanded to thirty. After 1973, a number of colleges of education were absorbed into the existing polytechnics, bringing with them additional expertise in the arts and humanities. The Education Reform Act (1988) gave the polytechnics their independence from local government from 31 March 1989. A new **Polytechnics and Colleges Funding Council** (PCFC) was responsible for their funding. Within two years, in May 1991, a White Paper *Higher Education: A New Framework* abolished the distinction between universities and polytechnics and the PCFC and the **University Funding Council** (UFC) would merge to become a single funding structure. The 1992 **Further and Higher Education Act** abolished the CNAA and allowed polytechnics the power to award their own taught courses and research degrees. From 1992, the thirty-four polytechnics in England and Wales and five in Scotland, with the approval of the Privy Council, changed their names to universities. (*see* Section 1, Essay 7)

positive discrimination The provision of resources to mitigate educational or other disadvantage caused by social and/or economic deprivation. This is often known as **compensatory education**. The **Plowden Report** recommended the identification of inner city districts which were to be recognised as educational priority areas (EPAs) for this purpose. Much of the emphasis is on pre-school facilities, nursery schools, the involvement of the parents with teachers and the development of community education. The issue is a political one and there are different views on the causes of inequality. As a result, the Plowden philosophy has not been fully translated into resources. (*see also* **Head Start**)

postgraduate A person studying for an award above that of a first, that is Bachelor's **degree**. This might take the form of a diploma or a higher degree, either at the master's or doctorate levels.

Postgraduate Certificate of Education (PGCE) A certificate taken by graduates, either immediately after their first **degree** course or (increasingly frequently) a few years later after some work experience. It is normally a one-year full-time course of educational studies; a minimum number of days of practical teaching in schools under supervision is normally prescribed. In recent years much greater emphasis has been placed on practical experience with the schools acting as equal partners with college tutors in the training process. (*see also* **teacher training**)

praxis A term used by many Marxist educationists, but especially Paulo Freire (1972). For Friere, real education is an individual's interaction with his environment. The task of a teacher is not to pass on a package of **knowledge** (the banking concept of education), but to go with the pupil and explore the relationship between experience and knowledge in a practical way. Praxis is, therefore, more than the opposite of theory. It is the exploration by an individual (or a group) of the environment in a way which produces 'real' knowledge rather than theoretical or second-hand knowledge.

precision learning See **objectives teaching**.

prefect Pupils who occupy posts of special responsibility in a school, usually chosen from the upper forms. They assist in various ways to the smooth running of the school. The term itself dates back only to 1865 in this sense. Although the prefect system is retained in many **independent schools**, only a minority of state schools now do so. Many different schemes exist which allow pupils to show leadership qualities and participate in the decision-making process. One example is where each class selects representatives for year-group meetings, which in turn select representatives for the **school council**, where a wide range of matters can be discussed. (*see also* **head boy/girl**)

preparatory school Often abbreviated to 'prep school', these are **independent schools**, either of the day or boarding type, which prepare their pupils for either the **common entrance examination** at 13 plus or, where, it still exists, the 11 plus examination. Some **public schools** retain their own preparatory schools, but most are independent of them. Where the target is the common entrance examination, the curriculum includes Latin and French.

pre-school education All education provision for children below the statutory school-starting age of 5, organised by local authorities or voluntary organisations. An official report by the Rumbold Committee, published in December 1990, into the quality of provision for the under-5s was not implemented, but education support grants for 1991–2 to help local authorities improve planning and coordination of pre-school provisions was a welcome move. (*see also* **nursery classes**, **playgroups**, **Plowden Report**)

pressure group Like-minded people who band together to press their claims on a particular issue or a set of issues to affect or modify the behaviour or actions of a body holding power. Since the 1960s, they have become a familiar part of the education scene. An early example was in the field of **pre-school education**, where the National Campaign for Nursery Education, formed in 1965, succeeded in persuading the government to make wider provision available. A number of groups have sprung up in recent years which have marked views on the need to bring about change in schools, such as the Campaign for Real Education, the **National Education Trust** and Parental Alliance for Choice in Education. Some pressure groups have a national organisation but rely on local branches to provide the momentum, such as the Campaign for Comprehensive Education and the **National Confederation of Parent-Teacher Associations**.

pre-test (post-test) In some experimental situations used in education a test is given to a student before starting a course or using experimental materials, and again at the end of such a course. The pre-test results are then compared with the post-test results and an estimate made of the effectiveness of the course or teaching programme or materials involved. The procedure seems to be a plausible one, but in practice all sorts of contaminating influences work to the detriment of simple interpretations or results.

pre-vocational education See **Certificate of Pre-Vocational Education**.

primary school Prior to the reorganisation following the Hadow Report of 1926, most elementary schools were divided into two parts – infants, taking in children from 5 to 7, and then boys' and girls' departments, from 7 to 14. The Hadow Report's suggestion, that 11 years of age was a more suitable time for the **transition** to **secondary education**, produced a distinctive unit, the primary school, consisting of an infants department, as in pre-Hadow times, and a junior department, with children of 7 to 11. By the 1944 Education Act, the **elementary school** finally disappeared, and was officially replaced by the **primary school**. This system still exists in most local education authorities, except where middle schools have come into existence.

A report by Professor Robin Alexander and two colleagues issued in January 1992, stressed the need for primary teachers to focus more firmly on the outcomes of their teaching and to have more specialist knowledge of their subjects. The first **Standard Assessment Tasks**, Key Stage 1, were taken by 7-year-olds in 1991.

primer Originally having a religious connotation, a 'book of prime' (or hours), the word now covers any book which deals with the elements of a subject. (*see also* **reader**)

principal Holder of the post of chief officer of a university, college or school. The title of the office varies from one university to another. In London, the post is largely administrative, as there is also a **vice-chancellor**. (*see also* **Committee of Vice-Chancellors and Principals**)

private school See **independent school** and **public school**.

probation Before September 1992, to obtain **qualified teacher status**, trained teachers were required by the **Department of Education and Science** (DES) to complete successfully one year's teaching in a maintained educational institution. **Local education authorities**, through their **inspectors** or **advisers**, were responsible for approving the majority of the probationers, and for providing courses and other assistance to support the new teacher. From September 1992, the responsibility rests with the school. This change took place at the same time as schools, rather than teacher-training departments, took the major share in the training of teachers. More emphasis is now placed on **induction** with greater opportunities for the new teacher to learn his or her profession in the classroom over a number of years. Previously, service in the independent sector was not allowed to count towards probation. Now new teachers have the choice of starting their career in either **maintained** or **independent schools**. (*see also* **teacher training**)

problem solving A style of teaching or learning where the aim is to encourage pupils to acquire **knowledge** and **skills** in the process of solving problems rather than simply learning about how other people have solved such problems.

Professional Association of Teachers (PAT) This Association, which has over 40 000 members, is best known for the pledge of its members never to go on strike. It also seeks a professional code of conduct for teachers. The Association claims to be non-party political. (*see also* **teachers' unions**)

professor Traditionally, the highest ranking teacher in a field of learning at a university. A professor may hold either an established post, carrying with it a named chair in a named faculty, or a personal title, awarded on the basis of the holder's academic standing. From 1969, polytechnics have appointed professors, but not necessarily based on the same criteria as universities. Generally, it was confined to senior staff but the title carried with it the extra salary. From 1992, when the two sectors of higher education were merged, similar criteria for professorships began to be exercised.

The term is also used for senior staff at specialist institutions such as the Royal College of Surgeons, Cranfield, and the London Music Colleges (*see also* **universities, history of**)

profile An attempt to provide an alternative form of **assessment** to school reports for pupils. Whereas the conventional report concentrates on performance in particular subjects, profiles assess a range of pupils' qualities, attitudes and behaviour, so that a much fuller picture of each individual may be given. It is claimed that they are particularly appropriate in the upper secondary school for potential employers and were included in the criteria for the **Technical and Vocational Education Initiative** extension (TVEI) programme as well as schemes for **records of achievement**. Criticisms are directed at the ethical and technical difficulties of profiles, the place of teachers' value judgements in assessments and their value if confined only to those who achieve few examination successes. It should be noted that profile schemes can be pupil-controlled as an alternative to teacher-based judgements: this involves the pupils in recording their experiences and achievements.

profile component (PC) A profile component is a cluster of **Attainment Targets** for the **National Curriculum** assessment.

programmed learning Programmed learning is based upon self-instructional materials. They are designed to allow pupils to progress at their own pace, step by step, through carefully structured sequences. The programmes may be either linear or branching, or a mixture of the two. They are normally presented in the form of a programmed text or in a teaching machine. More recently, programmed learning has been associated with computer-assisted instruction or **computer-assisted learning** (CAL). Some programmed learning is associated with the **behavioural objectives** school and/or the work of B. F. Skinner. (*see also* **individual learning, Skinnerian**)

Programmes of Study (PoS) Defined in the **Education Reform Act** (1988) as 'The matters, skills and processes which are required to be taught to pupils of different abilities and maturities during each Key Stage.' There is a description of Programmes of Study for each subject with reference to appropriate **Key Stages**. (*see* Section 1, Essay 7)

progressive education One of the most ambiguous terms in the whole of educational literature. For some, 'progressive' meant no more than a reaction against the nineteenth-century harsh discipline and unimaginative teaching methods. The reaction (at the end of the nineteenth-century and more particularly at the beginning of the twentieth-century) usually took the form of schools which did not use **corporal punishment**, which treated children as individuals and which moved away from **rote learning** as the main system of acquiring **knowledge**. After the 1944 Education Act, however, the word 'progressive' began to be used by those who supported **comprehensive schools** rather than the traditional **tripartite schools**. Comprehensive school supporters were described as progressive; those who wished to retain the grammar schools would be labelled traditional. This was particularly confusing since one strand in the English progressive education movement was the group of **independent schools** associated with the **New Education Fellowship**.

In the late-1960s and early-1970s, progressivism in education was attacked in the **Black Papers**. This attack was on so-called progressive methods in **primary schools**, which usually consisted of an **integrated** approach to the curriculum rather than a subject-based timetable; and in **secondary schools**, a more **child-centred** approach was attacked; in primary and secondary schools, the alleged lack of '**discipline**' was deplored. The abolition of the 11 plus system in primary schools and the liberalising of examinations at 16 plus in secondary schools was also criticised by the writers of the Black Papers. In the 1990s, these were probably still the major issues separating 'progressives' from traditionalists, but the label is sometimes applied indiscriminately. For example, an educationist might be a strong advocate of comprehensive schools, but someone who wishes to retain traditional examination. 'Progressive' is a term now best avoided unless carefully defined. (*see also* **New Education, progressive schools**)

progressive schools First pioneered by Cecil Reddie at Abbotsholme in 1889, the English progressive school movement was based on the notion of social reform through education. **Independent schools**, many of which are mainly boarding in character, represented miniature societies; Reddie and others looked to a reformed and enlightened system of schooling which eliminated **corporal punishment**, furthered team-spirit rather than individualism, was co-educational in composition and democratic in its day-to-day running. This move-ment received a second impulse after the First World War and again in the 1930s. Well-known schools associated with the movement include Bedales, Dartington Hall, King Alfred School and Summerhill. (*see also* **New Education, progressive education**)

project (1) An educational activity often based on pupils' interests, centred on a particular problem or issue. This method emphasised cooperative learning between pupils and teachers. W. H. Kilpatrick, a colleague of John Dewey in the USA, was instrumental in popularising this approach after the First World War. (*see also* **assignment, problem solving, team teaching, topic work**) (2) A name given to a small- or large-scale research programme, carried out by one or more persons, in some aspect of education. (*see also* **curriculum development project**)

prospectus All state schools are legally obliged to produce a prospectus setting out basic information for parents. The prospectuses vary from glossy brochures to much more modest efforts.

public school In England, an independent fee-paying school, of which there are about 200, most of whose heads are members of the **Headmasters' Confer-ence**. The majority of them are boarding schools. The origins of this type of school are complex and varied. Many were the result of the endowment of pious founders and were indistinguishable from grammar schools. Eton, Winchester and Westminster are typical examples. By the eighteenth century, a number of 'great schools' had emerged, including Harrow, Rugby, Sherborne, Canterbury and Shrewsbury. The Clarendon Commission of 1861 named nine public schools as the object of its investigations and thus marked off these institutions from other endowed schools. Some have close links with universities under the terms of their founders, for example, Henry VI established King's College, Cambridge, for Eton scholars and similarly, William Wykeham, founder of Winchester, endowed New College, Oxford. These schools are now called **independent schools**. In the USA and many other countries the term public school means state school.

punishment, corporal See **corporal punishment**.

punishment, psychology and philosophy of A good deal of work has been done by educationists on both the psychology of punishment and the philosophy of punishment. Much of the work on the psychology of punishment has been carried out from a behaviourist point of view and sees punishment as a way of discouraging certain kinds of behaviour and encouraging alternative preferred behaviour. In the philosophy of punishment, distinction is made between punishment as a means of reform. (*see also* **corporal punishment, Society of Teachers Opposed to Physical Punishment**)

pupil See **student**.

pupil-teacher ratio (PTR) The majority of local education authorities approach the allocation of teaching staff to schools at all levels by the use of a pupil-teacher ratio (PTR). At the primary level, schools are staffed on the basis of numbers of children and size of school; at the secondary level, local authorities have moved from a single PTR for all pupils to age-specific PTRs which take account of the higher staffing demands imposed by older pupils; special factors are increasingly taken into account. A major concern for parents is the size of classes. In 1992, almost a quarter of children in English primary schools were in classes of more than thirty. Whilst educationists are not unanimous on the importance of small classes, **independent schools** regard this as an essential basis for good teaching.

Pygmalion effect See **self-fulfilling prophecy**.

q

'Q' and 'F' levels In 1969, the Standing Conference on University Entrance and the **Schools Council** put forward proposals to replace GCE **'A' level** examinations. This consisted of two stages: a 'Q' or Qualifying examination, based on one year's study of five subjects beyond GCE **'O' level**, and an 'F' or Further examination, corresponding to one year's work beyond the Qualifying examination in not more than three subjects. These proposals were not adopted and were replaced by **'N' and 'F' levels**. (*see* Section 1, Essay 5)

quadrivium The school **curriculum** in the Middle Ages consisted of the so-called seven liberal arts. The first three – grammar, dialectic and rhetoric – formed the **trivium** and the other four – music, arithmetic, geometry and astronomy – made up the quadrivium. The whole made a course of seven years' duration. The term 'quadrivium' dates back as far as Boethius (AD 480–542). (*see also* **liberal studies**)

qualified teacher status (QTS) Qualified teacher status is granted by the Secretary of State for Education under regulations which set out categories of qualifications for teachers in maintained and other schools. The most common 'routes into teaching' of this kind are the possession of a **BEd degree** (or a BA/BSc which includes an approved education course), or a degree of a UK university together with a **Postgraduate Certificate of Education** (PGCE). In 1990, the Secretary of

State for Education announced two new categories: **licensed teachers** and **articled teachers**.

quality assurance A term introduced into the official language of education in the White Paper *Higher Education: A New Framework* (1991). Quality assurance is a general term which includes two more specific aspects of quality; **quality control** which is carried out by the institutions themselves; and **quality audit** which is an external check on internal controls (probably by means of an **academic audit unit**).

quality audit An aspect of **accountability** intended to specify procedures for monitoring standards. In England and Wales the White Paper *Higher Education: A New Framework* (1991) included a good deal of discussion of 'quality audit' in higher education and the possibility of establishing **quality audit units** (QAUs) in order to ensure maintenance of standards and comparability of standards between institutions. (*see also* **audit**)

quality control The aspect of **quality assurance** which is concerned with maintaining **standards** of teaching and student **performance**. Quality control is normally carried out by the institution itself. (*see also* **quality assurance, quality audit**)

quango (quasi-autonomous non-governmental organisation) A term of abuse developed in the 1970s to attack a particular kind of bureaucratic structure. Some quangos were educational organisations, and a few of them were very important. The overall number of quangos was reduced in the early 1980s and a number of educational organisations disappeared. This did not, however, prevent the Government from creating new quangos such as the **Council for the Assessment of Teacher Education** (CATE)

quota system A scheme operated by the Department of Education and Science until 1975, whereby local education authorities were allocated a quota of teachers as a means of ensuring fairness during a period of teacher shortage.

r

raising of the school leaving age See **ROSLA**.

Rampton Report One of the results of the discussions during the 1970s about the under-achievement of certain ethnic **minorities** was that a Committee of Enquiry was set up under the chairmanship of Mr Anthony Rampton in March 1979. Its Report was published in 1981 and became very controversial. One of the major findings was that children of West Indian parents under-achieved in schools whereas Asian minorities performed as well as, or almost as well as, native born children. The explanation of this seemed to be the conscious or unconscious racism of some teachers in English primary and secondary schools. Soon after the publication of the Interim Report, Anthony Rampton was replaced as chairman by Sir Michael Swann. (*see* **multicultural education, under-achievement**)

rank, ranking, rank order Ranking is the process of arranging individuals in order of achievement (e.g. **reading ability** or **intelligence** or performance on arithmetic tests). The highest rank is given to the person with the highest score and this person is numbered 1, the second highest 2, and so on. (In the USA, ranking is sometimes reversed so that 1 is the lowest rank.) If a list of marks is published in this way (rather than alphabetically) the list may be described as a rank order.

readability Since it is important that material presented to young pupils is not too 'difficult' for them, a number of educationists have attempted to develop measures of 'readability' which indicate the ease with which a passage or even a whole text may be read. Sometimes **reading ages** are assigned to texts in this way. The measures most frequently employed are length of words and sen-tences, but the familiarity of the language used and the style are also important. It is rarely possible to give an exact indication because two other factors are also very important and they are much more difficult to measure; the first is the number of abstract words and examples given; the second is the author's ability to motivate the child. It has been found that children can read 'above their reading age' if they find the subject matter sufficiently interesting. (*see also* **reading, readiness**)

reader (1) A volume consisting of extracts of the works of various authors on a particular theme. (2) A university title, in status between that of senior lecturer and a **professor**.

readiness A concept described by Jerome Bruner as a 'mischievous half truth'. The idea of readiness is that pupils should not be forced to learn certain **skills** (particularly **reading**) until they have reached a certain maturational stage, and are ready to embark upon that particular learning skill. Critics of the concept point out that it might encourage some teachers to avoid teaching children until they were 'ready', when they ought to be making them ready by teaching them the prerequisite abilities.

reading There has been much controversy in recent years on the question of reading standards in schools and the most effective methods of teaching reading. Standardised reading tests are based on the scores of large samples of children who have been tested on the recognition of increasingly difficult words, or the selection of appropriate words to complete sentences. Such tests have been criticised on the grounds that the format does not allow the assessment of a pupil's ability to handle continuous text or to make inferences.

Little is known on how a child learns to read. A variety of practices exist in schools with the majority using more than one method. **The phonic method** involves children learning the sounds of letters and building them into words. This is often combined with *look and say*, where pupils learn to recogise words and sentences by their shape and pattern and to compose words and sentences from banks of letters and words. Two other contrasting methods are the *real books* approach, which claims that children can acquire reading skills simply by being allowed to read attractively produced books, and the *Reading Recovery* scheme, which gives low-achieving children daily intensive help on a one-to-one basis.

The Comparative Reading Survey carried out on 1991 by the **National Foundation for Educational Research** (NFER) showed that the reading performance of 7- to 8-year-olds in England had fallen between 1987 and 1991 though not uniformly in all schools. Some factors influencing the scores were also listed. The majority of heads pointed to a similar downward trend in other subjects. The first national **Standard Assessment Tasks** in reading carried out in 1991 showed that 28 per cent of 7-year-olds did not reach **level** 2. However, an analysis of the results has shown that the same pupils performed differently on traditional reading tests and that disadvantaged schools had much higher numbers at the lowest levels. (*see also* **readability, readiness**)

reading age   A pupil's competence in **reading** measured against the average competence of children for his/her age. An 8-year-old pupil who was advanced in his/her reading ability might have a reading age of 10, whereas a less advanced 8-year-old might only have a reading age of 6 or 7. (*see* **IQ**)

reception class   The class reserved for 5-year-old new entrants into the infant section of a **primary school**.

record-keeping   Maintained schools are required to keep records of all pupils' academic progress, including the results of National Curriculum assessment at age 7, 11, 14 and 16.

record of achievement   A method of summarising a pupil's attainments and activities in school so that they can be passed on from teacher to teacher and from school to school. (*see also* **National Record of Achievement, school records**)

recurrent education   A policy based on the view that **compulsory education** should be regarded as the first stage in the educational process, followed if not by **further education** or **higher education**, by a series of returns to courses of education throughout the period of adult life. Recurrent education could be vocational or professional or entirely non-vocational, but there tends to be an association of recurrent education with the idea of updating professional skills. (*see also* **adult education, continuing education, in-service education of teachers, permanent education, PICKUP.**)

'redbrick' university Name coined by Bruce Truscot (pseudonym of F. Allison Peers) in his book *Redbrick University* (1943), to describe the characteristics of seven of the English civic **universities** established in the late-nineteenth and early-twentieth centuries. The term has now passed into general usage and is contrasted with **Oxbridge**. (*see also* **universities, history of**)

redeployment Voluntary or compulsory transfer of staff to another teaching post in another school. Because of **falling rolls** in schools, this practice has become more common. (*see also* **teachers**)

reductionism A belief held by some psychologists and others that it is possible to explain a complex phenomenon by breaking it down into smaller parts and explaining the individual constituents. Behaviourist psychology is said to be reductionist because it claims to explain the whole of human behaviour in terms of the two concepts – stimulus and response. Similarly, the **behavioural objectives** approach to **curriculum** planning is said to be reductionist because it reduces the learning process to a series of behavioural changes which can be measured. In psychology, an opposite point of view is held by **Gestalt** psychologists. In curriculum studies, the opposite point of view would be taken by those describing themselves as humanistic. (*see also* **behaviourism, objectives**)

registrar A senior post in a college or **university** whose holder is responsible for students' enrolment, student records, examinations, academic administration and the oversight of committees. Some institutions have both an academic registrar (concerned with enrolment) and a registrar with more general responsibilities.

registration of independent schools Since the 1944 Education Act, all **independent schools** providing full-time education for five or more pupils of compulsory school age have been obliged to register with the **Department of Education and Science** (now the **Department for Education**) or the **Welsh Office**. After a school has been given provisional registration by **Her Majesty's Inspectorate**, visits are made to satisfy the Department on the suitability of the premises, accommodation, staffing and instruction; as a result final registration may be granted. The **Children Act** (1989) requires the proprietors of **boarding schools** to safeguard and promote the welfare of their pupils. Since 1977, independent schools cannot apply to be registered as efficient. The Independent Schools Joint Council have a system of **accreditation** of schools based upon inspection.

regius professor University chairs which were endowed by the Crown. The first, at Oxford in 1497, was the professorship in divinity. There followed other chairs at Oxford and Cambridge in divinity, law, physics, Hebrew and Greek, and in other fields. These chairs are confined to Oxbridge and Scottish universities. Although the Crown may nominate candidates for these chairs, appointments are in fact, made on the advice of the Prime Minister or the Secretary of State for Scotland. (*see* **professor**)

regression (1) A term derived from psychoanalysis, but which has become common in educational and counselling circles. Regression occurs when an individual returns (regresses) to behaviour typical of an earlier stage of his/her emotional or intellectual development. Regression is said to tend to occur when an individual encounters a situation which is extremely painful. (2) Regression is a statistical technique for analysing relationships between two or more variables in order to predict or estimate values. (*see also* **regression to the mean**)

regression to the mean A phrase which is often found in discussions of intelligence and other desirable qualities. Where parents are tall (or intelligent) there is a tendency for children of those parents to be tall (or intelligent), but not as tall or intelligent as the parents – in other words, there is a tendency for offspring to be somewhere between the parents' score and the average score. This is, of course, a tendency and not a general rule. The same process applies with unintelligent parents: their children are likely to be below average, but closer to the average than their parents. (*see also* **regression**)

reification A term much used in sociology of education. It refers to the tendency of individuals, including social scientists, to treat ideas as if they existed as things. For example, the class structure is 'man-made' or socially constructed, but it is often referred to as if it had an independent existence. More controversially, some sociologists have suggested that **knowledge** is reified and that subject barriers are taken for granted when they ought to be questioned.

reliability A technical term which must be distinguished from **validity**. Reliability means the extent to which a test or an individual test item will give the same result on different occasions. For example, an individual test of **intelligence** should give the same result for a given individual on a number of separate occasions. If it does this, it could be said to be a 'reliable test' even if there were some doubts as to whether or not it was measuring real intelligence – that is a question of the validity of the test.

remedial education Such education tends to be of relatively short duration and limited to specific objectives, particularly remedying failures or difficulty in learning some school subjects, especially in basic education. Schools differ in their method of providing such education. In the **Warnock** conception of a range of alternative forms of special provision in ordinary schools, the remedial teacher would be part of a school's response to children with **special educational needs**.

report Most schools have kept parents informed of their children's progress by means of one or more reports during the year. These included the results of internal examinations and/or classwork throughout the year together. From summer 1992, schools were required to send a written report to all parents at least once a year, to include information on achievements in the **core subjects** of the **National Curriculum** and the results of **Standard Assessment Tasks** taken at 7, 11 and 14, results in other examinations or tests taken during the year; how the child's results in the Standard Assessment Tasks tests compare with those of other children of the same age; the child's general progress and his/her attendance record. Parents are also encouraged to explore with the school ways in which they can help to improve their children's performance. (*see also* **National Record of Achievement, school records**)

research and development (R and D) A style of research activity which focused on practical issues and where the intention is to produce results of a practical improvement kind as part of the research programme. It is closely related to the style of research described as **action research**. In **curriculum** studies, one stye of innovation is described as R, D and D (research development and dissemination). This is based on a concentric model of dissemination with an expert at the centre doing the research, pilot schools carrying out the development and, finally, the good news being disseminated to other schools. The model is now regarded as generally too simple to be of practical use in a curriculum development programme.

Research Fellow An individual, holding a post in an institution of **higher education** for a specific period of time, who is employed to investigate a particular topic or range of topics. Many of these posts are sponsored by bodies outside the institution.

research grant A sum of money made available to an individual or an institution in order to carry out research into a topic. The outcome is usually presented in the form of a report.

research project A systematic inquiry of some kind of limited duration designed to produce new knowledge or to test new materials or methods, or in some other way engage in scientific discovery or problem solving. The **Economic and Social Research Council** (ESRC) annually promotes funded research for a number of educational inquiries. The **National Foundation for Educational Research** (NFER) also engages in a series of such projects. (*see also* **curriculum development project**)

revenue support grant (RSG) (Previously rate support grant.) A grant from central government towards the cost of services for which a local authority is responsible – including education. The RSG is fixed as a result of negotiations between government and local authorities. In November/December the government issues to all local authorities **standard spending assessments** (SSAs) including a specific SSA for education. (*see also* **Local Government Acts**)

'rising fives' By law, parents are obliged to send their children to school at the beginning of the term after which their children reach the age of 5. **Local education authorities** may admit them to schools if there is sufficient accommodation before the statutory age. Such pupils are called 'rising fives'. (*see also* **nursery classes, nursery schools**)

Robbins Report A committee on higher education appointed by Harold Macmillan, the then prime minister, and chaired by Lord Robbins to review the existing patterns of higher education in Great Britain, and to advise whether there should be any changes in that pattern and whether any new types of institution were desirable. This enquiry stemmed from the growing numbers of sixth formers who were eligible for advanced education. The Report, published in 1963, assumed as an axiom ('the Robbins Principle') that courses 'should be available for all those who are qualified by ability and attainment to pursue them and wish to do so.'

Several important recommendations were made. University first degree courses should be broadened, increased in length to four years and more provision made for research and advanced courses. The status of **teacher training colleges** was to be effected by closer links with universities and the introduction of an appropriate degree. The Report recommended that they should be renamed **colleges of education**. The need to attract a higher proportion of first-class talent to technology was to be recognised by an expansion of postgraduate research and training. Colleges of advanced technology were to be granted charters as technological universities and the Report recommended the setting up of six new universities and the advancement to university status of ten other colleges.

The Report was immediately accepted by government, making £650 million available for capital expenditure, promoting colleges of advanced technology to university status, and creating some technological universities. The policy was a success; between 1965 and 1975, university numbers doubled and **polytechnics** increased by almost 50 per cent. Expansion continued into the 1980s and 1990s, culminating in the granting of university status to polytechnics in 1992. (*see also* **universities, history of**)

ROSLA (raising of the school leaving age) During the academic year 1972–3 the statutory minimum leaving age was raised from 15 to 16, as was envisaged in the 1944 Education Act and specifically recommended by the Newsom Report (1963). The 'extra year' caused many secondary schools to rethink what they were doing and to mount, in some cases, special courses for pupils who had previously left at age 15. To some observers it seemed that schools could be divided into two categories: those who regarded the extra year as a challenge and an opportunity to provide a full course of **secondary education** for all their pupils; and those schools who regarded the extra year as a problem and began talking of courses for 'ROSLA pupils'. (*see also* **school leaving age**)

rote learning Learning facts mechanically 'by heart', by a process of practice and repetition. A style of teaching which indulges in a good deal of rote learning without any attempt at understanding the material will now be criticised as old-fashioned.

Royal Commission Royal Commissions are appointed by the Queen in Council and are charged with the duty of reporting in terms of their order of reference. Eminent people are invited to be members for their knowledge of the topic to be investigated. The Commission's Report is published as a Parliamentary Paper. Their recommendations may form the basis for legislation. Evidence taken is usually printed as a non-Parliamentary Paper by Her Majesty's Stationery Office.

The great age of Royal Commissions in education was the second half of the nineteenth century. Before this time, **Select Committees** were the chosen instrument. With the **Bryce Commission** on secondary education in 1895, the series of Royal Commissions came to an end because of the comparatively lengthy time which they took to report. From the founding of the **Board of Education** in 1900, the work of the Commission was given first to consultative committees and later still to **Central Advisory Councils**. (*see also* **Parliamentary Papers**)

Royal Society of Arts (RSA)   Founded in 1754 'for the encouragement of Arts, Manufactures and Commerce' and incorporated by Royal Charter in 1847, the Society, an independent and self-financing body, carries out a number of functions. The RSA Examinations Board, a separate company with charitable status, offers examinations in a wide range of subjects in vocational areas. These include business and administration, teaching and training, languages, **information technology**, and retail and basic skills. The Society also mounted projects, such as those on profitable learning, education for capability and home-school contract of partnership. (*see also* **business education**)

Ruskin College   An **adult education** college established in Oxford in 1899, offering full-time courses up to two years in length. Many of the students are actively involved in trade unions. At a ceremony to mark the opening of a hall of residence, the then Prime Minister, James Callaghan, in October 1976, launched the **Great Debate** on education, calling in his speech for the improvement of **standards** in schools and the introduction of the concept of teacher **accountability**. (*see also* **Yellow Book**)

Rutter Report   A study, following a comparative survey of 10-year-olds in London and the Isle of Wight, of twelve inner London non-selective secondary schools which attempted to measure success by reference to pupils' behaviour both in and out of school, their academic achievements, and attendance rates. The team of researchers, led by Professor Michael Rutter, published their findings in 1979 in a book called *Fifteen Thousand Hours*. The Report concluded that schools could significantly affect children's achievements, compared with home and other influences. Schools with good attendance tend to have well-behaved pupils who perform well in examinations. The ethos of the school was found to be an important factor. Where teachers set good standards, provide good models of behaviour, praise and give responsibility to pupils, and where lessons are well prepared and organised, all these were indicators of a good school. Criticisms of the Report's findings have been made on a number of grounds. It is claimed that the schools selected were untypical, that some of the statistics were wrongly analysed and that it over-estimated the extent to which schools can overcome social influences. Nevertheless, the study raises a number of important issues especially on the relationship between life in schools and factors affecting achievement. (*see also* **effective schools**)

S

sabbatical   A period of paid leave for private study or research, varying in length from one term to one year. In the original sense of the term, a sabbatical year should occur once every seven years, but institutions differ widely in their practices. Sabbatical leave is commonly available in **higher education** institutions but much less so in schools. (*see also* **study leave, unpaid leave**)

sandwich course   A course consisting of a mixture of full-time studies and full-time work. Many **university degree** courses combine these two elements in such areas as engineering and **business studies**. The sandwich element can be either 'thick', with full-time employment of a year, or 'thin', consisting of two or three periods of time each lasting up to half a year.

scaling   The process of converting scores from one scale to another. Different procedures are used in different circumstances, for example: (1) The conversion of scores for a particular examination component from one scale (e.g. 0 to 60) to another (e.g. 0 to 100) to accord with the **weighting** of the component. (2) The adjustment of a set of scores to give the set a different mean and **standard deviation** (thus altering its weighting). (3) The adjustment of an individual examiner's scores to bring them into line with an agreed **standard**.

schema (*plural* **schemata**)   A technical term used by Piaget and other developmental psychologists to refer to a conceptual structure which is used to interpret information in the external world perceived by the senses. A schema is, therefore, a kind of hypothesis set up in the brain to make sense of reality. When a child (or adult) encounters a new situation which does not fit in with an existing schema, the individual will either be puzzled or adapt the schema or schemata to try to make better sense of reality.

scholarship   (1) **Knowledge** and **skills** of a high standard in an **academic** field. (2) An **entrance award**, carrying with it a sum of money, for students embarking upon **higher education**, who are regarded as worthy of exceptional support.

scholastic/scholasticism   Scholasticism was the medieval theological system which attempted to integrate Christian doctrine with Platonic and Aristotelian philosophy. 'Scholastic' can now mean: (1) pertaining to schools, universities or colleges; (2) pedantic or quibbling over detail.

scholastic agency (or agent) An employment agency for private schools which also provides advice for parents wishing to choose such a school.

Scholastic Aptitude Test (SAT) In the USA, batteries of **multiple choice** tests lasting about three hours are set at the end of high school courses to assist in the process of **selection** for colleges and universities.

school (1) Most commonly refers to an institution where children of school age are taught. (2) At Oxford, may describe a course of study leading to an examination for a first degree, for example philosophy, politics and economics, or more widely to describe all persons working in a subject, for example chemistry school. It also appears as part of a title of a college in other universities, for example the London School of Economics and Social Science. In the University of London, a school is a semi-autonomous college, as distinct from a Senate institute.

School Certificate Introduced by the Secondary School Examinations Council in 1917, the School Certificate was an examination taken by pupils at the end of a four-year **secondary school** course of study, usually at 16 years of age. No certificate was awarded unless passes in five subjects were obtained. Credits in five subjects bestowed **matriculation** exemption on successful candidates. It was replaced by the **GCE 'O' level** examination in 1951. (*see also* **General Certificate of Education, Higher School Certificate**)

school closure See **Section 12 notice**.

school council A council of students who are either elected or nominated within a school. It expresses views on school matters, though its terms of reference are normally laid down by the headteacher and staff. Such councils do not exist in all schools.

School Curriculum and Assessment Authority (SCAA) The 1992 White Paper *Choice and Diversity* recommended that the **National Curriculum Council** (NCC) and the **School Examinations and Assessment Council** (SEAC) should be replaced by a School Curriculum and Assessment Authority (SCAA).

school day The length of time a school is open for pupils and for which pupils of compulsory school age are obliged to attend. The **Education Reform Act** (1988) (Section 115) gave power to governing bodies to determine the length of the school day and to decide how the sessions should be organised (i.e. the length of lessons). Pressures arising out of the **National Curriculum** may encourage a longer school day. The number of hours covered by the teachers' contract (in **maintained schools**) is 1265 per annum.

school development plans (SDP) A concept intended to encourage schools to plan for future developments rather than to react to changes imposed upon them. SDPs should give schools more autonomy and control, but **accountability** demands that eventually they will be expected to demonstrate progress in accordance with their SDP.

School Examinations and Assessment Council (SEAC) One of two statutory bodies established under the **Education Reform Act** (1988) to give advice to the Secretary of State on the National Curriculum (the other being the **National Curriculum Council**). SEAC had to be consulted by the Secretary of State on National Curriculum assessment, but the Secretary did not have to accept its advice. SEAC has been responsible for commissioning the development of assessment instruments for Key Stage 1 and Key Stage 3 assessment, and has been criticised for the kind of assessment tests which have been produced. The first Chairman of SEAC was Philip Halsey who served from 1988 until 1991 when he resigned unexpectedly and was replaced by the more right-wing figure of Lord Griffiths, who had been a prominent member of Margaret Thatcher's Policy Unit.

In 1993 SEAC was abolished and together with the NCC, was replaced with the **School Curriculum and Assessment Authority** (SCAA).

school leaving age Under the 1870 Education Act, the newly formed school boards were required to draw up by-laws for the purpose of securing attendance of pupils between the ages of 5 and 13. The 1880 Act required unconditional attendance between 5 and 10 years and with exemption on the grounds of proven proficiency for those between 10 and 13. In 1893, the minimum leaving age was raised to 11 and in 1899 to 12 years of age. The 1918 Education Act raised the leaving age to 14; it was further raised to 15 in 1947 and to 16 in the academic year 1972–3. (*see also* **ROSLA**)

School Library Association (SLA) The Association promotes the development of school libraries and the use of books and other resources. It was founded in 1937 and its members include representatives of all levels of education, as well as publishers and public libraries. A joint board comprising representatives of the School Library Association and the **Library Association** validates courses for the Certificate in School Library Studies.

school meals service The poor physical condition of potential recruits for the Boer War led to the setting up of an inter-departmental committee on physical deterioration in 1904. Amongst its recommendations were the feeding of necessitous children and the establishment of school medical inspections. Accordingly, another inter-departmental committee the following year, headed by the President of the Board of Education, Lord Londonderry, examined these two aspects with special reference to the elementary school. In its report, the committee asked for better coordination of existing organisations providing food. However, in 1906 an Education (Provision of Meals) Act went further in stating that the **local education authorities**, not voluntary societies, should be responsible for provision. Local authorities were empowered to levy a rate of half a penny in the pound for this purpose. Both World Wars increased the demand for such a service. The 1944 Education Act made it obligatory for local education authorities to provide a school meals service. The 1980 Education Act removed this obligation, though the need for provision for pupils whose parents were in receipt of supplementary benefit or family income supplement was acknowledged.

School of Education See **university department of education**.

school phobia Some children develop such anxieties about attending school that they feel that they cannot leave home or be separated from a parent. It is difficult to distinguish between dislike of a school and a neurotic condition, so much so, that estimates of school phobia numbers varies from about 7000 in England and Wales (0.1 per cent of the school population) to twice that number. Some schools and **local education authorities** do not accept the existence of school phobia. An organisation has been set up to help genuine cases of school phobia: the Children's Home-based Education Association (CHEA). It produced a booklet *School phobia – how to attack it* (1989), which provides helpful advice, including the option of educating children at home. (*see also* **Education Otherwise**)

school psychological service Educational psychologists are usually employed by **local education authorities** to provide psychological support services to ordinary schools, **special schools** and **units**, to other agencies like health and social service assessment centres, and to parents. Psychologists have recognised initial and **postgraduate** qualifications in psychology and many are experienced teachers. Psychologists specialise in areas of treatment such as family therapy or behaviour modification, and may act in consultative and advisory roles. They are mainly occupied with children with learning problems and maladjustment in ordinary schools and work closely with remedial services and child guidance clinics. (*see also* **local management of schools**)

school records Confidential records should be kept of all pupils in maintained schools. They contain details of **academic** achievement and other relevant details which are passed on when pupils change school. In recent years there has been a tendency to make the content of school records more available to parents. (*see also* **Parent's Charter**, **record of achievement**, **National Record of Achievement**)

school refusal The condition of a child – a school refuser – whose dislike of school is so intense that he or she refuses to attend. It is often indistinguishable from **school phobia** although the neurotic anxiety of that condition may not be present.

school report An assessment of pupils' progress in written form, usually subject by subject, for the information of parents. Reports may be issued on a termly, half-yearly or yearly basis. The traditional report has been attacked mainly on the grounds that it does not give a rounded picture of a pupil. **Profiles** have been suggested as an alternative. (*see also* **parents and education, school records, National Record of Achievement**)

Schools Council In 1962, David Eccles, the then Minister of Education, established a small curriculum study group to give advice on the school **curriculum**. After some hostility from local education authorities and teachers' unions, a Working Party on Schools Curricula and Examinations chaired by Sir John Lockwood produced a Report in 1964 which reaffirmed the importance of the principle that schools should retain the responsibility for their own work, but that a Schools Council for Curriculum and Examinations was necessary for **research and development**. The Council took over the functions of the Curriculum Study Group and the Secondary School Examinations Council.

The Council funded many curriculum projects and published working papers and research reports. In March 1981 the Secretary of State for Education and Science announced that Mrs Trenaman had been invited to review the Schools Council and to make recommendations. Her Report (1981) concluded that the Council should continue with its present functions. It outlined a number of changes which should be made and recommended that the Council should not be the subject of any further review for the next five years. In April 1982 the Secretary of State announced his intention to disband the Council and replace it by two separate bodies – a **Secondary Examinations Council** and a **School Curriculum Development Committee** – appointments to both of which would be made by the Secretary of State. These arrangements were changed as a result of the Education Reform Act (1988) which created a **School Examinations and Assessment Council** (SEAC) and a **National Curriculum Council** (NCC) which were in turn replaced by the **School Curriculum and Assessment Authority** (SCAA) in 1993.

Science Research Council (SRC) A council set up by the Department of Education and Science to allocate funds for approved scientific research. Members of the Council were appointed by the Secretary of State for Education and Science and met regularly to scrutinise research proposals and to allocate funds to what they considered to be the most deserving projects. In 1992 when the Department of Education and Science was replaced by the Department for Education, the Science Research Council ceased to be the responsibility of the Secretary of State for Education.

Scottish Education Department (SED) The SED was established at the time of the 1872 Education (Scotland) Act, which transferred the administration of schools from church to lay authorities, through locally elected school boards. The SED was set up as a central controlling and coordinating body for education. A Secretary (since 1926, Secretary of State) for Scotland was appointed in 1885 and since then has been responsible for the development of the system. The Department's functions are the same as the **Department for Education** (DFE). (*see also* **Dunning Report, Munn Report**)

screening A process of identifying children with **learning difficulties**, especially in reading and mathematics. There are many tests available for assessing or diagnosing special educational needs associated with various disabilities such as impaired vision or hearing.

Secondary Heads Association (SHA) Set up in 1976, from the former **Headmasters' Association** and the **Association of Headmistresses**, the Association's 8000 members include heads and **deputy heads** from both the maintained and the **independent** sectors. All the major **public schools** are represented. The Association makes pronouncements of common concern to both sectors, such as examination and **curriculum** and is non-political in character. (*see also* **teachers' unions**)

secondary modern school The Hadow Report on *The Education of the Adolescent* (1926) recommended the division of secondary education into two types: the **grammar** school, for the most intellectually able pupils, and the secondary modern school, which would cater for most adolescents between the ages of 11 and 15. The **curriculum** to be offered in the latter was to concentrate initially on offering a good broad education, but in the later years of schooling a more practical bias was to be introduced into the curriculum. The White Paper on Educational Reconstruction in 1943, which set the pattern for **tripartitism**, recommended three types of school – grammar, technical, and modern – corresponding to supposed psychological categories of pupils. A Ministry pamphlet, *The New Secondary Education* (1947), claimed that it was 'impracticable to combine a system of external examinations . . . with the fundamental conception of modern school education', and teachers were encouraged 'to plan the curriculum of the school on purely educational lines.' Despite this, modern schools developed sixth forms and entered pupils in growing numbers for the **General Certificate of Education** (GCE) examinations: the **Certificate of Secondary Education** (CSE) examinations were introduced in 1965 for the bulk of the modern school's population. Dissatisfaction with the status of the schools was increasingly voiced by teachers, parents and politicians. National variations in the provision of grammar school places, the questioning of the validity of **intelligence** tests as a basis of selection and the lack of progress towards the 1944 Education Act's promise of equality of opportunity led to the reorganisation of secondary schooling on **comprehensive** lines.

secondary school Normally, schools providing education for children from the age of 11 years: either 11 to 16 or 11 to 18.

secondment The allocation of a teacher, on a temporary basis, to a course or another post away from his or her normal place of employment.

Secretary of State for Education (and Science) The **Robbins Report** recommended that there should be changes in the machinery of ministerial responsibility – that the Minister of Education should be replaced by a Minister for Arts and Science. Whilst agreeing to the need for changes, the government's solution was for a single **Department of Education and Science**, the enlarged ministry to have a secretary of state as its head. The Secretary of State had overall responsibility for the work of the Department and the formulation of general policy. He was also a member of the Cabinet. In 1992, Science was reallocated to the Duchy of Lancaster and the Department of Education and Science was replaced by the **Department for Education** (DFE).

Section 11 teacher Section 11 of the Local Government Act (1966) empowers the Home Office to provide money to assist local education authorities in the promotion of English among immigrant communities. For many years the government paid for 75 per cent of the cost of approved schemes (most of which involved additional 'Section 11' teachers in classrooms in schools with high proportions of non-English speaking pupils). The grant was reduced to 57 per cent in 1993 and 50 per cent for 1994. Some Section 11 teachers are **bilingual**; others are specialists in teaching **English as a second language**.

Section 12 notice When a local education authority intends to close a county school or change its character to a significant extent, it issues a public notice for two months to allow objections in accordance with Section 12 of the 1980 Education Act. Circular 2/80 states that local education authorities should give parents at least one term to make alternative arrangements and should allow at least a full twelve months between the publication of closure proposals and the date on which they come into effect. The **Secretary of State for Education** has, under the Act, to approve Section 12 notices. It should be noted that the establishment and alteration of **voluntary schools** are covered by Section 13 of the same Act.

security of tenure The contractual right of an **academic** (particularly in **universities**) to retain full-time employment until a specified retirement date. Security of tenure was normally granted only after satisfactory completion of a probationary period. In the early 1980s, the privileged position of academics with security of tenure was questioned by the Conservative Secretary of State for Education, Sir Keith Joseph, and others. Tenure for *new* appointments (or new contracts, for example, promotion) was effectively removed by Sections 202–8 of the **Education Reform Act** (1988).

Select Committee A Committee made up of named members of either House of Parliament with the purpose of taking evidence on a subject and reporting its findings back to the House which appointed the Committee. It has power to summon witnesses to attend, to give evidence and to produce documents. (*see also* **Parliamentary Papers**)

selection See **'eleven plus' examination**.

selective school A school for which pupils have to demonstrate a level of attainment or ability to gain entry, usually by means of some kind of test or examination.

self-concept, self-image An individual's self-concept is the way an individual sees himself or herself. Some research has been based on the hypothesis that children with a negative self-image tend to be **underachievers** at school. It has also been suggested that children from certain ethnic minorities have a negative self-image, and that this accounts for their under-achievement in school. The evidence for this is not conclusive. (*see also* **multicultural education, underachiever**)

self-fulfilling prophecy A term originally used in sociology by Robert Merton. It has become a feature of some discussions of schools and of organisational practices, such as streaming. In education, it is often associated with the term 'labelling'. If a pupil is believed by his/her teacher to be bright he or she is likely to improve; if pupils are thought to be dull, they will become dull. This is sometimes also known as the **Pygmalion effect**.

self-instruction A method of learning in which students use programmed learning or other materials. No direct help is given by a teacher although the course would normally be laid out with very specific goals. A **correspondence course** is not, strictly speaking, a self-instructional course, because students normally submit work which has to be marked and commented on by a tutor. Some correspondence courses might, however, include self-instructional materials or units. Some textbooks have been written on a self-instructional basis, that is, the content is so devised as to provide answers for the student and alternative routes should the student make mistakes.

semester Whereas most English schools and **universities** have academic years which are divided into three periods of work (**terms**) plus **vacations**, North American universities tend to divide the academic year into two working periods called semesters usually lasting at least fifteen weeks, with longer breaks in between. Thus, many courses in American universities are organised on a semester basis rather than as a whole year. Some English universities have adopted the American pattern.

seminar A meeting of students in a group with a **tutor** sometimes for the purpose of following up a **lecture**. Members of the group may present papers at the seminar to stimulate discussion or raise further issues. (*see also* **tutorial**)

semiotics (or semiology) The study of signs and symbols – especially in the context of human communication. It is often associated with structuralism in studies of literature. At school level it has been influential in new areas of the **curriculum** such as communication studies and media studies, especially for the analysis of film and television.

Service children's schools Schools provided for children of members of the Armed Forces in service garrisons and bases. Teachers are mainly drawn from Britain to staff the schools. The Service Children's Education Authority (SCEA), within the Ministry of Defence, is responsible for providing the schools overseas.

setting In the early days of **comprehensive** schools most headteachers organised the schools on the basis of **streaming**, that is, they allocated pupils to classes in terms of their supposed general **ability**. Pupils remained in those streamed classes for all or most subjects. Many considered streaming to be too crude and rigid a selection process, and adopted as a compromise the process of 'setting'. This might leave pupils in **mixed-ability** groups for most of their subjects, but allocate them to ability groupings for certain subjects where more homogeneous classes were thought to be necessary. Setting is most common in such subjects as modern languages and mathematics. (*see also* **family grouping, labelling**)

seventeen plus examinations During the 1960s and 1970s there was much discussion about the 'new sixth former', that is, a student who stayed on in a **comprehensive** school after completing the five-year course, but without sufficient academic success to undertake **GCE 'A' level** courses. Many such students simply retook **'O' level** examinations which they had earlier failed or even repeated **CSE** examinations in order to obtain improved grades. This practice was generally thought to be undesirable educationally and various proposals for alternative examinations were put forward. One of these was the Certificate of Extended Education (CEE) which was discussed in the Keohane Report. Other suggestions involved vocational preparation and courses designed by bodies such as the City and Guilds. In 1986 the **National Council for Vocational Qualifications** (NCVQ) was created and given responsibility for coordinating all courses into a series of 'levels'.

sixteen plus examinations The **Schools Council** recommended a merger of the **General Certificate of Education** (GCE) **'O' level** and the **Certificate of Secondary Education** (CSE) examinations. Eight years later, the **Waddell Report** concluded that such a system was feasible. In February 1980 a modified scheme was announced by the Conservative Government, with groupings of GCE and CSE boards, and strong **national criteria**. Four groups of examination boards were established in England. Examination boards were asked to draw up criteria for every subject, and a joint council for the **General Certificate of Secondary Education** (GCSE), establishing 16 plus national criteria, was formed by the GCE and CSE boards. The first awards for the new GCSE were made in 1988.

sixth-form college Unlike the **tertiary college** which caters for all students of 16 years and over in an area, the sixth-form college accommodates the traditional sixth-form intake and those requiring somewhat less academic courses. Many of the students aim to go on to **higher** and **further education**, and the college offers a range of examinations. In 1991 sixth-form colleges were removed from local education authority control. (*see* Section, 1 Essay 9)

skill A physical, social or mental **ability** acquired mainly as a result of practice and repetition. Skill is frequently contrasted with **knowledge**, but this is an over-simplification. It may be convenient to divide educational objectives into knowledge, skills and attitudes, but it should always be recognised that these are overlapping categories. (*see also* **social skills**)

Skinnerian An adjective describing the work of B. F. Skinner, an American psychologist. One meaning of Skinnerian applies to the **behaviourist** theory of **learning** and its particular application in schools; a more limited use of Skinnerian applies particularly to Skinner's work on **programmed learning**, and in this sense a Skinnerian programme is a linear programme (to be contrasted with a branching programme). (*see also* **behaviourism**)

'S' level An examination which may be taken by above average **GCE 'A' level** candidates who wish to go on to **higher education**. The standard is high and the result is taken into consideration only if the candidate has done sufficiently well in the 'A' level papers. (*see also* **General Certificate of Education** (GCE))

Social Science Research Council (SSRC) The Council was set up in 1965 by Royal Charter to encourage research, to provide advice and to disseminate knowledge concerning the social sciences. It also allocated funds for **postgraduate** students, and financed high-quality research proposals from the universities. In September 1981, the Council announced that changes needed to be made to encourage a more multidisciplinary approach to problems which were seen to be important in policy formulation. The SSRC suffered a cut of about 20 per cent in real resources between 1978 and 1982. In October 1982 following the recommendation of the Rothschild Report on the SSRC, the Secretary of State decided to continue the Council, but Sir Keith Joseph insisted on a change of title to **Economic and Social Research Council** (ESRC).

social skills The ability to communicate effectively with people in social and work situations. Many schools and colleges offer courses in this area, for example, preparation for interviews. In a wider context, it may be seen as one aspect of **personal and social education** (PSE), an umbrella term covering a number of curriculum areas concerned with values and personal developmental processes. (*see also* **skill**)

Society of Education Officers (SEO) A professional association for educational administrators of local authorities in England, Wales and Northern Ireland, formed in 1971. The Scottish counterpart is the Association of Directors of Education in Scotland. Its main objectives are to confer on matters relating to education for the benefit of members and through them of their authorities, and to make representations to government departments and other bodies. (*see also* **chief education officer**)

Society of Teachers Opposed to Physical Punishment (STOPP) A **pressure group**, set up to abolish the use of physical punishment in schools. The Society is controlled by teachers but has parental membership. **Corporal punishment** was banned in maintained schools in 1986.

spatial ability The kind of reasoning which manifests itself as the **ability** to see relationships between objects in space or occupying space. Individuals possessing high spatial ability will find it easier to read maps, find their way in unfamiliar territory, or do jigsaw puzzles and other manipulative tasks. Spatial ability is measured in some tests of general **intelligence**; there are also specific tests of spatial ability sometimes used for **vocational guidance**. (*see also* **intelligence tests, verbal reasoning**)

special agreement school A type of voluntary school, usually secondary, where the local education authority pays, by special agreement with a denominational interest, one-half to three-quarters of the cost of building a school or enlarging an existing one. Two-thirds of the governors are appointed by the voluntary body, the remainder by the local authority. The local education authorities control the teaching staff and the governors are responsible for religious instruction in the school. (*see also* **religious education, voluntary-aided school, voluntary-controlled school**)

special educational needs The concept of special educational needs has developed since the 1944 Education Act's definition of 'disability of mind or body'. It has come to be recognised that special educational needs should be based on educational and developmental considerations rather than on purely medical ones. In 1978, the **Warnock Report** concluded that 'special educational needs' was a relative concept, a sentiment echoed in the 1981 Education Act: 'a child has "special educational needs" if he has a learning difficulty which calls for special educational provision to be made for him.' The Act recommended that assessment should include educational, psychological and medical components. Duties were placed on local education authorities and schools to identify a secure provision for a wide range of special educational needs. Parents were also to be consulted when decisions about their children's special needs were being taken and on the choice of provision to meet these needs. (*see also* **exceptional children, giftedness, integration, parents and education**)

special school Special schools are provided by local education authorities and **voluntary organisations** for groups of children who have **special educational needs**. Until the 1981 Education Act, children were classified into categories and special schools made a response to one type of categorised child. The size of teaching group, pupil-teacher ratios and curriculum styles are some of the special requirements prescribed for special schools as outlined in regulations and circulars from the Department for Education (*see also* **assessment, Down's syndrome, educationally subnormal, school psychological service)**

spiral curriculum See **curriculum, spiral**.

split site A school or college which is situated on more than one site.

staff meeting A meeting of the staff or department of an educational institution to discuss matters concerned with the activities of the department or institution, such as **curriculum planning** and **timetabling**. The frequency of such meetings and the length of the agenda varies from place to place. (*see also* **head of department**)

staff:student ratio (SSR) The ratio between the number of teachers and the number of students in a **university**, college or school. (*see also* **pupil:teacher ratio**)

standard(s) There are two very different educational meanings of the term standard. (1) After the Revised Code of 1862, the work of **elementary schools** was divided into six Standards. Pupils began Standard 1 roughly at the age of 6, and given normal attainment, passed through the other five Standards year by year. Before progressing from Standard 1 to Standard 2, pupils would be tested (on a narrow and rigid curriculum) to ensure that the required knowledge had been satisfactorily mastered. Later in 1882, Standard 7 was introduced. (2) All educational institutions have 'standards' in the sense of a level of quality of work below which they do not wish to fall, and would probably wish to raise. In secondary schools, standards are maintained partly by means of external or **public examinations**. Individual institutions can be compared according to national examination standards. In **universities**, standards are maintained by a combination of examinations (local not national) which are **moderated** in terms of standards by the system of **external examiners**. Doubts about standards in schools was one of the reasons given for the introduction of the **National Curriculum** (with national assessment) in 1988. (*see* Section 1, Essay 4)

Standard Assessment Task (SAT) Standard Assessment Tasks are part of the National Curriculum assessment procedures. Originally conceived as normal classroom assignments with built in assessment, they have become largely pencil and paper tests. Since 1990 Standard Assessment Tasks have been renamed Standard Tests or Standard Tasks (STs). But they are still widely referred to as SATs.

standard deviation (SD) A term used in statistics to indicate a measure of variability among the values of a frequency distribution. For example, when indicating the range or scatter of scores from the mean or average, it is sometimes convenient to express the extent of scatter in terms of standard deviations. When discussing a range of scores it is rarely sufficient to know only the average or mean score; it is also important to know the standard deviation or 'scatter' of marks. (*see also* **standardised, Z scores**)

standard scale teacher A teacher who is not paid any **incentive allowance**. (*see also* **teachers' salaries**)

standard spending assessment (SSA) Throughout the 1980s and 1990s the Government was anxious to restrain local authority spending – including spending on education. The two mechanisms employed were by 'capping' – that is enforcing a limit on local rates (later council tax); the second was by specifying how money should be allocated – by means of the SSA. The SSA for education is determined by complex formulae and broken down into five spending categories (primary, secondary, post-16, under-5 and 'other'). (*see also* **Local Government Acts**)

standardised (1) Standardised marks or scores in a test would mean that they had been adjusted in such a way as to make them comparable with scores from a different test, perhaps by reference to a given mean and **standard deviation**, or by use of **Z scores**. (2) A standardised test is one that has been systematically piloted and then modified in order to ensure that it is both **valid** and **reliable**. Standardised tests would have norms which have been carefully established. It would also be standardised in the sense of having unambiguous written procedures.

Standing Advisory Council on Religious Education (SACRE) Local education authorities are required under the **Education Reform Act** (1988) to set up a SACRE to advise on religious education and worship.

statement The 1981 Education Act provided a legal appeal system for children with **special educational needs**. All local education authorities have a general duty to identify those children whose special needs call for the authority to determine the special educational provision that should be made for them. The process of identifying and assessing special needs is left to local education authorities who decide on the appropriate provision. This decision to accept or reject responsibility is known as making a statement. There are procedures for parents to appeal against the local authority's decision. (*see also* **remedial education, school psychological service, special school**)

Statement of Attainment (SoA) National Curriculum **Attainment Targets** are sub-divided at each **level** into SoAs. (*see* Section 1, Essay 7)

state school Refers to publicly **maintained schools**, as distinct from **independent** or private schools.

statutory instrument A form of delegated legislation, under an Order or regulation by the Queen in Council or one of her ministers, which has the force of an Act of Parliament. Statutory instruments must be laid before Parliament before coming into operation. (*see also* **Parliamentary Papers**)

streaming The assigning of pupils to classes on the basis of general **ability**. The number of streams depends on the size of the year group. Streamed classes usually stay together for the majority of subjects. It has been shown that streaming affects teachers' judgments of children's abilties and brings about a '**self-fulfilling prophecy**'. **National Foundation of Educational Research** surveys found that 50 per cent of large primary schools used streaming in 1963 but only 2 per cent employed this form of organisation in 1980. There is some evidence that a form of streaming for the basic subjects is becoming more prevalent in primary schools. (*see also* **family grouping, labelling, mixed-ability grouping, setting, unstreaming**)

student (1) Formerly a term reserved for those pursuing a course of study in an institution of **further** or **higher education**, for example, at a **university** or college. It is now often used interchangeably in schools with the term '**pupil**'.

(2) The non-ecclesiastical equivalent of **Fellow** at Christ Church, Oxford; also for those holding endowed studentships at either Oxford or Cambridge.

student-teacher A person undertaking a course of training to become a **teacher**. The term is also used to indicate the status of such a person whilst undertaking teaching practice in an institution. (*see also* **teacher tutor**)

Students' Union A society formed by students of a college or other institution to promote social activities and provide recreational facilities. In many colleges, representatives of the Union serve on official committees which are concerned with **academic** affairs. At Oxford and Cambridge, the Union is a club with well-known debating societies. (*see also* **National Union of Students**)

study leave A period of leave, usually with pay, made available to teachers in schools or in **further** or **higher education** to attend professional or **academic** courses. One of the ideas behind **recurrent education** has been the extension of this privilege to the whole population – hence 'paid study leave' as an area of negotiation for trades unions, especially within the **European Community**. (*see also* **sabbatical**)

study skills Ways in which students can become more effective in their studies by becoming aware of the learning processes involved. Courses in study skills often aim to encourage independent learning by presenting information, in a workshop situation and/or by lectures, on some of the following: note-taking, drafting, problem solving, contributing to group discussion, systematic revision for examinations, and ways of finding out information. Study skills are now being taught in schools and places of further and higher education and are particularly important for those involved in distance learning. (*see also* **correspondence course, Open University, PICKUP**)

sub-culture Every society has a culture. By definition all members of a society will share in some of the aspects of its culture. But within the whole society there may be groups who are identifiable by possessing distinctly different values, beliefs and behaviour patterns. In such cases it would be appropriate to talk of a sub-culture. In the UK it is possible to identify, for example, working-class sub-cultures and the sub-cultures of certain ethnic **minorities**. (*see also* **multicultural education**)

summative assessment The kind of assessment given at the end of a course, as a final judgement. (*see also* **formative assessment**)

summative evaluation See **formative evaluation/summative evaluation**.

Sunday school The Sunday school movement is usually associated with Robert Raikes of Gloucester who, from 1780, established classes for children of the poor who were in employment during the rest of the week. The movement, which saw its task as the inculcation of religion and the elimination of radical ideologies, quickly spread and was eagerly taken up by religious organisations. A century after the movement began over five-and-three-quarter million children in England were attending these schools.

supply teacher Teachers employed by a local education authority or school to cover the work of an absent member of staff.

Swann Report A committee was set up under the chairmanship of Sir Michael Swann in December 1965 to investigate the shortage of science and engineering graduates. The Report, published in 1968, showed that the best science and engineering graduates tended to remain at university rather than embark upon a career in industry. The Report was also concerned with the lack of good science graduates entering school teaching. It recommended some new kinds of **postgraduate** training, emphasising links between the academic world and the world of industry. Suggestions were also made about encouraging scientists to make contributions to the work of schools.

syllabus An outline, more or less detailed, of the ground to be covered in a **course**. The distinction between syllabus and **curriculum** is not always clear, but the following distinctions might be helpful. The lowest unit in terms of curriculum planning would be an individual **lesson**; this would be part of a **scheme of work** covering several lessons (perhaps half a term or a term's work); this would be related to a syllabus (perhaps a whole year's work) and a syllabus would be related to the whole curriculum. In the National Curriculum (1988) there are two closely related but distinct specifications: **Attainment Targets** (sub-divided into ten **levels** of achievement), and **Programmes of Study** for each subject setting out the **content** to be covered. The Programmes of Study are closer to the traditional concept of syllabus.

t

tariff questions Where an examination paper consists of different questions pitched at different levels of difficulty, each with different mark values. Candidates can select from those questions which they consider will gain them the most marks.

Task Group on Assessment and Testing (TGAT) The Task Group on Assessment and Testing – a non-statutory group appointed by the then Secretary of State for Education, Kenneth Baker, in 1987 – was set up to advise on **National Curriculum assessment**. It was chaired by Professor Paul Black and produced the TGAT model. (*see* Section 1, Essay 1)

taxonomy Classification, especially in relation to general laws or principles of classification. In education, the word is most usually associated with the work of B. S. Bloom and his *Taxonomy of Educational Objectives* (1956).

teacher Many changes in the training, appointment and conditions of service of teachers have occurred in recent years. There are a number of different entry routes into the profession – **Postgraduate Certificate of Education** (PGCE), **Bachelor of Education degree** (BEd), **Open University** scheme, **licensed** and **articled teacher** – and the training is largely school-based. Since the **Education Reform Act** (1988), which introduced the local management of schools, teachers are appointed, promoted and dismissed by schools rather than the **local education authority**. Teachers' pay and conditions of service are now subject to variations by governing bodies and local education authorities. The introduction of the **National Curriculum** in 1988 and the compulsory testing of pupils have also affected the way in which teachers operate at both primary and secondary levels. In January 1992, there were 394 900 full-time equivalent teachers employed in the maintained nursery, primary and secondary schools sectors: approximately one-half of this number were employed in the nursery and primary and the other in the secondary sector. (*see also* **teacher training, teacher tutor, teachers' aides, teachers' centres, teachers' salaries, teachers' unions**)

teacher appraisal Sound teacher appraisal consists not only of the teacher's performance, but in the context of the department of the school or institution itself. A Department of Education and Science Circular suggested that a full appraisal should have six stages: an initial meeting between the appraiser and the appraisee; classroom observation; collection of other sources of information; self-appraisal; an appraisal interview; and preparation of the appraisal record. The **headteacher** should decide who does the appraising, with the head having two appraisers appointed by the **chief education officer**. The Circular stated that appraisals should be carried out every two years.

Much depends on the purpose of the appraisal: whether it is perceived as a threat to the teacher's professional integrity or as a cooperative venture to improve competency. To what extent appraisal reports should be taken into account in making pay recommendations is not always made clear, though a number of heads are on formal performance-related pay agreements. (*see also* **teachers' salaries**)

teacher support staff This may take the form, depending on the type of school, of administrative help, such as secretaries or classroom help, nursery nurses or helpers. Included under this heading are schoolkeepers, cleaners and kitchen staff. (*see also* **teachers' aides**)

teacher training There are five main routes into school teaching:
(1) *Postgraduate Certificate of Education (PGCE)* This is a one-year course for **graduates** or those with an equivalent qualification, the majority of whom train for secondary schools.
(2) *Bachelor of Education degree (BEd) or Bachelor of Arts (BA) with professional train-*

ing   This is a three- or four-year course leading to a professional degree. There is also a two-year in-service BEd degree for practising teachers without a degree. (3) *Licensed teacher scheme*   This was started in 1989 for candidates over 26 years of age, with at least two years in higher education. They are recruited by local authorities and spend most of their two years in schools. Qualified teacher status may be awarded at the end of it.
(4) *Articled teacher scheme*   This was launched in 1990, and is open only to graduates. Local authorities and colleges form consortia to run the scheme, which is largely (about 80 per cent) based in schools. From 1993, the articled teacher scheme was limited to the primary sector.
(5) *Open University scheme*   This was started in 1984, and is aimed at those graduates already in full-time non-teaching employment. The course is eighteen months in length with much of the studying done by **distance learning**. Students undertake two periods of supervised teaching practice.

Much criticism of the nature of teacher training has been voiced by politicians in recent years. Greater emphasis on school-based experience has been called for, with good classroom teachers taking on the mentor role. From September 1994 all secondary PGCE students spend at least twenty-four weeks out of thirty-six in schools. The schools taking part in the scheme have first to acquire approval by the **Council for the Accreditation of Teacher Education** (CATE).

teacher tutor   Institutions concerned with initial **teacher training** sometimes involve practising teachers in the work of student teachers, especially for professional aspects of the course and school **teaching practice**. These part-time tutors, often referred to as teacher tutors, are normally senior and experienced members of staff who may receive a small payment or honorarium for their services. (*see also* **mentor**)

teachers' aides   A term used in the **Plowden Report** on primary schools (1967) to describe a person without formal teaching qualifications who is employed in infant or primary classes. Aides assist teachers in classroom work and supervision. (*see also* **dilution**)

teachers' centres   Centres run by **local education authorities** to promote professional development in the education service from the primary to the tertiary sectors. They are general purpose institutions but provide a focus for **In-service Education of Teachers** (INSET) programmes and house resources for consultation by teachers. Many teachers' centres provide the base for the activities of advisory and support staff, though in some authorities such staff may be located in the local education authority offices. Only a few authorities still offer specialist teachers' centres, for example, for service teaching. The head of a teachers' centre may have a title such as centre manager, warden, or centre leader. There is an association for professional development in education, which issues a newsletter for leaders and also arranges conferences. The provision of teachers' centres is not mandatory and the number of centres is diminishing.

teachers' salaries Arrangements and regulations governing teachers' pay are set out in the Schoolteachers' Pay and Conditions Document which is revised annually by the **Secretary of State for Education**.

With the introduction of **local management of schools** (LMS), governors now have considerable flexibility in determining the salaries of teachers. However, now that schools are responsible for their finances, this may, in certain circumstances, place some constraint on teachers' salaries. For qualified teachers, there is a basic **standard scale**, consisting of ten points. **Governors** have the discretion to place newly qualified staff higher up the scale. Apart from the annual service increment, individual teachers may be awarded one or more additional increments at any time. Incentive allowances, which in practice are allocated to named posts, may also be given for a range of conditions, for example undertaking of additional responsibilities, outstanding ability as a teacher, offering a shortage subject. The salaries of **heads** and **deputy heads** are calculated on a different basis. The group size of a school (apart from a special school) depends on its unit total, which is calculated from the number of pupils and their ages according to a nationally determined formula. The group size varies from one for a primary school with below 150 pupils to six for a large secondary school. There is a salary spine consisting of fifty-one points for all heads and deputy heads, with a range of points within each group. Governors decide at which point, within each range, heads and deputy heads should be placed. This may be decided by considerations similar to those appertaining to the determining of assistant teachers' salaries. (*see also* **teacher appraisal**)

teachers' unions Bodies organised on a national scale to safeguard the interests, salaries, working conditions and welfare of their members. They also promote views on educational issues and consult with national and local government and other organisations; they are represented by many bodies concerned with formulating educational policies.

There are a number of different bodies which represent the teaching profession in the UK. For schools, there is the **National Union of Teachers** (NUT), the largest union; the **National Association of Schoolmasters and the Union of Women Teachers** (NAS/UWT); the **Association of Teachers and Lecturers** (ATL); and the **Professional Association of Teachers** (PAT). Headteachers are represented separately by the **National Association of Headteachers** (NAHT); and the **Secondary Heads Association** (SHA). In further and higher education, there is the **National Association of Teachers in Further and Higher Education** (NATFHE); the **Association of Polytechnic Teachers** (APT); and the **Association of University Teachers** (AUT). In Scotland, 80 per cent of all teachers from nursery to further education belong to the **Educational Institute of Scotland** (EIS). Recent attempts to explore mergers between unions have not been successful.

With the reorganisation of educational institutions at both school and higher education levels, unions are widening their range of membership. The former

Assistant Masters and Mistresses Association is now called the **Association of Teachers and Lecturers** (ATL), to cater for the staff in the independent sixth-form and tertiary colleges.

teaching methods Approaches to teaching methods vary between subjects and phases of education. For instance, it was long accepted that for younger children, the **child-centred** approach was most appropriate, emphasising discovery learning and the use of project work. Since the introduction of national testing and the questioning of standards in the basic subjects, there has been a tendency to concentrate more on effective methods of teaching, as in **reading**. New developments in teaching methods can arise from **curriculum development projects** such as the Schools History Project. (*see also* **child-centred education, teaching style**)

teaching practice A period of time during a **student-teacher's** course devoted to gaining classroom experience. Assessment of performance is carried out by supervisors in conjunction with the school. The length of practice varies according to the type of course, though from 1994 with the **Postgraduate Certificate of Education** (PGCE), some two-thirds of the course (twenty-four weeks) has be taken up with this activity. (*see also* **teacher tutor**)

teaching style The ways in which teachers differ in presenting materials to their pupils, in particular, the kind of social relationship established within the classroom. Teaching styles may be categorised in a number of different ways: for example, formal, informal; authoritarian, democratic; didactic, enquiry based; child-centred, subject-centred. (*see also* **teaching methods**)

team teaching A method of teaching where a team of teachers works together with a large number of children. This form of organisation is often used where a **project** or a **topic** is being pursued, with individual teachers taking responsibility for particular aspects of the work. (*see also* **teaching methods**)

Technical and Vocational Education Initiative (TVEI) An initiative introduced in 1983 for full-time 14- to 18-year-olds which emphasised **vocational and technical education** and preparation for working life. The project, under the auspices of the **Manpower Services Commission** (MSC) was financed by the Department of Employment, by-passing the Department of Education and Science in order to circumvent the legal restrictions of the 1944 Education Act. The pilot phase, costing £46 million was carried out for five years in the first instance by volunteer **local education authorities**. The programme, designed to continue until 1977, absorbed £134 million in the first seven years. In 1991, the National Audit Office criticised the scheme on the grounds that the pilot phase did not address the needs of local education authorities and was of limited value in assisting authorities to plan their TVEI extension projects. A survey, *Experiencing TVEI*, published in 1992, revealed that only 10 per cent of schools had established regular employer involvement in curriculum development or direct work with students, as tutors or mentors.

technological baccalaureate A new examination with a four-part curriculum structure starting at 16 plus: A – exploration and development of individual potential; B – a common curriculum within a technological and commercial context; C – an elective curriculum related to aesthetic or performing arts, the humanities or recreation; D – an extension curriculum suited to the individual students post-qualification intentions. Three certificates are offered: the technological baccalaureate; with credit; with distinction. (*see also* **baccalauréat, international baccalaureate**)

technology Technology may be defined as 'the application of scientific knowledge to the solution of practical problems.' In education the term is used in two very different ways:
(1) A 'new' subject introduced into the National Curriculum in 1989, it combines art, craft, design and technology (CDT), home economics, business studies and **information technology** (IT). The aim of technology is to develop technical skills, knowledge and understanding through working with materials and systems. It is often carried out through projects or topics.
(2) Educational technology often means no more than **visual aids**, but it should refer to the techniques and understanding of the whole process of learning as well as the 'hardware'.

tenure The existence of tenure, particularly at universities, has long been seen as a prerequisite for academic freedom. Good reason for dismissal has to be shown by the employing body and the findings challenged in a court of law. The **Education Reform Act** (1988) provided for a revision of university statutes to weaken rights of tenure. There are great variations already between universities, varying from strong tenure to no tenure. In all institutions, new members of staff are increasingly offered short-term contracts. (*see* Section 1, Essay 7)

term The academic year of schools and colleges in the UK is normally divided into three periods: autumn, spring and summer, though some universities still use older names, for example, Oxford terms are Michaelmas, Hilary and Trinity. The length of both school and college terms vary, though the former are usually of longer duration. Some institutions are now working in **semesters** rather than terms.

terminal examination An examination taken after the completion of a course of study. An external terminal examination is a requirement for each **General Certificate of Secondary Education** (GCSE) subject assessment.

tertiary college A college catering for all 16 to 19 education, full- and part-time, in an area. It brings under one roof both the range of courses found in normal sixth forms in schools and the **vocational** and **technical** courses offered in **further education**.

testing Evaluation of a student's understanding of a lesson, module or course. The new requirements of the National Curriculum for testing at 7, 11, 14 and

16 has produced the claim that such tests impose much strain, especially on the younger age groups. National testing is becoming more popular as countries become more interested in ways of raising educational achievement. (*see* Section 1, Essay 5)

thesis A treatise, based on research, submitted for an award or qualification, such as a Master of Arts (MA) or Doctor of Philosophy (PhD). It is similar to a **dissertation**, though a thesis may be considered as contributing original knowledge to a **discipline**. (*see also* **graduate**, **postgraduate**, **viva**)

three Rs The Revised Code of 1862 altered the system of government grants to schools. The money which had been paid to certificated teachers was now given to the **managers**, who paid the teachers according to the average attendance of pupils and their achievements at examinations conducted by **Her Majesty's Inspectorate** (HMI) – hence the title of this system '**payment by results**'. The subjects tested were the three Rs – reading, writing and arithmetic, with plain needlework for girls. This system led to greater pressure by teachers on pupils and at the same time led to a narrowing of the **curriculum**. From 1867, other subjects were allowed to be offered for grant purposes and a liberalising of the Code continued until the end of the century. The term is still used to refer to these three subjects.

timetabling Refers to the groupings of pupils, the **curriculum** and the allocation of teachers in an institution. Traditionally, timetables explained *when* things happened rather than reflecting the aims of the organisation. A more analytical approach to planning in schools and resource allocation is now favoured which takes into account types of pupil grouping and curriculum philosophy.

topic work A method of teaching, particularly in **primary schools**, which aims at developing children's conceptual development through a study of a particular topic over a period of days or weeks. Some topics may attempt to cover the whole **curriculum**, but many are confined to subjects such as history, geography and social studies. (*see also* **assignment**, **project**)

Training and Enterprise Councils (TECs) The eighty-two locally based TECs established in 1991, took over many of the functions of the former **Manpower Services Commission**. Members of TEC boards consist of leading businessmen in the area, who dispense a government-funded budget to finance courses for **youth training** in **further education colleges**, to participate in **vocational** and **technical** initiatives in schools and to take a close interest in local authorities' careers service. There is also close liaison with **local education authorities**; many TECs having representatives from this constituency on their boards. The objective of TECs is to offer every young person the opportunity to attend vocational education courses, gain relevant qualifications and improve their work skills. In Scotland the equivalent is carried on by twenty-two local enterprise companies (LECs). (*see also* **training credits**)

training credits An initiative launched by government in 1990 whereby 16- and 17-year-olds who have left full-time education are given training credits or **vouchers** to buy the training of their choice under the **Training and Enterprise Councils'** scheme.

transition from primary to secondary school In most, but not all **local education authorities** there is a transition at the age of 11 from primary school to secondary school for the majority of pupils. This can create problems of two kinds. First, there is, in many authorities, a lack of continuity between the **curriculum** of the primary school and the curriculum of the secondary school; second, the regime of the secondary school is likely to be much more formal and puzzling for the 11-year-old than the regime of the primary school, where the pupil probably had only one teacher for all subjects rather than a different teacher for six or seven periods every day. Partly to counteract the difficulties of this transition, **middle schools** were set up in some authorities and, at one stage, it was suggested that primary and secondary schools should pay attention to the 'middle years' so that greater continuity would be achieved. (*see also* **Great Debate, Plowden Report**)

triangulation A research technique, particularly associated with the work of John Elliott, in which evaluation is carried out by means of a threefold process. The teacher has a view of what he/she wants to do (and of how successfully he/she has achieved it); this may be different from the view or views of **pupils**; in addition, an independent, neutral observer may have yet further views. The hypothesis is that by open discussion of these three points of view the teacher's performance and competence may be improved. Triangulation in this sense is part of the 'teacher as researcher' model. (*see also* **participant observation**)

tripartite system Refers to the threefold classification of secondary schools postulated by the Spens Report (1938), that is **grammar, technical** and **modern** schools. Later, in 1943, the Norwood Report, basing its findings on psychological evidence, claimed that there were three types of minds corresponding to the schools – the **academic**, the applied scientific, and those with the ability to handle concrete things rather than ideas. No mention of types of schools was made in the 1944 Education Act; but **local education authorities** were allowed to establish various kinds of secondary schools with **selection** tests determining pupil allocation. The system was largely replaced by **comprehensive schools**. With the advent of the **grant-maintained school, city technology colleges** and a revival of the **grammar school**, there is once more diversity in the structure of secondary education.

tripos An honours **degree** course of study at the University of Cambridge. The name is derived from the three-legged stool on which medieval undergraduates used to sit. A student must pass two tripos examinations to qualify for a Bachelor of Arts (BA). The majority of triposes are in two parts: it is possible for the student to take both parts of the same tripos or one tripos followed by part 1 or 2 of a different tripos.

truancy A problem of long standing; in fact since **compulsory education** was introduced in the last century. Truancy is often associated with low levels of **literacy** and **numeracy** as well as boredom. The **Children Act** (1989) introduced a system which gave **education welfare officers** responsibility for working with parents to ensure that their children return to school. Another approach which is being adopted is for a local authority to cooperate with industry in providing part-time work where the pupils receive basic **skills** lessons and **counselling**.

tutor There are several kinds of tutors. In **higher** and **further education** it is the person responsible for the supervision of students' **academic** work, often operating through **tutorials**. A tutor may be designated as an **advisor** to students, acting as a **counsellor**. In schools, tutors may be in charge of a tutor group which encourages pupils to become integrated into the school community as well as to achieve their own academic and personal potential. Finally there is the private tutor, employed to **coach** an individual to achieve success in an examination or to remedy weakness in a subject. Tutorial colleges exist for the same purpose.

tutorial A meeting between a **tutor** and one or more students, frequently based on a paper or essay submitted by a student. Such meetings normally take place throughout the student's course. Tutorials are very common in institutions of **further** and **higher education**, though with the large expansion of student numbers, it has been argued that other more economical teaching methods should be used.

tutorial college See **crammers**.

TVEI See **Technical and Vocational Education Initiative**.

U

underachiever A pupil whose performance at school is identifiably below what would be expected from his or her known **ability**. Underachievers probably fall into at least two main groups: first, individual pupils whose achievement does not come up to their performance on **IQ** tests; second, groups of students (e.g. working-class pupils or children from ethnic **minorities**) whose work is generally below average when there is no reason to believe that their **intelligence** level is below average. (*see also* **intelligence test, multicultural education, self-concept/ self-image**)

undergraduate A student following a course leading to a first degree. (*see also* **graduate, postgraduate, university entry requirements**)

UNESCO (United Nations Educational, Social and Cultural Organisation) One of the sub-divisions of the United Nations, founded in 1946 to promote international, cultural and educational cooperation. It has its own constitution and budget. Its permanent headquarters are in Paris. It is administered by a Director-General and an international Civil Service of about 800. Member states are required to establish national citizen commissions, to advise UNESCO on policy, and to encourage participation in activities that flow from UNESCO programmes. UNESCO-sponsored activities can be classified as follows: (1) emergency aid and reconstruction; (2) advancement of knowledge; (3) promotion of human welfare; (4) the encouragement of international understanding. In the early-1980s there was some criticism that certain UNESCO activities were becoming 'political'; in 1984 the USA (which contributed 25 per cent of the UNESCO budget) withdrew from membership, and the UK followed in 1985.

uniform, school Often justified on the ground that it demonstrates a school's corporate identity and helps in the enforcement of discipline. School uniform is generally compulsory in the older **independent schools**, such as Eton and Harrow, though less so in state schools. Heads and governors decide on the wearing of uniforms, their design and up to what age they should be worn.

unit Some schools may contain a special unit where children with **special educational needs** receive specialist help and support.

Universities and Colleges Admission Service (UCAS) The clearing house for admissions to higher education which was formed in 1992 from a merger of the **Universities Central Council on Admissions** (UCCA) and the Polytechnics Central Admissions System (PCAS). UCAS is also responsible to the **Committee of Vice-Chancellors and Principals** for public relations about admissions.

universities, history of The oldest universities in the UK are Oxford and Cambridge, both founded in the thirteenth century. Scotland established three universities (Aberdeen, St Andrew's and Glasgow) in the fifteenth century and one at Edinburgh a hundred years later. Durham was the first of the revived universities to be built in the nineteenth century (1832), closely following the Oxbridge pattern. At almost the same time in London, a secular institution, University College, was founded with an Anglican rival, King's College, which stressed religious instruction. The University of London was established in 1836 as a degree-awarding body to affiliated colleges in various parts of the kingdom, including University College and King's College.

The provincial civic universities of the second half of the century were often the result of local benefactors, who favoured a science based **curriculum**, and the **university extension** movement. Owens College, Manchester, was the first, opened in 1851. Between 1874 and 1902, university colleges were founded at Birmingham, Bristol, Exeter, Leeds, Liverpool, Nottingham, Reading, Sheffield and Southampton. All were eventually granted full university status. During this period, the University of Wales, a federal body, came into existence.

Between the two World Wars, only two new colleges were founded – at Hull and Leicester.

After 1945, there was a dramatic expansion of university provision. The University College of North Staffordshire was the first in 1949, followed by East Anglia, Essex, Kent, Lancaster, Sussex, Warwick and York in the years 1961–5. In 1963, Newcastle became a university in its own right, formerly being associated with Durham. The final phase of expansion followed the **Robbins Report** (1963) recommendation that the nine colleges of advanced technology should became full universities – Aston, Bath, Bradford, Brunel, Chelsea, City, Loughborough, Salford and Surrey; at the same time Strathclyde, Dundee and Heriot-Watt were founded in Scotland. Northern Ireland has Queen's, Belfast, and the University of Ulster at Coleraine. The only private university in the UK is the University College of Buckingham; established in 1976, it offers courses for two-year honours degrees.

In 1992, the **binary** line distinction between **polytechnics** and universities was abolished, thus adding considerably to the total number of universities and university places in the UK.

University Central Council on Admissions (UCCA) The Council was set up in 1961 as a clearing house to handle all applications for entrance to universities in England (except the Open University and Buckingham), Scotland, Wales and Northern Ireland. The Council plays no part in the selection of students but forwards candidates' application forms to universities. Up to five universities can be named on the form. An unsuccessful candidate may take advantage of either the continuing applications procedure which provides for further chances or the clearing scheme, which operates every september in a final attempt to place candidates. The UCCA scheme does not cover postgraduate applicants, who apply direct to universities. In 1992, UCCA was replaced by the **Universities and Colleges Admissions Service** (UCAS). (*see also* **clearing house**, **entry qualifications**, **open admission**, **Open College**, **undergraduate**, **university entry requirements**)

university college A college of **university** rank which is unable to award its own degrees. Most of the civic universities were at one time university colleges, but they have since achieved full university status. (*see also* **federal university**, **universities, history of**)

university day training college One of the recommendations of the Cross Commission (1888) was that day training colleges should be established in connection with local universities or university colleges. The Education Department's Code for 1890 sanctioned this arrangement for training elementary school teachers, and fourteen day training departments were opened; the course was to be of three years' duration.

university department of education (UDE) A university department, specialising in teacher education. UDEs grew out of **university day training colleges**, which were established in 1890 to enable **student-teachers** to follow a three-year course and take a **degree** if they wished. They were at first called university training departments (UTD), but after the Second World War most had assumed their present nomenclature. Some are called **schools of education**. (*see also* **in-service education of teachers, teacher tutor**)

university entrance requirements The normal (minimum) entrance requirement for admission to a **university** is the possession of two **GCE 'A' level** passes. Individual departments may stipulate more detailed achievements above the minimum. Many universities also operate special entry systems for mature students as well as access courses for those without 'A' levels. The **Open University** accepts students without formal qualifications. (*see also* **entry qualification, open admission, undergraduate**)

university extension A movement which began in the second half of the last century, instigated mainly by James Stuart, then a Fellow at Cambridge, which attempted to set up a 'peripatetic university' in towns where none existed. Following the success of his lectures on gravitation in a number of northern towns in 1867, he persuaded Cambridge to found a range of courses in 1873 in the region surrounding the University. Three years later, the University of London followed and in 1878, so did Oxford. The success of the movement led to the establishment of university colleges such as Sheffield and Nottingham; it also brought into prominence the lack of university education provision for women. Today's **extra-mural** departments of universities are another outcome. (*see also* **universities, history of**)

University Grants Committee (UGC) Established in 1919, the Committee's main terms of reference were to 'enquire into the financial needs of university education in the UK and to advise the government as to the application of any grants that may be made by parliament towards meeting them.' After 1964, on the recommendation of the **Robbins Report**, the UGC became the responsibility of the **Secretary of State for Education and Science**. One of the provisions of the **Education Reform Act** (1988) was to abolish the UGC and replace it by a **Universities Funding Council** (UFC). The UFC was in turn replaced by the **Higher Educaiton Funding Council** (HEFC) in 1992 following the recommendations of the White Paper *Higher Education – A New Framework* (May 1991) and the 1992 Act. (*see* Section 1, Essay 9)

University of the Third Age (U3A) The first Universite du Troisieme Age was founded in Toulouse in 1972 as a summer school for retired people; the university staff did the teaching. The English version began in 1982 and was different from the French inasmuch as the teachers were not necessarily professionals and received no fee. The main aim of U3A is to provide educational opportunities for older members of society (the over-50s) to enable them to have a better quality of life.

university training department (UTD) See **university department of education**.

unstreaming   This is the product of a diametrically opposite philosophy to **streaming**. Pupils here are randomly assigned for teaching purposes without reference to **ability**, or are deliberately placed in **mixed-ability groups**. (*see also* **labelling, setting**)

V

vacation   A period of time when an educational institution is not in session. The major breaks in the UK are at Easter, in the summer and at Christmas. Formerly, the term was used mainly in connection with universities. (*see also* **semester, term**)

validation   Universities are empowered by their charters to award **degrees**. This privilege includes the right to validate degrees in other institutions – for example, in **colleges of higher education**. The validation procedure normally consists of the formal submission of plans and syllabuses, visits to the site, and ensuring that the teaching staff are adequately qualified. The university would also monitor the **standards** of the awards.

validity   An intelligence test or examination rarely measures exactly what it is intended to measure. For example, a test of **creativity** might give results which are superficially plausible but which, on further investigation, turn out to be no more than a test of **intelligence**. The validity of many tests of attitude is often called into question: asking students to say what they would do may not be a valid measure of what they would actually do in real life. (*see also* **reliability**)

value added   Part of the result of educational policies of the 1980s encouraging parental choice of school has been the attempt to find ways of providing evidence of school quality. One obvious, but unreliable, device is to publish the examination results (**GCSE** and **'A' level**) of schools, and since the establishment of the **National Curriculum** in 1988, the publication of National Curriculum assessment results in **league table** form. An objection to this practice is that such 'raw scores' do not give an accurate picture of school quality or of the teachers in it. Raw scores tend to indicate the social class of the pupils. To avoid this trap, some assessment experts advocate that examination results should only be published in a 'value-added' form – that is, measuring the difference that the school has made by comparing, for example, 'A' level results with GCSE results two years before; in that way it is claimed that the contribution of the school can, to some extent, be indicated. Eventually it will be possible to extend that kind of analysis by comparing individual results at age 11 with performance at 14, 16 and 18. There are more complicated methods of 'value-added' comparisons such as **multi-level analysis** models.

verbal reasoning One aspect of general **intelligence**. Verbal reasoning tests (often used for **eleven plus selection** procedures for **grammar schools**) focused upon this aspect of intelligence rather than **spatial ability**. It is the aspect of intelligence which is most difficult to separate from environmental factors.

vertical age grouping See **family grouping**.

vice-chancellor The vice-chancellor is the chief academic and administrative officer of a university. He is often the chairman of many important university committees and is ex-officio member of all of them. He is involved in the appointment of senior university posts and is the channel of communication with bodies such as the **Committee of Vice-Chancellors and Principals**. Vice-chancellors vary in their style of leadership. It should be noted that in the University of London, the vice-chancellor is assisted by a **principal**, who shares the administrative load. (*see also* **chancellor**)

village college The brain-child of Henry Morris, County Education Secretary (Chief Education Officer), for Cambridgeshire (1922–54), the village college was envisaged as a community centre of a neighbourhood. Its aim was to 'provide for the whole man, and abolish the duality of education and ordinary life.' Thus Morris's first college, opened at Sawston in 1930, contained a school, an **adult education** centre and a community centre. Morris had hoped that twelve such colleges would be built for the county though in fact only five – at Sawston, Linton, Bottisham, Impington and Bassingbourn – were completed. After the Second World War, this notion was revived in the form of the **community school** or college. (*see also* **adult education**, **community education**)

village schools Characterised by their smallness, village schools have come under pressure in recent years. A Department of Education and Science Report *Better Schools* (1985) pointed out the need for a school to be large enough to offer a full curriculum to its pupils and for classes to be of economic size. Since then, the advent of the **National Curriculum** and **local management of schools** (LMS) present further problems. Although village schools are popular with the community, administrative and financial considerations are becoming increasingly important in determining their survival. (*see also* **falling rolls**)

virement The power to transfer money from one budget heading to another.

viva Short for *viva voce*. An oral examination most frequently used in connection with the award of higher **degrees** but also applies now to many other different examinations.

vocational education and training See **National Vocational Qualifications**.

vocational guidance Giving advice to young people and adults about the occupations most suitable to their aptitudes and personality. **Aptitude** tests are extensively used in the diagnosis of special abilities and inclinations.

vocational preparation See **National Vocational Qualifications**.

voluntary-aided school A type of voluntary school where the governors control the admission of pupils and the type of religious education given, though parents have the right for their children to be taught according to the **agreed syllabus**. The church authority concerned appoints two-thirds of its governing body, who are responsible for the capital expenditure on alterations or enlargement of a school, but the **Secretary of State** makes a contribution of 85 per cent towards the expenditure. The **local education authority** maintains such schools and pays the salaries of the teachers. Approximately one-half of the total of voluntary schools in England are of this type and some 2300 of the 5000 in this category are Church of England. (*see also* **special agreement school**, **voluntary-controlled school**)

voluntary-controlled school In this type of voluntary school the local education authority is responsible for the total expenditure and maintenance of the building. It appoints two-thirds of its governing body and the teaching staff, though governors are consulted on the appointment of heads and on teachers giving denominational religious instruction. Most controlled schools belong to the Church of England. (*see also* **religious education**, **special agreement school**, **voluntary-aided school**)

voluntary school Originally owned by voluntary bodies, usually religious, but now in receipt of public funds. They may be of three kinds: **aided**, **controlled** or **special agreement**, as distinct from those schools which are entirely within the province of the local education authority. Approximately 30 per cent of **maintained schools** in England are voluntary schools. (*see also* **religious education**)

Voluntary Service Overseas (VSO) An organisation established in 1958 and dedicated to assisting development in the world's poor countries. Each year around 700 men and women set out to work on projects in more than forty developing countries. The average age of a volunteer is 33, with the youngest in their early twenties and the oldest in their late sixties. The range of skills sought and requested includes: agriculture and natural resources, education, technical trades and engineering, social development, and business and commercial development. Volunteers are normally paid the equivalent amount of someone who does the same job in that country on a permanent basis.

W

Waddell Report In 1970, the **Schools Council** recommended a single system of examining at 16 plus and, after some experimenting, repeated its belief in such a system in 1976. The then Secretary of State for Education, Shirley Williams, agreed that a Steering Committee should be formed to make an intensive study of 'outstanding problems'. The Committee, under the chairmanship of Sir James Waddell, reported in July 1978. Entitled *School Examinations*, the Report concluded that a common examination was educationally feasible and could be introduced without causing major difficulties. It recommended a seven-point grading system, with the first three grades representing the **General Certificate of Education** (GCE) **'O' level** pass grades of A, B, and C and the other four representing **Certificate of Secondary Education** (CSE) grades 2, 3, 4 and 5. An ungraded category was to be included for those who did not gain a certificate. An important organisational change was that GCE and CSE boards were to be regionally grouped, four in England and one in Wales. Schools were not to be limited in their choice of examining board by regional considerations. GCSE courses began in 1986 with the first examinations taken in 1988. (*see also* **examination boards, national criteria, sixteen plus examination**)

Warnock Report The Committee of Enquiry into the education of handicapped children and young people, chaired by Mary Warnock, was set up in 1973 and reported in 1978. It recommended that the Department of Education and Science's statutory categories should be abolished, that services should be planned on the assumption that one in six children at any time attending schools would need help, and that intellectually impaired children and children with remedial problems should be referred to as **children with learning difficulties**. Attention was drawn to the need for more parental involvement in children's education and for greater opportunities for young people aged between 16 and 19 years. **Special needs** were an essential element in initial **teacher training** and in-service training courses. Although the issue of **integrating** children with special needs into ordinary schools was fundamental to the work of the Warnock Committee, the Report did not make specific proposals as to how this should be achieved. A Government White Paper, *Special Needs in Education* (1980), accepted the proposal to abolish categories of handicap as a basis for planning services. This was implemented in the 1981 Education Act, but no concessions were made on the running down of special schools or the redistribution of resources to help develop ordinary school-based provision. **Special schools** were to remain. (*see also* **integration, remedial education, special educational needs**)

weighting The contribution which an examination component makes to the distribution of candidates' results. If the scores for one examination component are more widely spread (i.e. have a greater **standard deviation**) than that for a second component, the first will exercise a greater influence on the overall attainment order of candidates, even if both components have the same mark allocations. Its *actual* weighting will be higher than its *intended* weighting.

welfare assistant Often employed by local education authorities to help teachers with children who have **special educational needs**. Welfare assistants have no teaching qualifications and, as the title indicates, are especially concerned with the pupil's physical needs.

Welsh Office Up to 1970, the Department of Education and Science was responsible for education in Wales. In that year, primary and secondary education was transferred to the Education Department of the Welsh Office, under the Secretary of State for Wales. Eight years later, non-university institutions and public libraries in the Principality were also transferred. (*see also* **Department of Education Northern Ireland**, **Scottish Education Department**)

White Paper The name given to the majority of government discussion documents, derived from the colour of the publication. A White Paper describes official policy towards an issue and is often a prelude to legislation, for example, the White Paper *Choice and Diversity* (1992). (*see also* **Parliamentary Papers**)

women's studies Courses at any level of education (**secondary school**, **undergraduate** or **postgraduate**) which are intended to emphasise the contributions made, for example, in history, English literature or philosophy, by women. (*see also* **girls' education**)

workcards Cards, often devised by the teacher, giving information on a particular subject or **topic**, with follow-up work arising out of it. Workcards are used as a means of individualising instruction, as, for example, in a mixed-ability setting. (*see also* **individual learning, teaching methods**)

Workers' Education Association (WEA) Founded in 1903 by Albert Mansbridge as a means of developing the intellectual capacity of working men [*sic*], the WEA was an alliance between universities, trade unions and the Cooperative Society. Up until 1945 the WEA provided courses for many thousands of workers and was associated with the Labour Party. After the Second World War, the WEA became identified with middle-class leisure pursuits, but efforts have been made to return to the original purpose, for example, day release courses for shop stewards in aspects of trade unionism run in association with the Trades Union Congress.

By 1992 WEA activities were subsidised by direct government grants amounting to about £2 million, with another £1 million being received via the **local education authorities**. From April 1993, however, government grants were channelled through the **Further Education Funding Council** (FEFC), and the Association has to compete for funds rather than having amounts earmarked as was previously the case. In addition, local education authorities are unlikely to be able to continue their previous level of support. The long-term future of WEA courses (like many other kinds of adult education) seems doubtful.

World Education Fellowship See **New Education Fellowship**.

y

Yellow Book A confidential report on standards in education compiled by civil servants in the **Department of Education and Science** in 1975 for the then Prime Minister, James Callaghan. It voiced many criticisms of primary and secondary schools which were reflected in Callaghan's **Ruskin College** speech in October 1976. It proved to be the basis for the subsequent 'Great Debate', which included, amongst other things, discussion on the need for a **national curriculum**.

Youth Opportunities Programme (YOP) The **Manpower Service Commission** organised a number of schemes under the Youth Opportunities Programme for 16- to 19-year-olds who were unemployed. The two main schemes were the Work Preparation and Work Experience courses. Participants could spend up to a year on such courses and receive a training allowance. Approximately a quarter of a million youths took part in this scheme in 1981–2. It was replaced in September 1983 by the Youth Training Scheme, now **Youth Training**.

Youth Service The 1944 Education Act placed responsibility upon local education authorities to provide adequate facilities for recreation, social and cultural activities for young people between the ages of 11 and 25. In the same year, the McNair Report made recommendations for the supply, recruitment and training of youth leaders. Since then, reports such as Albemarle (1960) and Thompson (1982) have pointed out the inadequacies of the Service and made recommendations for its improvement. Much of the Service depends on the efforts of unpaid volunteers.

In November 1990 at a ministerial conference, a *Core Curriculum for the Youth Service* was unveiled. Its recommendations included the establishment of nationally agreed learning outcomes of the core curriculum for the Youth Service and a set of input, process and output indicators were listed. Priority groups were to be identified locally and the type and mix of youth work provision was to be locally determined.

Youth Training (YT) In December 1981, the Government White Paper entitled *A New Training Initiative: A Programme for Action* was issued. It proposed radical reform of training as a whole. In its present form, YT offers places on a vocational programme of up to two years for 16- to 18-year-olds known as the 'guarantee group', that is, those not in work or in further education. The programme, which is aimed for the most part at the **National Vocational Qualification** (NVQ) level 2, is delivered through the eighty-two **Training and Enterprise Councils**. The providers of the programme include employers, **colleges of further education** (youth sections), private training providers and workshop type schemes for those with **special needs**. **Day release** may be provided for those on the programme to attend further education colleges. Providers are funded for the number of weeks training delivered, plus an element for attainment of outcomes by the trainees. (*see* Section 1, Essay 9)

Z

zeitgeist Literally 'spirit of the time' (German). The dominant ideas of a particular period, for example, the 1920s or the 1980s reflected in politics, philosophy, literature, art and architecture – even education and the **curriculum**.

zero-based budgeting A budget which is prepared by ignoring previous spending priorities and begins with a completely clean slate to decide a school's requirement.

z-scores A form of **standardised** score on a test which is obtained by expressing the raw score (actual score) in terms of the relationship of that score to the mean or average score. The difference is expressed in units of the **standard deviation**. For example, a raw score that was above the mean score by one standard deviation would have a z-score of +1; a raw score below average would have a minus z-score.

Section 3

ACRONYMS *and* ABBREVIATIONS

AAU	Academic Audit Unit
ACAC	Curriculum and Assessment Authority for Wales
ACC	Association of County Councils
ACE	Advisory Centre for Education
ACFHE	Association of Colleges for Further and Higher Education
ACRG	Access Course Recognition Group
AERA	American Educational Research Association
AFC	Association for Colleges
AFE	Advanced Further Education
ALBSU	Adult Literacy and Basic Skills Unit
A level	Advanced Level Examination (GCE)
AMA	Association of Metropolitan Authorities
AMG	Annual Maintenance Grant
AMMA	Assistant Masters and Mistresses Association
APL	Accreditation of Prior Learning
APR	Age Participation Rate
APS	Assisted Places Scheme
APT	Association of Polytechnic Teachers
APU	Assessment of Performance Unit
APVIC	Association of Principals in Sixth Form Colleges
ARELS	Association of Recognised English Language Schools
AS level	Advanced Supplementary Level Examination
ASB	Aggregated Schools Budget
ASE	Association for Science Education
ASLIB	Association of Special Libraries and Information Bureaux
AT	Articled Teacher
AT	Attainment Target (National Curriculum)
ATD	Art Teachers Diploma
ATL	Association of Teachers and Lecturers (formerly AMMA)
AUT	Association of University Teachers
AVA	Audio-Visual Aids
AVA	Authorised Validating Agencies
AWPU	Age Weighted Pupil Unit
BA	Bachelor of Arts
BAAS	British Association for the Advancement of Science
BCIES	British Comparative and International Education Society
BEd	Bachelor of Education
BEI	British Education Index
BEMAS	British Educational Management and Administration Society
BERA	British Educational Research Association
BL	British Library
BPS	British Psychological Society
BSc	Bachelor of Science

BTEC	Business and Technology Education Council
CAL	Computer-Assisted Learning
CASE	Campaign for (the Advancement of) State Education
CATE	Council for the Accreditation of Teacher Education
CATS	Credit Accumulation and Transfer Scheme
CBET	Competency-Based Education and Training
CBTE	Competency-Based Teacher Education
CCTV	Closed Circuit Television
CCT	Compulsory Competitive Tendering
CCW	Curriculum Council for Wales
CD-ROM	Compact Disc – Read Only Memory
CDT	Craft Design and Technology
CE	Common Entrance
CEA	Conservative Education Association
CEDEFOP	Centre Europeen pour le Developpment de la Formation Profes-sionelle
CEE	Certificate of Extended Education
CEO	Chief Education Officer
CERI	Centre for Educational Research and Innovation (OECD)
CertEd	Certificate in Education
CFE	College of Further Education
CEWC	Council for Education in World Citizenship
CGLI	City and Guilds of London Institute
CHE	College of Higher Education
CI	Chief Inspector (of Schools)
CILT	Centre for Information on Language Teaching and Research
CIPFA	Chartered Institute of Public Finance and Accountancy
CLEA	Council of Local Education Authorities
CNAA	Council for National Academic Awards
CPS	Centre for Policy Studies
CPVE	Certificate of Pre-Vocational Education
CRE	Commission for Racial Equality
CSE	Certificate of Secondary Education
CSV	Community Service Volunteers
CTC	City Technology College
CVCP	Committee of Vice-Chancellors and Principals
DE	Department of Employment
DENI	Department of Education Northern Ireland
DES	Department of Education and Science
DFE	Department for Education
DipEd	Diploma in Education

EA	Education Association
EC	European Community
ECCTIS	Education Counselling and Credit Transfer Information System
EFL	English as a Foreign Language
EIS	Educational Institute of Scotland
EIU	Economic and Industrial Understanding
EMU	Evaluation and Monitoring Unit (of SEAC)
EO	Education Otherwise
EOC	Equal Opportunities Commission
EPA	Educational Priority Area
ERA	Education Reform Act (1988)
ERASMUS	European Action Scheme for the Mobility of University Students
ERIC	Educational Resources Information Centre (USA)
ESL	English as a Second Language
ESN	Educationally Sub-Normal
ESRC	Economic and Social Research Council
ET	Employment Training
ETS	Educational Testing Service (USA)
ETV	Educational Television
EWS	Education Welfare Service
FAS	Funding Agency for Schools
FE	Further Education
FEU	Further Education Unit
FEFC	Further Education Funding Council for England
FHE	Further and Higher Education
FTE	Full-Time Equivalent
GA	Graded Assessment
GCE	General Certificate of Education
GCSE	General Certificate of Secondary Education
GED	General Education Diploma
GLC	Greater London Council
GMS	Grant-Maintained School
GNVQ	General National Vocational Qualification
GPDST	Girls' Public Day School Trust
GRE	Grant-Related Expenditure
GRIDS	Guidelines for Review and Internal Development in Schools
GRIST	Grant-Related In-Service Training
GTC	General Teaching Council
GTTR	Graduate Teacher Training Registry
HE	Higher Education
HEA	Health Education Authority

HEC	Health Education Council
HEFC	Higher Education Funding Council
HMC	Headmasters' Conference
HMI	Her Majesty's Inspectorate
HMSO	Her Majesty's Stationery Office
HNC	Higher National Certificate
HND	Higher National Diploma
HOD	Head of Department
HOY	Head of Year
IAEP	International Assessment of Educational Progress
IAPS	Incorporated Association of Preparatory Schools
IB	International Baccalaureate
IE	Instrumental Enrichment
IEA	Institute of Economic Affairs
IEA	International Association for the Evaluation of Educational Achievement
IHE	Institute of Higher Education
IIEP	International Institute for Educational Planning
ILEA	Inner London Education Authority
INSET	In-Service Education of Teachers
IPPR	Institute for Public Policy Research
IQ	Intelligence Quotient
ISCED	International Standard Classification of Education
ISIS	Independent Schools Information Service
IT	Information Technology
ITE	Initial Teacher Education
ITT	Initial Teacher Training
KS	Key Stage (National Curriculum)
LA	Library Association
LCCI	London Chamber of Commerce and Industry
LEA	Local Education Authority
LEATGS	Local Education Authority Training Grants Scheme
LEC	Local Enterprise Companies (Scotland)
LISE	Librarians of Institutes and Schools of Education
LLB	Bachelor of Laws
LMS	Local Management of Schools
MA	Master of Arts
MACOS	Man – A Course of Study
MBA	Master of Business Administration
MEd	Master of Education

MSc	Master of Science
MSC	Manpower Services Commission
NACEIC	National Advisory Council on Education for Industry and Commerce
NAFE	Non-Advanced Further Education
NAGC	National Association for Gifted Children
NAGM	National Association of Governors and Managers
NAHT	National Association of Head Teachers
NAIEA	National Association of Inspectors and Educational Advisers
NAPE	National Association for Primary Education
NAS/UWT	National Association of Schoolmasters/Union of Women Teachers
NATE	National Association for the Teaching of English
NATFHE	National Association of Teachers in Further and Higher Education
NCA	National Curriculum Assessment
NCB	National Children's Bureau
NCC	National Curriculum Council
NCE	National Commission on Education
NCET	National Council for Educational Technology
NCPTA	National Confederation of Parent-Teacher Associations
NCVQ	National Council for Vocational Qualifications
NEC	National Extension College
NFER	National Foundation for Educational Research in England and Wales
NGO	Non-Governmental Organisation
NIACE	National Institute of Adult Continuing Education
NNEB	National Nursery Examination Board
NRA	National Record of Achievement
NTS	Non-Teaching Staff
NUS	National Union of Students
NUT	National Union of Teachers
NVQ	National Vocational Qualification
ODA	Overseas Development Agency
OECD	Organisation for Economic Cooperation and Development
OFSTED	Office for Standards in Education
O level	Ordinary Level Examination (GCE)
ONC	Ordinary National Certificate
OND	Ordinary National Diploma
OU	Open University
PAT	Professional Association of Teachers
PBTE	Performance-Based Teacher Education
PC	Profile Component (National Curriculum)

PCAS	Polytechnics Central Admissions System
PCFC	Polytechnics and Colleges Funding Council
PE	Physical Education
PESC	Public Expenditure Survey Committee
PGCE	Postgraduate Certificate of Education
PhD	Doctor of Philosophy
PI	Performance Indicator
PICKUP	Professional Industrial and Commercial Updating
PL	Principal Lecturer
PLR	Public Lending Right
PoS	Programme of Study (National Curriculum)
PRP	Performance-Related Pay
PSE	Personal and Social Education
PSHE	Personal, Social and Health Education
PT	Part-time
PTA	Parent-Teacher Association
PTR	Pupil-Teacher Ratio
QA	Quality Assurance
QAU	Quality Audit Unit
QE	Qualifying Examination
QTS	Qualified Teacher Status
QUANGO	Quasi-Autonomous Non-Governmental Organisation
R and D	Research and Development
RE	Religious Education
RoA	Record of Achievement
ROM	Read Only Memory
ROSLA	Raising of the School Leaving Age
RSA	Royal Society of Arts
RSG	Revenue Support Grant (formerly Rate Support Grant)
SACRE	Standing Advisory Conference on Religious Education
SAM	Skills Analysis Model
SAT	Scholastic Aptitude Test (USA)
SAT	Standard Assessment Task (National Curriculum)
SATRO	Science and Technology Regional Organisation
SCAA	School Curriculum and Assessment Authority
SCDC	School Curriculum Development Council
SCEA	Service Children's Education Authority
SCI	Senior Chief Inspector (HMI)
SCOTVEC	Scottish Vocational Education Council
SCRE	Scottish Council for Research in Education
SCSE	Standing Conference for Studies in Education

SCUE	Standing Conference on University Entrance
SD	Standard Deviation
SDP	School Development Plans
SEA	Socialist Education Association
SEAC	School Examinations and Assessment Council
SED	Scottish Education Department
SEN	Special Educational Needs
SEO	Society of Education Officers
SGCT	Scottish General Teaching Council
SHA	Secondary Heads Association
SL	Senior Lecturer
SLA	School Library Association
SMILE	Secondary Mathematics Individualised Learning Experiment
SMP	School Mathematics Project
SoA	Statement of Attainment (National Curriculum)
SPG	Special Purpose Grants
SRC	Science Research Council
SRHE	Society for Research into Higher Education
SSA	Standard Spending Assessment
SSR	Staff-Student Ratio
STOPP	Society of Teachers Opposed to Physical Punishment
TA	Teacher Assessment
TA	Training Agency (Previously MSC)
TC	Training Commission
TEC	Training and Enterprise Council
TEFL	Teaching English as a Foreign Language
TGAT	Task Group on Assessment and Testing (National Curriculum)
TQM	Total Quality Management
TUC	Trades Union Congress
TVEI	Technical and Vocational Education Initiative
UCAS	Universities and Colleges Admissions Service
UCCA	Universities Central Council on Admissions
UCET	Universities Council for the Education of Teachers
UDE	University Department of Education
UFC	Universities Funding Council
UGC	University Grants Committee
U3A	University of the Third Age
UKRA	United Kingdom Reading Association
UNESCO	United Nations Educational, Scientific and Cultural Organisation
UVP	Unified Vocational Preparation
VA	Voluntary Aided

VC	Voluntary Controlled
VC	Vice-Chancellor
VSO	Voluntary Service Overseas
VET	Vocational Education and Training
WEA	Workers' Education Association
WEF	World Education Fellowship
YOP	Youth Opportunities Programme
YT	Youth Training
YTS	Youth Training Scheme

NB An updated and comprehensive list of acronyms is published regularly by the Librarians of Institutes and Schools of Education with the title of *Acronyms and Initialisms in Education*. The fifth edition (1991) was compiled by John Hutchins. Copies are available from: Publications Secretary LISE, Education Library, University College, Swansea.